D1082951

Political Power in the Ancient World

Political Power in the Ancient World

MARIO ATTILIO LEVI
Director of the Institute of Ancient History
Milan University

Translation by Jane Costello

WEIDENFELD AND NICOLSON
20 New Bond Street London W1

Printed and bound in England by
Hazell Watson and Viney Ltd
Aylesbury, Bucks

CONTENTS

1 THE LAW OF THE STATE AND THE LAW OF THE GODS 1

2 GREECE AND THE ORACLES 27

3 THE SOCIAL TRANSFORMATION 61

4 THE ATHENIAN REVOLUTION 81

5 GREECE AND HELLENISM 105

6 ROME AND ITALY 128

7 ROME AND THE MEDITERRANEAN 149

8 THE ROMAN EMPIRE 165

CHAPTER ONE

*

THE LAW OF THE STATE AND THE LAW OF THE GODS

MANY of the fundamentals of civilised life in the classical period of history were the result of political developments in ancient Egypt. Our earliest information about the Egyptians suggests that they did not share our concept of the state as a community of men living in its own territories, and governing itself by its own laws and customs. Their concept was much simpler: that of the King, who was himself identified with the state and the law. Without the King there could be no order and discipline, no security, and no central authority to undertake the public works that would benefit the whole society, spiritually or materially.

The King of Egypt was God. Not his image, his representative, his delegate or protégé, but Horus the Hawk-God, the personification of Heaven, who had descended to Earth from on high. The supreme deity was Ra, and Horus was his son, present in each of the succeeding Pharaohs. This continuous chain of incarnations was described by the Egyptians as 'autogeneration', for each new king was the son, not of the dead king, but of himself, as God. The King of Egypt was more than a deified prince: he was God himself, unchangeable and eternal, present among men. Just as the sun in its course between sunrise and sunset is born and dies, yet is always the same vital and regenerating force, so the king was always the same God, unchanging and yet always different.

From the theological point of view, this was a static situation. Only developments in the religion itself could produce changes in the Egyptian kingdom. When Amun became dominant and identified himself with Ra, Horus became the son of Amun-Ra, while at the same time identified with his father by the process of 'autogeneration'. It was not long before Amun-Ra was given a Queen, and the King-god's birth and upbringing were assisted by minor deities.

Although the Egyptian ideas of God and the nature of kingship were quite different from ours, they have something in common with those of the classical world, which was close enough in time to Egypt to be influenced by her in many ways. The complete identification of the deity with the state gave to the will of the state, that is, the will of the sovereign, quite a different character from that of 'the Law' as we mean it today. Whatever the King of Egypt wanted, came about not just because it ought to, but because it was brought about by the act of willing it to. There was no difference between the act of willing and the act of implementing that will. Disobedience of the king's will was sacrilege.

It was by the will of the Pharaoh that the months succeeded one another, that the Nile swept down to the sea, and men were born and died. Thus everything that exists was the result of his will, because its existence was right and just. He was the standard by which everything, spiritual and physical, was measured; the source of the concept of justice, 'ma'at', which was of the same nature as himself, and which he alone could know and interpret to man.

Justice caused the seasons to follow one another, and it also led men to respect their parents, and to avoid the impure foods. Every act of justice was just because it conformed to 'ma'at', and therefore belonged to an order of things which God had willed, but which also bound God to observe it and to make others do the same. 'Ma'at' was a limitation imposed on God by himself. Just as, in theological terms, God begot himself in the form of the king, so 'ma'at' became the Law that even the King-god had to respect, and which was therefore separate from him as the son was separate from the father.

Since the Law which the Pharaoh submitted to and

expressed in his nature was of divine origin, the idea of dynasty as we understand it did not exist, for it was the mystical birth of the God that determined the succession, not human marriage or kinship. The sacred rites – the 'coronation' – in which the Pharaoh was acknowledged and venerated as God, were the essential thing. Once they had been observed, the distinction between the Pharaoh's religious obligations and his civil and military functions disappeared. When as head of the army he repressed marauding tribes along the caravan routes, or invaded neighbouring states, or when as supreme judge he punished wrongdoers, his function was to prevent man's sinfulness from marring the good order which was the will of the Gods and therefore his own will. The Pharaoh's duty was to bring peace, security and happiness to the faithful by a continuous effort to work for the destruction of his enemies, whose hostility consisted in their disbelief in his divinity. Whatever opposed 'ma'at' was sacrilege and arrogance, so that the conquests were themselves attempts to convert the subject races and liberate them from the powers of evil. The warrior Pharaohs were missionaries of a faith in themselves, the beneficent deities.

In matters of administration and internal politics, the ruler's wish could only be received as a revelation of the divine will. The theology of the Old Kingdom, which included the theory of monarchy, held that what the King wanted inevitably happened, and that what he did not want could not survive. However, it is clear from the evidence of the Pyramids that after his death on earth, the God-king had to account for his actions, to save himself from the flames of the Underworld, his fate if he had not acted honestly and justly, according to 'ma'at'.

Thus there was a distinction between the Father-god and the Son-god even in the earliest period of Pharaonic history: the Son, in the act of being born, received 'ma'at', and carried it within himself during his cycle on earth, but was responsible to it for any betrayal or forgetfulness of what was his own superhuman faculty. This ancient dichotomy led to the realisation that the divine ruler was not infallible, since he too could act in a way incompatible with absolute and transcendent justice.

The doctrine of a theocratic monarchy was formed and elaborated at the time of the fusion of the two kingdoms of Upper and Lower Egypt, but at the same time forces were at work to create an aristocracy of courtiers and priests, who assisted the ruler and thus limited his absolute power by making their collaboration necessary to him. The most splendid epoch of the Old Kingdom coincided with the period of the Pharaoh's theocratic omnipotence, before he was surrounded by administrators of his policies and priests of his cult. He owned all the country's weath. Everyone worked for him and was paid by him. Administering so centralised an empire called for delegation on a vast scale, and there grew up from among the men who made the Pharaoh's work possible a class which, being indispensable, entrenched itself more and more firmly, with growing powers, until it became dominant. In a land in which private ownership did not exist, this class acquired privileges which destroyed the equality of all men before the king, and so the principle of common liberty within the bounds of the religion was nullified.

Because the only principle which made one man's superiority to another comprehensible was a religious one, the ruling aristocracy had to share in the ruler's divinity. So the theocratic monarchy acquiesced in the beginning of its own destruction, and the Old Kingdom was plunged into anarchy, in which the unity of the State was shattered in a contest between the leading aristocratic clans, each claiming to share in the divinity which was, during the period of absolute Pharaonic rule, the very foundation of the state and legal system.

It is clear that the Egyptian philosophy of this period developed the concept of the relationship of the Pharaoh and 'ma'at' which was illustrated in the Pyramids, and continued to maintain that the Pharaoh was a god, but introduced a new idea; that it was possible for him to err, and to act other than rightly and justly. The Middle Empire restored the absolute power of the Pharaoh, based on grades of officials who gave the Egyptian state a governing class without aristocratic privileges, so that a new equality of subjects before the Ruler was created, and the only differences between men were those of office. However, the religion underwent profound changes after the introduction of the cult of Osiris, according to which human life followed a cycle of birth, death and rebirth, like everything else in nature. This meant that the Pharaoh was no longer uniquely immortal and divine amongst men, since the nature of all mankind was seen as sharing in the survival after death which gave men something in common with gods.

Perhaps it was because of this realisation, which lessened the difference between the Pharaoh and his subjects, and destroyed his claim to a nature in every way unlike and transcending theirs, that the Middle Empire crumbled in a period of foreign domination.

This period of insurrection was also one of religious reforms, in which the influence of Asiatic examples led Egyptian theology towards monotheism. According to this theory the Pharaoh was no longer a god, but simply the emissary and protégé of the one God. But the Pharaonic monarchy could not tolerate this position for long, and returned to the more ancient and traditional form of faith, in which the Pharaoh was one of the gods present among men. However, a tentative revolution had been achieved, a reform based on profound upheavals in the religious thought of the time, and these events left deep scars. Documents of the New Empire give written evidence of a closely reasoned doctrine of the relationship of the Pharaoh with the gods of the Upper and Lower Worlds: he had to answer for his deeds on earth, like common men, but was still a god, though of an inferior kind to the others, from whom his divinity derived.

Thus a thousand years of Egyptian history, down to the Persian conquest, show a deep contrast between the original principles of the Pharaoh's absolute divinity and his subjects' equality in submission to him, and the elaborate political and legal modifications of these basically religious ideas. Because of these very principles, which were implicit in 'ma'at', it became necessary to admit that whoever shared the ruler's power also shared his divinity, since without this the concept of the division of power was incomprehensible. So political conflict revolved round the central theme that the power which one man could have over another came from the gods alone. At the same time this conflict tended to diminish the gap between the Pharaoh and his subjects.

The path of political reform started from the separation of 'ma'at' from the ruler who had been its interpreter. Once men had admitted the existence of a justice to which the Pharaoh must submit after death and, as a consequence, that the Pharaoh did not have completely free will, and that what he willed was not necessarily just, the way was open to fundamental reforms in the concept of sovereignty. It was possible to concede that the Pharaoh could act unjustly, and also that the victim could find re-established beyond the tomb the justice which had been infringed in this world.

As long as theology held that the Pharaoh's word was Law itself, and determined all the laws of the world, then there was no need of a written legal code. But once justice and truth were seen as principles towering above even the Pharaoh, written laws became necessary, conforming to the supreme Law which the Pharaoh had to obey. There are historical traditions of the existence of written Codes, but we have no contemporary evidence.

A basic principle of Egyptian life was that the Pharaoh, being God, was the owner of everything that existed, and that no form of private ownership or personal right could take precedence over his. When the idea of 'ma'at' became separate from the ruler's divine person this situation no longer existed, and recognition of the rights of the individual began to be identified with the principle of 'ma'at'.

There is a dominant theme running through the three thousand years of political struggle which made up the historical experience of the great Egyptian nation, and which modified the course of history through the development of the states which came under Egyptian influence; this is the conflict surrounding the theological doctrine of the divinity of the ruler. The state of Egypt arose as a theocracy in the strictest meaning of the word; as a unified religious organisation in which every aspect of life was governed by the Law, and where the infallibility of the Ruler's will was the basis of faith. Thus it was inevitable that any political question should be treated solely in theological terms. The struggle over the divine nature of the ruler, and the struggle by those who indirectly shared his powers for recognition of their share in his divinity, were the elements which shaped Egyptian political evolution.

The Pharaoh's administration had its centre at the royal palace, the 'Great House', from which the whole life of the country was regulated. The ruler had religious, military and administrative duties, for all of which he needed assistants, as indispensable as the limbs of his body, and it was from among these that there grew up, inevitably, a dominant class of governors and administrators. In the early period it was a group of feudal nobles who performed this function, later it was religious, civil and military officials, but in either case a large group of men held a position in between the Pharaoh and his people, endowed with powers and therefore with privileges which they owed to their intermediary position. There were of course various grades and hierarchies in this privileged order, but in every case, though in a variety of ways, the source of all power and authority and financial reward was the king.

The privileged classes thus held their positions because the ruler's authority could only be expressed through the intervention of an elaborate network of officials; on the other hand the ruler was essential because from him alone did the officials derive the authority to carry out their duties. Without a ruler, Egypt fell literally into anarchy, since appointments, concessions, rights, duties all became meaningless and motiveless. In losing its sovereign, the structure of society lost its key-stone. This explains why the divinity of the sovereign as the foundation of the state lasted not only throughout the 3000 years of Egypt's independence, but remained intact during the Persian and Graeco-Macedonian conquests; not even the Romans could convert the Pharaonic-Ptolemaic system into their normal provincial administration.

The crises through which the Egyptian state passed were all determined by the existence of the Pharaonic monarchy. Rebellions by feudal or priestly aristocracies, extensions of power and independence by officials; these were not negations, but limitations of the royal authority. The greatest revolution of Egyptian history was the attempted substitution of the monotheistic cult of Atun for the polytheism of Amun. The Pharaoh was trying to free himself of the heaviest burden on his authority, the order of the priests of Amun. The king should have the right to appoint the chief priest, but he was elected in fact by methods which left little or no scope for the ruler's discretion, and the Pharaoh himself became the priests' puppet. With a religious reform and the introduction of monotheism, the monarchy too would have been on a reformed basis, more like those of Asia Minor in that the Ruler would no longer be a god, but the elect of the one God. However, the battle ended with the triumph of the high priest of Amun, and the monotheistic religious revolt failed.

So Egypt continued to be the land to which the ancient and modern worlds owe a characteristic, fundamental and unchanging solution of the problem of political organisation: that in which men are bound by religious faith to obey the laws, and to respect the authority which is the source of the laws and responsible for their enforcement. The identification of Ruler with deity, the recognition of a divine nature in the representative of political power, the character of an act of faith given to any of society's activities, the division of humanity not into compatriots and foreigners, but into believers and unbelievers, were all aspects of a solution of men's political problems to which they have often returned in the course of history.

Perhaps Egypt and Mesopotamia had a very early period of common history; certainly the two countries had close links and affinities, and there were times when their evolution seemed like two aspects of a common political development.

The structure of the state of Egypt was to some extent determined by the Nile, which not only irrigated the land, but united it and forced it to stay united, because the common source of wealth, if divided into hostile sectors, would become the source of common destruction.

Mesopotamia had no such well-defined form, and the basis

of its political organisation was more socio-economic than geographical; its centres were urban groupings, each with its commercial hinterland. The state was less defined, geographically less united than Egypt, and the tendency of the people to a monarchical form of government was simply expressed in the formation of local monarchies.

But even these had characteristics which lined them with the Egyptian theocracy. The king's power was derived from Heaven; not, however, because he was a god amongst men, but because he was the mediator between God and man. The Lord of the World was the great god venerated by the people of the region, while the king was his delegate, acting in his stead in the government of the faithful, exercising the functions both of high priest and of deputy for the god himself.

Thus there was a fundamental difference between the Egyptian and the Mesopotamian monarchies. The Pharaoh necessarily saw himself, potentially or in fact, as the universal king, for the man who did not acknowledge him as king did not acknowledge him as God; such a man was an infidel today, but tomorrow might be converted or compelled to change his mind for the sake of his present happiness and future salvation. The Mesopotamian king had a more limited power; the more or less restricted authority which the god allowed him. The God was, of course, the one true God and Lord of all men, in the eyes of his faithful, but the king could be delegated by him to rule over a mere village, although by the will of God he could also rise to govern the whole of mankind.

Since the authority of the Mesopotamian king was only delegated and not his own, his relations with the priestly caste were different, even if he himself were the high priest, from those of the Pharaoh with his priests. The Mesopotamian monarchy had to create its own defences by rooting its power firmly in the judicial origin of its authority, in all its cultural and religious aspects. The king was appointed by God, who manifested his choice in mysterious ways, and the king's power depended on general recognition of his legitimacy. His position was essentially a priestly one, in that the god had marked him with the seal of destiny as intermediary between God and man. Given the more limited and delegated nature of the authority allowed him by Mesopotamian tradition, clearly the king could not claim the particular characteristic of the Pharaoh at this phase, that of being the 'living law', the incarnate expression of the very principles of law, truth and justice. Perhaps it was precisely this Mesopotamian influence that led Egypt to admit the existence of an abstract and eternal idea of justice to which even the Pharaoh had to conform. In any case the Mesopotamian monarchy could not evade the obligation to give the people a guarantee that it would support the basic principles of the code of law that God desired man to follow, and which it was therefore man's duty to interpret and apply.

In Egypt, justice was an aspect of the divine nature; in Mesopotamia, it was a command from God, who could illumine man by inspiration. Legislation was an act of piety, since it consisted of assembling, arranging and writing down God's will, to bring it to the knowledge of all. The written laws that have come down to us from the Mesopotamians are pronouncements of God's will, and to enforce them was the religious duty which justified the king's power and position and underlined his sacerdotal character. So in Mesopotamia as well as Egypt, government was based on religious obedience, but the king could not speak as a god, only in the name of a god. Even the isolated cases where the king was attributed with divine qualities did not break the general rule: the religion might, in particular circumstances, include the adoption by a man of the attributes of divinity, but the man did not identify himself with the god by this means; he limited himself to representing him in order to contribute all the more to the glory of the god himself. This was one of the priestly aspects of the position of the king, who appeared before his subjects as the living pledge of the protection that God offered to the faithful, by giving them a leader who was his representative, and could ask and obtain his protection and generosity to the believers.

It is impossible to distinguish, in the Mesopotamian monarchy, the king's religious functions from his administrative and military ones. As in the case of the Pharaoh, his actions as king were a religious performance. As military leader he was simply executing God's will; it was God who directed the battle and fought it, using the king as the arm and weapon of an armed and warrior God. Victory thus assumed the nature of a confirmation of the divine will that the king should remain the leader of his people, and was therefore a factor which supported the legitimacy of the king's power.

As civil leader, the king governed, like the Pharaoh, from his palace, administering the land, which belonged to God, as if it were his own, or as if he were the agent of an absent landlord. As head of the legal system, the king administered justice in God's name. An aspect of his position as high priest was that he always appeared as the living image of God: in the local artistic tradition, for thousands of years, he was shown as taller than other men, with a characteristic stance, and symbols on his throne which marked him as the ruler, while around him the people, in armour or civil robes, were drawn up like an impersonal, uniform chorus, distinguished only by racial differences of dress or appearance. Under God, one man alone was clothed in all the dignity that linked mankind with the superhuman world: the king, the elect of the Gods, delegate of the supreme Lord of all men and all creation. Apart from the King, mankind was simply the mass, the crowd, the flock entrusted to a shepherd whom God had chosen.

However, the political situation of the successive monarchies of Mesopotamia differed fundamentally from that of the Kingdom of Upper and Lower Egypt. The Babylonian or Assyrian king was also forced to use assistants in carrying out his duties, and all our evidence suggests that the royal palace was the centre of a complex organisation of officials in a variety of grades and departments. The ruler's estates, and those of his relations, his household, the state and the temples, were each administered by different departments with their headquarters in the palace.

Although the king was also the religious leader, the temples had a financial and administrative autonomy rarely achieved in Egypt without a struggle. The fact that the king was only God's representative increased his dependence on the priests and lessened his authority over his subjects, while the nature of the country made the need for strong armed forces greater than it was in Egypt, and so made the king more dependent on the collaboration of the military sections of the administration, and more vulnerable to domination by them.

The geographical difference between Egypt and Mesopotamia had other effects as well. The navigability of part of the Nile, and the sea coast of other parts of the country, made communications easier in Egypt than in Mesopotamia. There, lack of access forced the central government to keep a less strict control over some parts of its territory; in many peripheral regions, around temples or powerful local landowners, minor kingdoms grew up with submission to the king and his administration dependent on the possibilities of his direct intervention in their affairs.

In the eras of the Sumerian and Accadian monarchies, the region made up of Mesopotamia and Babylon became increasingly centralised under a monarchy which aspired to universality. The title of the King of Accad, 'King of the Four Countries of the World', meant the same as his other title, 'King of the Universe'. The centre of political power passed from the populated area of southern Mesopotamia, Sumeria, to that of the central area, Accad, only to return in greater strength to the South with the supremacy of Babylon, in a period in which the Mesopotamian state came to maturity, producing written and systematically organised legal codes. At this time the Mesopotamian monarchy came to be shown in works of art in the way mentioned just now, a way which distinguished it from the Egyptian monarchs.

So the relationship of the king to the god led to a written code of law, which limited the king's power and allowed the subject certain precise and defined rights. The subject was no longer simply at the king's mercy, for the written law, which laid down both a duty and a guarantee, was the basis of a sort of contract between the two sides; the subject acknowledged and obeyed the king, but only within the limits defined by statutes which bound the king as well. Thus the Babylonian codification of the second millennium BC was a crucial point in the history of political ideas.

The decline of the Accadian kingdom had been accompanied by the growth of local autonomy in the outlying regions and in the cities, and the consolidation of the aristocracy in opposing central control of its religious, military and judicial powers. With the supremacy of Babylon, increasing centralisation was necessarily hostile to the privileged classes, and the codification of the laws was a declaration of war by the King, for in giving written laws the monarchy ranged itself against the priestly paternalism of the old system and against the local ruling clans of privileged aristocrats. By guaranteeing equality for all in the eyes of the law, and so giving a pledge that he would limit the scope of his own free will, the King gained the support of the new classes which, in liberating themselves from the oppression of local aristocrats, became the support and stay of the centralised monarchy. The local dynasties which succeeded in remaining in power were forced to accept the status of viceregal governors, and to adapt themselves to the same discipline as other officials – referring administrative matters to the King and receiving not just general directives, but precise instructions on specific cases.

In this bureaucratic system of public administration the King had to rely on the co-operation of a large governing class of priests, officials and army officers, who because of the essential importance for the survival of the state, finally became the new privileged class, and the support of the monarchy. However, the King was the source of their authority, the apex of the hierarchy, the supreme administrator and judge. The masses subservient to the new dominant class, the world of men excluded from the privileges of the few, turned to the King for bounty, justice and concessions, and saw in him and in his priestly authority an expression of the divine justice which would correct all the injustices in the world and all the inequalities between men.

The decline of the Babylonian monarchy, marked by great movements of population which the state could neither prevent nor control, was followed by the Hittite domination of Asia Minor. This was, as far as we know, the first large-scale political contact of the Mediterranean world with the Indo-European aristocracy which had come from East of the Bosphorus to dominate the Hittites. Experts in the breeding of horses and in their use in war, this warrior aristocracy conquered Asia Minor and Mesopotamia and attacked Egypt, finally sharing with the Phoenicians the command of the eastern Mediterranean. The religious and legal position of their monarchy was another new and important political experience for the pre-classical world. There was still no distinction between religious and civil law, the gods intervened in human affairs, the King was their protégé and took his authority from them; but the gods did not speak through the mouth of the King, or inspire him directly or any particular way. They had to be consulted by priests and interpreters of what were considered to be signs from heaven.

The King was the chief of the lords of the kingdom; he was the favourite of the gods who were the only lords of mankind, but he governed with the help of an assembly of aristocrats, from whom he tried to distinguish himself by emphasising his relationship with the gods and imitating the characteristics of the old Asiatic and Egyptian monarchs. But the Hittite rulers managed only to establish a position of friendship and familiarity with the gods; their divinity was recognised only in apotheosis after death, and even the succession to the throne had to have the approval of the aristocratic assembly. Although the subject peoples of the area had for centuries been used to a theocratic monarchy with its insistence on centralisation for unity and defence, it was clear that the Hittite monarchy could not avoid giving a controlling position in the empire to the leaders of the warrior class which had created it.

The reason for this situation is understandable: the Indo-Europeans who conquered Asia Minor and Mesopotamia were a small warrior caste who owed their success to their military superiority as horsemen in a world which knew only infantry fighting. The Hittite King was the leader of this armed aristocracy, but he could not hope to keep himself in power without their support. They lived as lords in a foreign land, whose costume, alphabet, and official language they had been forced to adopt. Thus the King was the instrument of the class which he led but which limited his power, and he could not attempt to oust the aristocracy and to found his power on the local subject peoples, since from their point of view he was simply a foreigner and an oppressor.

So the Hittite priest was a leader, representative and high priest, but true sovereignty was in the hands of the assembly, which could delegate its powers to the feudal lords who governed the outlying regions, conducted negotiations with the temple authorities, and promulgated laws, inspired by the traditional law of the subject society, whose structure was still Babylonian. The King acted as head of the priesthood and of the army; he performed the necessary religious rites, and was expected to foresee and placate divine wrath and to lead the armies to victory. The empire was made up of a network of pacts of alliance, protection and vassalage. The directly dependent races were more vassals and tribute-payers than truly subjects in common, the state really consisted of the ruling nucleus of warrior overlords, inherently foreign to the land they had conquered. The significant feature of this system was that although the Hittite state had a religious base and official gods from whom it derived protection and authority, obedience to the law was not an article of faith. The legal code was the work of man, even if divinely inspired; to break the law was not sin, sacrilege or heresy, and so even the scale of punishments was quite different from that imposed where crime was defiance of God's will.

The Hittite oligarchy could not escape the penetrating influence of the higher standard of civilisation enjoyed by the people they had subjugated. The achievements of the earlier Mesopotamian civilisations could not be ignored; family relationships did not change, the institutions of the law and of commerce remained intact, the use of money and of official price controls continued. However, the Hittites introduced a great industrial and military innovation: the working of iron.

The ancient Mesopotamian deities seem to have had much in common with those of Indo-European origin, and the fusion, under the Hittite empire, of many of the numerous gods of both conquering and conquered races may reflect a superficial unification of the civilised subjects and their more primitive overlords, their superiors only in the arts of war. Perhaps this unification might have been consolidated by a political revolution which abolished the aristocracy's privileges, raising the King to the position of a deity, and so making him King of the whole population. But the revolutionary process was blocked by the Hittite nobles, who fought against centralisation in any form, to preserve their own status, thus weakening the state by preventing its growth into a strong theocratic military organisation. The rise of Assyrian power in Mesopotamia at this time, the Phrygian invasions of Asia Minor, and other tribal migrations, led to the fall of the Hittite monarchy before it could transform itself into something more in tune with the political and religious needs and traditions of the civilisation it had conquered.

While Asia Minor lost its unity under the attack of tribes from beyond the Bosphorus, the Assyrian monarchy resumed its expansion in Mesopotamia, where it had until this time been a sometimes hostile neighbour to the Hittite kingdom. In the years that followed the Hittite collapse, the Assyrians progressively increased their influence to the Mediterranean coast and to Egypt.

The Assyrian King, the leader of a warrior race which ruled by force until it was conquered itself, was incapable of inventing an elaborate political system different from the one he found already functioning, and which did not conflict with the essentially military nature of his position. He too relied on the system of strong centralisation that had been characteristic of Mesopotamia before him. He was the delegate of the great god Assur; he represented him before the people and was the intermediary between God and his subjects. Having thus created a stable monarchical tradition in the Mesopotamian style, the Assyrian kings made themselves repositories and preservers of the Babylonian traditions, founding in Nineveh a library in which all the official acts of state were to be preserved; and not only those of the Assyrian kingdom, but also the old Babylonian decrees, of which they had new copies transcribed: a detail which reveals their anxiety to secure continuity of the Mesopotamian tradition. This is also clear from their style of architecture and art, and from their administrative system. As a warrior race the Assyrians applied with great severity the discipline of war, and created an autocratic type of administration, financed by tributes extorted from the subject races and by the spoils of victory.

Thus the Assyrian kings endorsed the most customary system of state organisation in Mesopotamia, evolved through thousands of years of monarchy: a system in which the King's legitimacy was based on divine choice and protection, and in which the King's power was made real to the people by a religious, military and civil bureaucracy, based on the palace and deriving its authority from the King.

In the region of Babylon, the seat of the monarchy on which the Assyrian kings modelled themselves, rebellion against the new rulers was fomented by the Chaldeans, who with the aid of the Medes of the Iranian plateaux succeeded in supplanting the Assyrians in Babylon. Meanwhile the Medes extended their influence in the North, and the Lydians in the West, occupying most of Asia Minor. Of these three powerful and prosperous monarchies the Lydian, which is the best known to us, had a strongly centralised administration on Mesopotamian lines. Greek tradition, which describes the Lydian kings as cruel tyrants, gives a picture of their struggle to impose their royal authority on the feudal lords. The significance of this struggle clearly escaped the Greeks, while the affinity of their political traditions with those of the Hittites or Phrygians, who had held Asia Minor before the Lydians, set their sympathies on the side of the nobles in the conflict, for they saw neither the need for an absolute monarchy nor the basis of its claim to legitimacy.

This lack of understanding became more serious as contact between Lydia and the Greek world increased, and the Lydian King, by the use of Greek artists, soldiers and labourers, opened the way to an exchange of ideas and influences. Lydia was certainly the first bridge for communication between the lands west of the Aegean and the great civilisations that had grown up in the eastern Mediterranean, in Asia and Egypt. One of the first results of this contact was economic and social; the Lydian monarchy allowed its administrative and trading classes a high standard of living, and through their example the living standard in the Greek states also began to rise, especially in the Hellenic territories on the Aegean coast of

Asia Minor, which shared directly in the benefits of a powerful and pacific monarchy of the Asiatic type.

The peaceful co-existence of Lydia, the Medes and the Chaldeans in Mesopotamia, and the benefits which as a result spread to their neighbours, among whom were the Greeks, all came to an end with a great new invasion from the Iranian plateaux, when the Persians bore down on these lands with irresistible violence, crushing all opposition with the dynamism of a people driven on by the impulse of a new religious faith. The Persian conquest began with the kingdom of the Medes, followed by Lydia and the Greek cities of the Aegean coast. With the conquest of all the lands between the Caspian Sea and the Persian Gulf, they re-created their own form of the ancient unified monarchy in Babylon, adding to it Egypt and Cyrenaica, and so building an empire broader than had ever before been achieved.

At the head of the Persian aristocracy was a king who derived his authority from his race's god, Ahura Mazda. But the 'Great King, the King of Kings' rarely claimed divine origin, but laid emphasis on being of Aryan stock; of the peoples of the Iranian plateaux. By pressing this ethnic derivation as its title to nobility, the Persian monarchy showed affinities with other races akin to its own which had ruled this area in earlier times: the Persians too had a warrior class which supported the monarchy and made victory possible, and its importance and influence in the state were sufficient for the King to wish to be identified with it. The power of the state had been the creation of the warrior class, and membership of that class was in itself evidence of the King's legitimacy. As for the other factor, divine approval, the Persians were a nation of horsemen, and the warrior chosen to rule them was the one whose horse, the sacred animal, the key to Persian power, more precious than man himself, was the first to salute with his neigh of joy the rising sun. This was the sign of God's choice, and it was the choice which justified the sovereignty.

Like the Hittites, the Persians ruled their empire with a compromise between the Aryan aristocratic traditions and the theocratic ideas of the Orient. Among the Indo-European tribes, a king was often leader of the cavalry, but the Oriental peoples would have seen in a king without divine origins simply an arbitrary oppressor. So a conflict arose – and it was not merely ideological – between the aristocratic concept of a nucleus of conquerors who installed themselves by force as governors of an empire, and the idea of a theocratic, universal monarchy, a gift from the one, true God for the guidance and benefit of humanity. The two opposite poles in the conflict were Pharaonic Egypt and the Thrace of the horse-breeding warriors.

The constitutional and political position of the Persian sovereign is an enigma to those who do not see the double nature of his situation, which was a conspicuous example of the meeting and collaboration of two civilisations at different stages of development.

The Persian King could not be simply a solemn, immutable symbol of sovereignty, inhuman, superhuman. The fact that he was one of the aristocracy himself meant that he had to be the paragon of military skill and courage, of physical perfection, humanity and friendship to the class of warriors who claimed to be, in a certain sense, his peers. On the other hand, as the incarnation of sovereign majesty, the fount of power and authority, the King had to be hedged in with the strictest protocol, to protect him from the approach of anything irreverent or degrading; while his need to protect his own rights made him inflexible against any attempt to question his authority. Thus two contrasting images of him were formed: that of the lovable leader, outstanding for his mental and physical excellence, and that of the hated tyrant, devoted to preserving his own power and position by means of absurd and unfounded superstitions. In his life and actions the two elements existed side by side, and sometimes came into conflict.

In the administration of the state, the King alone was the source of legitimate power, and every command and law had to proceed from the King himself. As in other states with a similar organisation, the King was the apex of a hierarchy of officials, but in this case he was assisted in his dealings with them by their leader, the minister, known to the Greeks as the 'chiliarches'.

In relations between the provinces and the capital, a more adequate network of roads than existed would have been essential to any sophisticated state organisation. The administration had to rely on a system of centralised control as the only way of preventing the disintegration of the empire. To a policy of direction from the centre the Persians added, as their precursors had done, a system of inspections and checks on provincial efficiency. Centralisation was increased by the adoption of Aramaic as the official language; the development of a single language for administrative purposes gave a privileged position to those who spoke it compared with those who spoke only Persian, or one of the many other racial languages of the empire.

These policies were far from being in the interests of the aristocratic class. The life of the state now depended on an official body of men who had nothing at all in common with the Persian warrior lords; neither language, nor traditions, nor ideals. The official class found itself in ceaseless conflict with the privileged Persian aristocrats who were, however, gradually being absorbed into official positions in the state. The most effective solution of the problem was the creation of the 'Satraps', thirty or so governors of regions within the imperial territories. The relative autonomy and almost regal position permitted to the Satraps by the King created a danger of their making a bid for independence and autonomy, but this risk was compensated for by the increasing fusion of former war-lords and bureaucrats, which led to the bridging of a political schism which could seriously have compromised the unity of the state.

The King tried to counter the centrifugal tendencies of the Satraps by giving them neither command of the local garrisons, nor control of their own chancelries, which depended directly on the 'chiliarches' and so on the royal court. But the centrifugal tendency was a direct consequence of the geographic and racial formation of the empire, and all earlier regimes had found themselves in the same situation: the cohesion or disintegration of the state was always dependent on the authority and influence of the central power.

The Persian kingdom still revealed in its organisation the particular characteristics of its origin: in the reliefs at Persepolis one can see long processions of bearers of tribute and ranks of armed men; these together were the main source of the King's power. The tribute-bearers are distinguished by their different costumes and accoutrements, which reveal their nationalities. They are the representatives of each of the Satraps, who were all bound to pay tribute to the King. Two races alone were not tributaries; the Persians and the Medes, but they were bound to provide special military contingents for the army. This was the salient characteristic of the Persian state, that it preserved the nature of an empire conquered by two races with the aid of their gods and the guidance of their kings. These two races were the subject of the King, but the dominators of the conquered peoples.

The Satraps' tribute, in precious metals and in kind, especially horses, provided the state with the finances necessary for survival, both in the central administration and in the satrapies. On the other hand the privileged races which had provided the forces for conquest of the empire could not – and perhaps did not wish to – sustain the whole weight of the defence of the state. So the King had to impose military and naval levies on the subject peoples as well, forcing them to take up arms for the defence and extension of a state which kept them in servitude.

As in all parts of the ancient world, the condition of the populations bound by military obligations to the state had a considerable influence on its political situation. Ancient society, especially in the eastern Mediterranean, was dependent on the efficiency of its armed forces to prevent invasions, to safeguard the liberty and labours of the individual, and to guarantee the very existence of the state. The state was relieved of the problem of the social value of the various trades and professions by the use of slave labour and the absence of large-scale industries producing goods which required transport. The socially important ranks in a state like the Persian were those of the officials of every grade, the priests and

Satraps, the chiliarch and the scribes, and the army; for the state could only survive so long as it had a religion to safeguard the legitimacy of its authority, ranks of officials to secure its continued functioning and an armed force which would enable it to defend itself, both internally and externally, and to extend its dominion. Only these three groups had real importance for the life of the state, and only they could have much influence on the state's direction and policy, interpreted by the Ruler.

The fundamental contradiction in the structure of the Persian state was the fact that the social importance of some groups in the state did not correspond with the real value of the services they rendered to society. The cavalry, the archers and the Iranian royal guard certainly provided the first and most powerful onslaught of an attack on the enemy; these detachments were provided by the Medes and the Persians, and were sufficient to furnish the main strength of a perfectly efficient army, willing to face any other armed force of the Mediterranean world. However, the King had to demand military contingents from races for whom the preservation of the Persian empire could not compare in importance with the value of the demands made on them, while the Persian and Median contingents, who made an important but not an exclusive contribution to the preservation of the state, gave to those races a position of absolute privilege. This disparity of treatment was one of the great injustices which made it necessary for the state to use force, or the threat of force, to impose the rule of law.

This situation limited the King's power, for it obliged him to keep a proportion of his troops in arms to prevent risings and to impose his authority. In fact, the non-Persian troops were not necessary simply for real war, in which the first ranks of the army were provided by the Median and Persian contingents, but the solid basis of the army, the supporting forces and non-combatants, could only be furnished by the subject races. Frequently revolts in several areas of the empire, especially in Babylonia where a long tradition of autonomy still left its traces, was one of the aspects of a situation which became still more serious when the King had to undertake campaigns which demanded the use of naval forces.

After the conquest of Egypt, it was only because of the Phoenicians that Carthage escaped Persian domination, and the Universal Monarch's dream was frustrated by the survival of a great commercial and maritime power. For it was the Phoenicians who provided the Persian King with the fleets that he lacked, and they refused to help him in an expedition against the greatest of their own race's colonies. During the Scythian expedition the Ionian cities began to realise their importance as the providers of the Persian empire's naval power, and it was a few years after this that the rebellion began which was to lead to the Graeco-Persian wars. As these two episodes showed, the functioning of the entire Persian empire could be threatened by injustices imposed by its origins and structure, and the difficulties increased in proportion to the political and military importance of the levies made on the subject races.

When the Greeks spoke of the Persian armies as slaves driven on like flocks of sheep in terror of the King's torturers, they may have been clothing reality in poetic exaggeration and polemic, but they were right in general about a situation which they were in a better position to judge than even the subject races. The value of the levies on individuals or towns was not given its due recognition by the state. This reduced the status of the men who composed the levies to that of slaves, not entitled to any reward for their services.

Because of its peculiar construction, the Persian empire preserved the character of a conquest by a minority, held together only by the implicit threat of force, and neither could nor would change into a unified state like the Egyptian. Egypt was held together by a common religion and obedience to the super-human royal power. Before the Pharaoh there were no privileges – at least in theory – since before God all men were equal, and when privileges were introduced and gradually became more noticeable, they brought with them conflict, disorganisation and rebellion. But the King of Persia could not put his people on an equal footing without compromising his own position – which he did in any case by the conspicuous lack of justice in his legal code.

The distinction which the Persian King made, with no justification but the wishes of the military nobility, between the Medes and Persians and the rest of the population, was perceptible even in the features of his policies which have been the most widely praised, though perhaps the least understood. The comparative freedom of the subject races to organise their religious, commercial and private lives was not, as is often believed, the result of an enlightened tolerance, but sprang from the belief that the Medes and Persians were the only important and active part of the political community, its subjects by right, while the rest were merely passive members. The apparent tolerance they enjoyed was the favourable aspect of an inferior condition, for the King was unconcerned that the races which did not of right share in the community of his true subjects had a religion and way of life different from theirs. This discrimination between 'the people' and 'the population' arose from the position of the Medes and Persians as an occupying force ruling the country and making a barrier between the King and his new subjects, but from the moment when the state first made use of the armies and navies of the subject races it no longer had any justification. The fact that the military contingents demanded of the Medes and Persians were of higher calibre than those of the other races did not justify their privileged position, which not only invalidated the King's claim to administer justice to all, but could by now only have a hereditary explanation, indefensible now that the empire needed the efforts of all its subjects to keep it united and safe.

The Persians amazed the ancient world by their conquests. They were a nation of warriors, with a new strategy based on speed of attack with cavalry and light infantry, inspired by their faith in their divine vocation to fight for the triumph of the power of good over that of evil, sure that they would win and bring the laws of Ahura Mazda to the whole world, stupefying it with the speed with which they crumpled monarchies that had seemed as solid as rocks. In a few years the Lydian state, envied and admired by the Greeks, had vanished, and so had those of Babylon and Egypt, after thousands of years of ascendancy. The Persian boundaries reached to places never visited by Assyrian or Egyptian warriors.

Once the empire was established, Persia continued to inspire amazement and awe by her wealth and stability. The causes of weakness in the Achaemenid monarchy were, at least in part, the same as those which led to the downfall of Lydia and threatened the Hittite kingdom, but they escaped the observation and analysis of contemporaries. In particular it suffered from the existence of a chosen class with unjustifiable privileges, the need to delegate power in the provinces and the lack of internal communications leading to a diffident organisation overloaded with controls. In Persia, other elements aggravated the situation; above all, the lack of the navies she needed to control her extensive coastline and her trade abroad. On the other hand the King, surrounded and almost besieged by the ranks of Medes and Persians whom he was forced to appoint to positions of power in his administration, had control of at least one of the elements of power he needed: money.

The descendant of the conquering heroes who had led to victory the finest cavalry and the best archers of the ancient world, proclaiming the triumph of good and of the will of God, having reached the heights of power was without the power to choose what means he would use to secure his position, but had to rely on being the richest man in the world. So the Persian kings treasured up their gold in thousands of tons, making its distribution in their realms deliberately scarce, so that places where the awe of their majesty did not extend could be reached by the corrupting power of gold.

The experience of the eastern Mediterranean was full of lessons for the Greeks and Romans of the classical world, who saw in Egypt, in Asia Minor and Mesopotamia, formidable and dreaded powers. In the Levant two political experiences had confronted one another and mingled: that of the state in which sovereignty was the law of God, and whose leader was a god or his protégé, and that of the state where an aristocracy settled among a conquered race and governed it by right of conquest. These two concepts met and co-existed in a compromise, in the case of Persia, but a fusion of two such contradictory systems was impossible, and the compromise suffered from the defects and inconsistencies of both.

The fundamental difference between the two systems lay in their origins and inspiration. The divine monarchy of the Pharaohs represented an absolute standard of justice, the complete equality of all men before a king who was God and so not only lord but father of all his subjects. In practice, the King had to rely on three groups of assistants, priests, soldiers and bureaucrats, who became an indispensable and therefore dominant class with all the privileges inherent in a position of such significance in the social structure. The theoretical system of absolute equality could not resist indefinitely the pressure of reality, and when the privileges of a dominant class outlasted the reasons for their predominance, injustice and disorganisation led to civil war and revolution. This happened several times in Egyptian history, and the 'renaissances' which followed phases of her evolution clearly represented crises in the reorganisation of political relationships and their adjustment to social reality.

In the kingdoms of Asia Minor and Mesopotamia, the situation could never have the theoretical clarity that it had in Egypt, nor was it ever possible to create a perfectly centralised administrative system like the Egyptian. But the most important feature of the Hittite or Persian type of monarchy was that the conflict between an aristocratic and a theocratic, monarchic theory of government made compromise not accidental, as in Egypt, but essential and inevitable, so that conflict, disharmony and injustice were permanent features of the political situation.

The power and example of the eastern Mediterranean countries had a lasting influence on the cities of the Greek peninsula, sometimes directly, sometimes as a result of particular situations in the world of Greece and the Aegean.

CHAPTER TWO

*

GREECE AND THE ORACLES

THE Greek peoples settled in the peninsula in remote times, and the influence on their already mature civilisation of the states of Lydia and Egypt was only one element in the first, splendid flowering of their social organisation there: the kingdom of Crete, which recently deciphered evidence has shown to have originated amongst a race whose language was akin to Greek.

The imposing relics of the Cretan civilisation have proved the existence of a state as old as the Egyptian Middle Empire, but with a different development, with an emphasis on naval activity and trade, as well as on agriculture and manufacturing processes. Excavations have revealed the traces of great palaces which were the residences of kings and rulers, centres of control and administration, and at the same time places for the collection and preservation of goods brought as tribute. As in many other parts of the Mediterranean and Mesopotamian world of that time there is evidence of widespread trade and exchange of ideas. The Cretan palaces show marked similarities to the royal palaces of other parts of Asia Minor, in which Mesopotamian and Hittite influences are more directly perceptible. The progress of archaeological work in Asia Minor, the great discoveries relating to the Hittites and others in those parts, even the new light that has recently been cast on the Mycenaean Greeks, all help us to understand Crete better.

As the fifth-century Greeks were aware, Crete was essentially a commercial and maritime civilisation. The various settlements discovered suggest that there were many different communities on the island, each with its own leader, but it seems likely that Cnossos was the seat of the supreme overlord. The Cretan documents written in Linear 'A' have not yet been deciphered; when this has been achieved we shall be in a better position to understand the origins of the Cretan civilisation and thus of the language itself. Until then we shall have to be content with thc most widely held theory, that the Minoan Cretans came from Asia Minor, and controlled some of the Aegean islands and coastline. Every Cretan centre shows evidence of wide distinctions between the richer and the poorer classes, above all between the ruling classes and the ruled. What little we understand of the linear 'A' tablets shows that they deal mainly with book-keeping – accounts of goods handed over as tribute and stored in the palaces. The ruling classes before 1500 BC lived in or around the palaces, and had quite a high standard of living, and some customs and practices of which we have no evidence in other parts of the world at that time.

Cretan religion was centred on a female deity, the 'Lady of the Beasts' (Potnia Theron), shown as a goddess standing between two rampant lions, and possibly also connected with an elaborate statuette of a woman in the act of grasping two snakes. We have evidence of rites of consecration and sacred symbols of sovereignty, horn-shaped objects and the sign of the two-headed axe, from which the name of labyrinth (from 'labyrs', axe) was given by the Greeks to the Cretan palace. Crete lived in peaceful prosperity on her sea trade which covered the whole Mediterranean area, and on industrial products of a high quality, and until about 1700 BC she was not seriously threatened by invaders. But in 1500 BC the island fell into Achaean hands, the palace of Cnossos was destroyed, and the paleo-Greek language disappeared from the eastern Mediterranean. The old chronology which recognises three Minoan periods of Cretan history is thus invalidated, in that the latest of the three refers to the Achaean period.

The brightest memory left to the Greeks of the Cretan naval empire, apart from recollections of the wealth she acquired from her widespread trade, was of her efficiency in policing the seas and repressing piracy. Even up to historical times, piracy was considered an inevitable consequence and necessary risk of sea travel, and the coastal cities lived on plunder. The 'right of plunder' was made the subject of negotiations and agreements which were based on a tacit acknowledgement of the existence of such a right. Only a country with supreme naval power could control piracy, but it could do it more effectively if it could provide other ways of earning a living.

At the head of the Cretan empire was the Minos, who ruled from Cnossos after establishing himself as the leader of the old tribal organisations and other local dynasties. The names and titles of the Minos, his priestly offices and divine attributes reveal the sacred character of the monarchy. Greek tradition, referring to the Minotaur, seems to imply an identification of the King with the bull-God, and we might infer from this a time when the Minos was believed to be an immanent god, like the Pharaoh. However, more precise and complete evidence than the confused Greek legends has made it clear that the bull-God was an anthropomorphic manifestation of a celestial being, the Zeus of the classical world, and the Minos was thought of as his chosen protégé, delegate and friend.

So it is clear that the Minoan monarchy had characteristics in common with those of Asia Minor and Mesopotamia, rather than with the Pharaonic system. This is made more clear by the fact that the King held his office not for life, but for nine years only, a term which could be renewed if the pact between the Minos and God were renewed in a complex form of mystical communication between them which took place on a mountain-top. This periodic investiture emphasised the subordinate position of the Cretan monarchy to the will of an aristocracy of priests and army officers.

As in Egypt and Asia, the palace was the vital element in the sovereign's position, not simply because he lived there, but because it was the instrument of his administrative system – private dwelling, council chamber, temple, government offices and law courts, admiralty and army headquarters. Thus the palace had become a very important factor in the daily life of the monarchy and equally in the theory of his position in the state: it was to the King what the sanctuary was to the god.

Of the characteristics that distinguished the Minos from the kings of Egypt, Mesopotamia and Asia Minor, the chief was the supreme importance of his judicial function over all the others, even over his priestly duties. Since the King was the elect of God, he was the manifestation of divine justice: in this the Cretan belief was similar to that of the Levantine monarchies. Law and justice consisted in the words spoken by the King, for the King could think and will only what was just. But the Cretans also held a belief quite different from the Oriental idea, and closer to what was to be found in Hittite and Lydian thought: that it should be possible to obtain direct expressions of God's will through the mediation of people qualified to do this. The Minos, by virtue of his appointment by God and his periodic investiture and mystic encounter with his Lord, was the qualified interpreter, the mouth through which God's justice was made known to man.

So clearly, legitimacy, in Crete, had a religious foundation in the sense that it was by God's will that the King held power, and man's duty was to obey the laws because they conformed with the will of God. But the monarch was always a man, and his position as the elect of God set him above other men without changing his nature. His inferiors in dignity and power received their authority from him, and with it part of his dignity: if the King wore three necklaces as a sign of his sovereignty, the commander of the armed forces wore one.

The power of Crete crumbled very soon after it reached its greatest splendour, because the Greeks who settled in the islands off the Aegean shores learnt navigation from the Cretans and added to this skill the vigour of their tactics in war. This was the Mycenean-Achaean civilisation, until recently known only through excavations, chiefly in the Peloponnese, while Homeric tradition, which had influenced the whole of classical Greek culture, was concentrated on a single episode: the Trojan wars. The deciphering of the Hittite cuneiform and of the ancient Greek linear 'B' tablets has shed much more light on the work of excavation which has so far been done. By comparing these discoveries with others made in various parts of Asia Minor, especially in Mari, Alalakh, Ugarit and Cyprus, a picture has been built up of a conquering power, extending its influence beyond Mycenae, beyond Tiryns and Pylos, even beyond the Aegean region. Certainly the Greek coast and islands were areas of Anatolian influence, or perhaps only Cretan, if the Cretans are proved to be of Asiatic origin. Greek place-names ending in *-nthos* and *-ssos* at least suggest Anatolian influence, and are common in Crete.

There is, moreover, the legend of Theseus to suggest that Attica was subject to Cretan impositions not later than the so-called middle Minoan period, that is before the fifteenth century BC. It was against these forces that a warrior race moved down into Greece; of Indo-European origin, it had political institutions, administration and methods of war not unlike those of the Hittites.

In centres of population they built palaces, unlike the Cretan in being fortified, so that perhaps they should be called castles, with elaborate monuments and tombs. Their political organisation was based on the populated centres, villages or cities, over which there ruled a local overlord, the 'Basileus', who held authority from the 'Anax' or supreme overlord, whose position was like that of Agamemnon in Homer: Lord of the heights of Mycenae. Land was distributed on a graded system of ownership depending on social class. At the top was the warrior class, who were the aristocrats, followed by the local administrators, then the priests, the foot-soldiers, and finally the manual workers. Economic and social life was strictly controlled, for the 'Anax' and the 'Basileus' had a monopoly of metals, and had also at their disposal great stocks of every sort of merchandise brought as tribute to the palace.

The Ruler's guests received gifts according to their rank, while anyone appointed to a public office had immediately to reimburse the Ruler with gifts representing what he expected to gain for himself from the right to collect tribute in his turn. The great majority of linear 'B' tablets so far deciphered are registers and accounts of such transactions, of the organisation of the stores and of economic controls. Raw materials were supplied to workmen who had to return a predetermined quantity of the finished product.

All the land belonged either to the King, the temples, or the nobles, or was common land, that is it belonged to the villages. Arms and chariots could be personal or royal property; the lists of warriors indicate which owned war-chariots, as other lists give inventories of armaments in the public arsenals.

The local dignitaries too, like the 'Basileus' of a village, could be 'honorary members' of the lists of warriors who fought from chariots. The Achaeans imitated the Cretans in the building of fleets; they drove Cretan influence out of the mainland and then, around 1450 BC, they occupied Crete. The Indo-European type of military order had its period of ascendancy; in about 1270 BC, after a long war, the Achaeans captured and destroyed Troy, and after twenty years occupied Cyprus, taking over the copper mines on the island. Groups of Achaeans settled in Asia; a few years after the fall of Cyprus, about the time when Hattusas, Ugarit and Alalakh were taken, the Achaeans for several decades practically dominated the Hittites, who officially considered them to be one of the 'great powers' of the ancient world, until in 1162 BC they were heavily defeated by the Pharaoh Rameses III. About twelve years later a new race, the Dorians, fell on the Peloponnese from the north, destroyed Mycenae, and superseded the Achaeans as rulers of the Greek peninsula.

Whereas the kings of Crete displayed their wealth and power in the security of their island, so that their palaces had no fortifications, and the emphasis was all on comfort, splendour and efficiency, the new rulers of Greece had to defend themselves, and so devoted all their effort and care to building secure dwellings, not palaces, but castles, not manors, but forts.

A race whose leaders had to think first of the defence of their lives and possessions could not develop the same kind of civilisation, customs, language or tastes as those of its predecessors, whose life was easy and prosperous, devoted in private to trade and sailing, in public to religious ceremonies and open-air spectacles. General public participation in any entertainment, a system by which the wealth of the powerful benefited even the poorest, created in the Cretan civilisation that vision of life which even now we can see in the colours of the murals and the details of arts and customs that have come down to us.

Crete was in a state of social evolution quite different from that of the Achaeans and Ionians at that time, and the new Greek invaders could only assimilate as much as their state of development allowed them. The wealth of gold in the Mycenaean tombs proves the quantities of booty taken by the city's warriors, but the fortress was built with an eye to solidity rather than decoration. The ceramic style they developed had nothing in common with the Cretan, although the occasional technical trick may have been picked up; taste was satisfied with geometric designs, and there were no buyers for the refinements of the Cretan decorative arts.

The civilisation of the new Greek invaders was founded on the pre-eminence of the warrior caste; their leaders wear their arms even in the grave. They lie enclosed in breastplates, shields as tall as themselves lie beside them, and of their life apart from war they have left only records of hunting, the fighting man's amusement in times of peace. In such a society, as in Persia, the leader's position above the rest depended on his superiority in war, and religion itself could only mark a military leader as one whom the gods considered their friend and worthy of their aid.

The success of the Greek immigrants was the success of a military structure confronting a people grown unaccustomed to war. But the collapse of Crete had other causes: the Cretan navy had eliminated piracy from the whole of the Mediterranean, and all her energies were inevitably concentrated on increasing her trade. It was pointless to train recruits for naval warfare when the very possibility of piracy had been excluded. The Cretans found themselves unprepared for an encounter with a warrior race capable of assimilating the first lesson of the Minoan civilisation – the art of shipbuilding and the technique of navigation.

This unexpected new sea power took the Aegean world by storm. Fighting like pirates, the sailor-warriors brought about the collapse of a state born from the destruction of piracy, but once they were victorious, the sea under their control and the initiative theirs, they found themselves incapable of succeeding to the Cretan empire. The first result was that the conquerors became nothing more than pirates: their castles and fortifications show that in destroying the Cretan empire they had removed the security of even their own homes and lives.

Soon, however, conditions began to improve. The obvious pre-eminence of their armed and naval forces in the Mediterranean encouraged the new Greeks to travel again the routes used by the Cretan ships, to revisit the ports and commercial bases and to try to reforge the links of trade: on the frail foundation of the Minos' ruined empire the Greeks were building their civilisation. As soldiers and conquerors, even in their architecture and arts, they looked to the Oriental monarchs, with their taste for the monumental – great walls of stone covered in bas-relief, the heraldic lion as the symbol of sovereignty – rather than to the peaceful nation they had conquered.

The Achaeans created an empire of small communities, like Mycenae, and did not initiate any more complex political development. The effort of conquest, the defence of new territories, and the transformation from semi-nomads into pirates and navigators, took all their energies and made it essential for power to be in the hands of the arms-bearers, indispensable to victory on land or sea. Only the belief that they needed the aid of the gods to gain victory linked the political life of a society like the Mycenaean with religion: the warrior-king of the Mycenaean era based his claim to power on his might and success as a fighter. He ruled not because the gods wanted him as their delegate, high priest and supreme judge, speaking with divinely inspired truth and justice, but because he was the most valiant and successful of the warriors, whom the gods assisted by allowing him the military supremacy which was the origin of his power.

This, then, was a world of ethical, political and religious concepts quite different from those of Babylon and Assyria, and although the same fundamental characteristics had existed in the Hittite and Persian monarchies, the pressure of tradition and the influence of the Asiatic environment had led these to lose their original Indo-European characters, and to assume a fideistic and theocratic form.

As far as we can judge from archaeology and poetic tradition, the Mycenaean-Homeric state was limited to the supremacy of a group of warriors over a society already organised on other lines. The tradition that Attica and other parts of Greece paid tribute to the Minos suggests that there was a period of history in which the peninsula was subject to Minoan domination: the Mycenaean castles and royal tombs, the new manifestations of taste and civilisation, like the use of images from war and hunting for decoration, show the influence of the conquering warriors over the lands that had been in the Minoan orbit. Instead of being a tributary of the protective power of Crete, Greece had to toil to secure the wealth and well-being of groups of armed men who settled on the land, fortifying themselves in castles and enjoying the spoils of war, the tribute of subjects and the produce of hunting.

In the society organised by the Achaean conquerors there was a dominant group, the active element with full political rights, and a dominated group of those who had hitherto paid tribute to Minoan Crete, excluded from active participation in the state. The fall of Crete, in whose empire naval and commercial activities had been the most important, the return of piracy, the lack of security and the end of political unity all put the towns and villages of Greece at the mercy of the army, which defended and at the same time subjugated them. The political struggle developed into the story of the relations between these various fortified centres, each with its own king and commander. Whatever went on outside the world of soldiers and fighting was politically irrelevant and had little effect on the life of the community. The ordinary people continued to live in the world bequeathed to them by Crete, clinging to such religious beliefs as the divinity of the creative power of nature, venerated in the cult of the Minoan and Mediterranean mother-goddess, the Great Mother or Potnia.

The cult of physical perfection was, however, something new, arising from the ideals and aims of the military Mycenaean state. The Homeric poems reflect the life of the Achaean overlords of that time: the mighty warrior caste, now securely dominant, aspiring to a nobler state, struggling to secure for itself the position that had belonged to the Minoan monarchy. The Achaeans too now had a naval force, the instrument of expansion. The social organisation was semi-feudal; the army was made up of contingents from the cities and islands, each with its own leader, the local king. The whole was then under the command of the supreme King, who was the strongest of all, and so rather the 'leader of Kings' than the 'King of Kings.' This loose monarchic unity suited the structure of a complex society which felt the need of a common direction, to co-ordinate its efforts and discipline its internal relations.

We lack the information we need to get more than a glimpse of the evolution of Achaean and Mycenaean Greece. After the transformation of society under the warrior bands, the high standard of living achieved under Cretan control encouraged the Greeks to make a fresh attempt to follow the same paths. Once again they crossed the ocean and cast their eyes on the Asiatic coast of Egypt. To succeed in these projects they had to unite their efforts, and so the search for unity was born.

The legitimacy of the 'leader of Kings' had the same foundation as that of the local kings. Divine favour, assumed by the local kings and therefore by their chief, gave the Ruler not simply military command, but also the other essential priestly and judicial prerogatives of the ancient King. As interpreter of the divine will and mediator between God and man, the Myceneaen king too inherited characteristics of the Cretan, Asiatic and Mesopotamian monarchies: divine sanction was a privilege granted to a whole family and passed on by inheritance. But this approach to a theocratic type of monarchy was held in check by the military aristocracy, exercising control through the assembly of elders which collaborated with the King in every decision he made.

The Achaean form of unity of fighting groups was the factor that determined Greece's position in the eastern Mediterranean. The Trojan expedition, and the colonising journeys of the Homeric heroes who returned from Troy, remained afterwards in men's minds as a nostalgic memory of a happy and glorious time, and proof of what the Greeks could have done if they had succeeded in co-ordinating their forces and had not dissipated them in brawls and raids on one another. In the Mycenaean-Homeric period the Greeks gained complete control of the Aegean and a firm foothold on the Ionian coast, strengthened by the Trojan victory.

As a result of the prosperity brought by their succession to the Minoan naval empire, the population of Greece began to find the supremacy of the warrior groups intolerable. The Achaean king was the prisoner of his army, and could only put forward policies which cited their interests as well as his own; he could not reform or extend the basis of his position.

In the richer, more civilised communities with greater resources, the groups which were just rising in the social scale were quicker to supplant the military upper class, and at the same time caused the downfall of the Mycenaean-Homeric type of monarchy, whose decline was due to the almost total disappearance of the fleets and of trade between the cities of Greece.

The aristocratic caste in its decline preferred to live on its stores of booty, and came to lack adventurers and active soldiers, while the naval power of the Phoenicians and the Greeks of the Ionian colonies created such competition that the mainland Greeks could no longer hold the command of the sea. At the beginning of the historical era in Greece, navigation was considered an occupation far inferior to the life of a small-scale farmer.

The development of this new rural capitalism completely transformed a society of semi-nomadic fighters into a state ordered in the interests of the landowners, who became the sole, or most important, means of production of wealth for the community.

Following the social transformation, whose effectiveness varied from city to city, came a varied, but less rapid transformation of political life; centuries separated the evolution of power from the military to the landowning aristocracy in the different regions of Greece.

Whereas the old military aristocracy had enjoyed collecting gold and treasure, hunting, owning fine armour, the new landowning class left to others the job of looking after their lands, and preferred to live in the city, imitating the wealthy classes of Asia Minor in their passion for the arts and for the cultured life; at one time military success and the booty of war were a man's title to honour; now the new upper classes, with a different idea of human perfection, preferred athletic and intellectual prowess.

But the political situation remained in some ways unchanged. Military strategy still depended on the warriors in their chariots, cavalry and heavy-armed infantry. All demanded a great deal of capital, for armour and for buying and stabling the horses, and so only the rich could provide the army that the state needed. Victory was decided by warriors lumbering on to the field of battle, in a chariot or on horseback, weighed down with so much armour that they lost any power to manoeuvre, but were sure of being able to resist the shock of the enemy's attack without wavering, and to give blow for blow with plenty of weight behind them.

So their wealth gave the rich not merely control over essential products, but also the burden and privilege of military duty, the only way of safeguarding the community. Political and social power gradually came into the hands of those on whom the state depended for survival, and the closer the connection between the two, the more efficient was the state organisation.

If political relations reflected the economic importance of the new class wherever they had come to power, Greek life in the period after the Homeric-Mycenaean monarchy was not regulated by the distribution of wealth. Cities and populations obeyed laws and customs which did not correspond simply to this type of relationship, and men, singly or collectively, conformed (as they still do) to rules and principles into which there entered other things as well as force and social importance.

Above all veneration and fear of the gods was an active element in the whole life of the country. Not all the gods were common to all the Greeks, but the religion was in general the same for all, and into it had flowed, through thousands of years of change, elements of Mediterranean religion and mythology, inherited from the Minoan world, as well as elements introduced by the Indo-Europeans through their migrations. The feeling of religious community overcame the independent tendencies of the various cities. Added to this was the blood-tie, which created a community with a tribal leader, ancestors, religion, and which, for reasons inherent in the religion, imposed duties and social relationships which cut across economic barriers. His place in the tribe determined a man's rights and status, imposed obligations, created ties and bonds of solidarity according to religious custom.

So the laws of religion and consanguinity limited the social domination of the richest, and the political and military domination of the strongest. Public life remained based on the Indo-European principle of entrusting the government to the assembly of arms-bearers, and in transforming the military into the aristocratic government, leaving unchanged the powers of the council of elders. The arms-bearers believed, and wished it to be generally believed, that the gods had bestowed on them the right to supremacy. The landed aristocracy, however, had the authority to govern and make laws only when it was sure of a divine will guiding its decisions, and felt that the community was equally sure of the existence of divine laws to which its own legislation conformed.

This was the only justification of the privileges of the few. The masses saw the rich and aristocratic as superior human beings. The Greeks were used to the idea of heroes; human beings whose especial virtues made them closer to the gods than other men were, beings whose beauty, power, influence and cultivation made even their physical appearance different from that of other men. The aristocrats had curled and perfumed hair, elegantly trimmed beards, wore trinkets of gold, embroidered and quilted robes, armour which was more the work of the goldsmith than of the blacksmith. They lived in luxurious houses, competed in horse-races and athletic contests, accompanied their singing on musical instruments, and seemed to be so favoured by the gods that they need only concern themselves with being agreeable and living glorious and happy lives. The petty tradesman or farmer, who shivered with cold beneath a cloak that barely covered him, who lived on a few figs or olives and coarse bread, burdened with debts, without education or any of the comforts of life – how could he have failed to imagine that the aristocracy was a race nearer to the gods than to himself, a race which was divinely predestined to organise the state and everything in it to suit itself?

Thus religion became an instrument of power for the aristocrats, as it had been for the Homeric kings. But it also limited their power, for they were bound by it to observe the traditional principles of rights and obligations which could not be transgressed without arousing feelings of sacrilege.

Close contact with the land and greater stability of their way of life only emphasised the fact that the Greeks of this period were essentially townsmen. Already in the Mycenaean era the social structure was based on small units of men and land from which the warrior nobles drew their power and their wealth. The end of the Mycenaean era and the fall of the monarchies strengthened the centrifugal tendencies that had been held in check by the need for a single military command and the co-ordination of land and sea forces. As Greece developed an agricultural civilisation, the need for unity disappeared, while for many centuries she lacked even the external enemy who would have drawn the cities together to defend their independence.

Divine laws and ties of blood were strong enough to keep the Greeks from open war amongst themselves. The ruling aristocracies were bound by kinship, and the priestly orders were ruled by members of their class. The pan-Hellenic festivals were opportunities for meeting together, organising their affairs and settling their disagreements. To make sure that in decision of general importance the Greeks should be guided by the will of the gods to act according to the universal principles of right and justice, Greek society had its characteristic institution, the oracle.

In Egypt the manifestation of the will of God was the word of the Pharaoh-God; in Mesopotamia the word of the delegate of the gods. In the Indo-European world there was no such direct way of discovering God's will, and men had to use divination to understand the signs sent by God. Such practices were already known to the Hittites, and by various paths had reached the Etruscans, especially in the form of the interpretation of signs from the heavens, from animals and plants, and from dreams, all of which had been practised in various forms by the Semitic races. Oracles, however, were 'non-technical', in the sense that they did not demand special skills for their interpretation, since they allowed the required answer to be received by direct inspiration, by a person with the gift of hearing it.

The oracle needed a minister, or at least someone to mediate between God and the questioner. In the theocratic monarchies, the king was himself a god who spoke the divine truth, and so was himself the oracle, or else was the equivalent of the minister who pronounced the words of God.

Politically, the minister of the oracle was the interpreter of the gods in their direction of the details of human daily life; only the complex and particular circumstances of Greek religious, social and political life, which left it poorly adapted to theocracy, prevented a government of priests based on the oracles.

Oracles were a constant feature of Greek life and religion, in common with other Indo-European races. A typical oracular institution was the one at Delphi, whose cult of Apollo had deep Dionysiac roots. The influence of the Asiatic Sun-God was felt in the Greek mysteries and oracles from the earliest times, and this determined the origin of the divinity of Dionysos, who was the Thracian and Greek manifestation of the Sun-God. The Dorians were not disposed to accept the Sun-Dionysos cult, because they, like other related peoples, were deeply devoted to the cult of the Sun-Apollo. So in the Delphic oracle the god who spoke to mankind was a Sun-god in whom the Phrygian-Thracian cult of Dionysos met the Achaean cult of Apollo and was overcome by it.

The Homeric poems do not attach much importance to oracles: more attention is paid to the interpreters of heavenly signs or individual dreams. This is understandable when there were still kings whose characters seemed nearer to the gods than to men, so that the divine will and the source of law was personified by the ruler.

With the fall of the monarchies and the military heroes

from the government, the landed aristocrats who succeeded them felt that they lacked legitimacy, since there was now no direct connection between the ruling class and the gods. On the other hand, the collapse of the monarchies was a loss to men accustomed to look to the king as their guide, so that for reasons both political and religious they found a way not to feel abandoned by the gods, or deprived of the means of learning their will.

While formal symbols of sovereignty still survived in order that their duties as priests should not be interrupted, oracles were arising in many places. Cities and states would consult them as much as individuals, wishing to know the gods' will in order to conform to it. The Delphic oracle stood out from the others because of its universal character, as the union of two concepts of the same Sun-God, so that it was better able than any other oracle to correspond to the religious ideals of all the Greeks as well as the races who shared their civilisation.

The oracle's functions were varied and complex. Its word was necessary to free a man or a whole people from religious impurity or any sort of sin which might bring misfortune and ruin on a city or a family. The oracle could raise a man to the status of a hero, sanction the founding of local cults, make pronouncements on any theological or religious question. But where it had a really political function, as the origin of constitutions and legal codes, was in sanctioning and directing the foundation of colonies, thus giving each colony the religious character which bound it to its parent-city. The oracle censored the choice of site, and all colonies had to offer to the God of Delphi the 'golden summer': a periodic tithe, in gold, of the value of their crops. Apollo bore the titles 'the Pythian' (the God of the oracle); 'the Archegetes' (the guide or leader); and 'the Decatephoros' (the one who holds the tithe). These three attributes: of giving man knowledge of the divine will, of guidance, and of taking the tithe of the harvest, are attributes of a divine ruler as legislator, commander and king.

In the colonies especially, where there was no continuous line of political legitimacy, legislation was closely bound up with oracular utterances. An oracle consulted about all important political decisions obviously had in its own way a very dominant position in a state; in new countries, without traditions, precedents or customs, only the aura of oracular sanction could popularise the work of a legislator who was creating out of nothing the legal code of a community with which earlier custom often conflicted. In places which already had inhabitants, the oracles insisted on conformity with the traditional law of that land, and their approval was necessary for the founding of new cities by a colony, and other decisions of outstanding importance.

The supremacy of Delphi, due to the fact that Apollo, as the Sun-god, had allegiance of much of the non-Hellenic world, was so great that even the Kings of Lydia and Persia consulted its oracle. Dionysos might have precedence over the maternal Earth-gods of the Mediterranean world because of the prestige of the sun cult throughout the Eastern Mediterranean, but the persistence of the Achaean cult of Apollo forced the oriental Sun-god to take a subordinate place in matters of art, learning, mystery and oracular utterances.

The large number of oracles is evidence of the gravity of the crisis which the fall of the monarchies had caused in the Greek world. Solidarity between the kings and the assemblies of warriors had created what little unity there was in the Homeric monarchies: the existence of the 'Warrior King' who at least provided a unified command in times of war. In the period after the fall of the kings, the differences between city and city in Greece were more conspicuous.

As well as venerating the Sun-Gods of diverse origins, Dionysos and Apollo, the Greeks worshipped celestial gods, like Zeus, Earth-Gods, like Athene and Demeter, of Asiatic and Mediterranean origins, and as a result of the country's military and political history, the Nordic deity of the warrior's greatest asset, the horse, which became associated with the Sea-God, since the Aegean Greeks felt that the sea, even more than the horse, was the source of power. This multiplicity of cults, some pan-Hellenic and some local, is evidence of the rifts between various parts of the Greek world, the pan-Hellenic cults being the only elements holding the state together. Even in Hesiod's poems the gods are the custodians of the great moral principles, some of which, like Diké, became the deified abstractions with which men filled the gap left by the fall of the monarchies, in their search for a secure justice, inspired by the divine source of conscience and morality.

Religion, apart from the oracles, provided the Greeks with other unifying elements. If the oracles were the basis of political legitimacy, over-riding the decisions and laws of man, the collective religious ceremonies were opportunities of strengthening the sense of cultural and racial unity. The Games, in which the athletic and intellectual gifts were exalted, have already been noted in Crete, and were a feature of an aristocratic society in which men had to glorify individual excellence to justify the gap between the privileged few and the masses. The theocratic monarchies did not encourage this sort of exhibition (where it was not a case of continuing earlier traditions) because their aim was to reduce all men to one level before a single superhuman ruler. But in the Greek world the aristocratic tradition had continued from the days of the warrior nobles, and the exaltation of the individual for physical excellence, athletic ability, beauty and intellectual superiority had always been a characteristic of its civilisation.

The Games were not only an occasion for periodic meetings of the inhabitants of various parts of Greece, to honour individual prowess. Their particular value lay in the selection not merely of the best of each city, but the best of the whole of Greece, emphasising the country's unity.

The honour that went to the victor's city of origin was purely secondary; it consisted only of an acknowledgement that one or more of the finest representatives of the Greek people was born in that city. The victors had to be free of any sin or religious impurity; only those who were pure, and therefore just, could enter the contests; afterwards the victorious ones met in the culminating and supreme moment of the whole ceremony, when they made a libation to the gods in the name of the Greek people. The victor's prize, which had no intrinsic value, was in fact a sacred symbol, a wreath.

The true significance of the days of contest lay in this moment: the selection of the best, most perfect, most god-like men to offer up a tribute or a sacrifice. Thus Hellenic unity was strengthened by the system of trials which selected and prepared men to perform the holy rite of bridging the distance between gods and men, men whose human perfection approached divinity and conquered the heights that set the gods above man. The political importance of the Games lay in this very feature, that they gave men the conviction that they had no need of kings or priests in order to be befriended and listened to by the gods. Greek political development was rooted in the two fundamental religious ideas of the Games: the unity of the Greeks in origin and religion, and the concept of aristocracy which held that there was 'something god-like' in certain men: the Games enabled this divine element to be recognised in anyone of Greek blood and birth.

The Olympic games were the oldest and the most illustrious. It is significant that the Greeks measured time according to the cycle of the Olympiads. The recurring event adopted as the measure of the passage of time must be something fundamental for man. The Olympiads could perform this function at a certain period in Greek history when the Greeks felt that from time to time they were set, before the face of the Peloponnesian Zeus, to the selection of the finest examples of their race, and to the most solemn consecration of their pact with God, the source of law and of political power.

The other Games had a local character, and did not become pan-Hellenic like the Olympics, but they survived because of the necessity to maintain bonds with the other gods as firm as those strengthened between Zeus and his people at the Olympics. It was the Delphic and Delian Games in honour of Apollo that confirmed the importance of intellectual qualities amongst the elements of individual excellence.

Of course within the pan-Hellenic unity the political and military pre-eminence of a city or a clan determined the relative importance of the divinity to whom the Games were offered, and so of the Games. This was the case with the Isthmian Games at Corinth, in honour of Poseidon, and with the Panathenaic Games at Athens in honour of the Goddess of the Acropolis. Each deity had its panegyrics, which were periodic meetings of devotees, and panegyrics might be introduced by contests to choose the people to take part in the rites of the cult. In the case of some cities and some gods, choice was based not on contests and races, but other criteria, such as virginity, birth into privileged families, even a man's date of birth. But the culminating event of the celebration, whether of local or pan-Hellenic panegyrics, was always the act of offering, by which the pact between gods and men was renewed; in Athens the Panathenaics were the occasion of the ritual offering of the people to their goddess.

All the rules governing participation in the games reveal the politically unifying quality of these festivals. The requirement that candidates should be of free birth and pure Greek descent sprang from the ancient aristocratic limitations on the right to full citizenship, and set the seal of divine approbation on the laws regulating the right to citizenship that each city made when forming its constitution. The law which protected from attack ships carrying participants in the pan-Hellenic Games, at a time when piracy was open and legitimate, was the source of all the laws governing maritime trade, repressing piracy and fixing legal procedures between city and city. A law such as this was of value to those who observed it – the Greek cities; but by the very existence of such a law the Greek community, as the community of the faithful, acquired the character of a political unit, a law-making organ.

Because the aristocratic system did not evolve at the same speed everywhere in Greece, traces of the different stages of development were visible even in historical times, in the Greek ethnic community. These traces are seen best not in the constitutions of cities, or in the distribution of government offices between various administrative and political bodies, but in the laws which the Greeks themselves considered to be the most significant and important of all; those governing the right to citizenship, which were the real limit to the political development of the state in Greece. Thus Sparta, where a few thousand descendants of the primitive conquerors made up the only group to enjoy full political rights and obligations, was the relic of a phase in the evolution of political life that went back to the early days of the Achaean conquest.

The Greek city, the Polis, did not have the equality now

attributed to it of a single, abstract, and uniform creation of Greek political life. Above all, the Polis required the survival of a force to regulate Greek life unilaterally, in spite of the fall of the Homeric-Mycenaean monarchies. This force was supplied by the oracles, which made laws and moral judgments based on a transcendent will, and gave an occasion for common religious ceremonies which reinforced the awareness of a racial unity. It is this that justifies the statement that the Hellenic 'state' was not the Polis, but a community with the character of a federal State with a religious basis, in which the Greeks preserved, less effectively, the unity of the Homeric-Mycenaean monarchy. The almost sacred importance of the Homeric poems in the history of Greek culture can be seen as one of the elements of this unity, and one of the factors in its survival.

On the other hand, the cities did not have the same territorial or legal characteristics, and their differences were the fundamental reason for the diminished effectiveness of the Greek community as a political force after the Mycenaean era. Some of the cities conflicted so violently with others on such subjects as citizenship, religion, economic system, and the position and interests of the ruling class that this in itself made local autonomy inevitable.

In the colonies, systems of government matured with greater freedom, and yet with greater difficulty, than on the mainland, precisely because of the absence of tradition. But the Greeks of the homeland had to deal with different circumstances and at the same time with conditions developed over long periods of time; old and new aristocracies, capitalism based on inherited wealth, traditional links between certain families and the Gods. Thus when the royal castle and warrior nobility of some cities had lost the importance to the state that justified their power, another ruling class was already at hand to take over the government of the state.

Even when we consider the Polis as an architectural unit, there is no definition which united them all. There might or might not be a wall; altars, temples and market places were not essential to the Polis as a political organisation, but exist in any human community of any importance. Harbours, canals, cross-roads were not inevitable – the Polis was not a Polis even by virtue of having an army or a fleet.

The Greek city, in fact, was simply the common home of a group of Greeks who were agreed to organise their own lives by laws which were not contradictory to the general principles of their religion, and so of the morality of the pattern of life that the religion imposed. All the rest was inessential; indeed the nature of this system of law, its extension beyond the frontiers of the local community, whether encouraged or merely accepted, all shows that the Polis was not a 'sovereign state' in our sense of the word, but more like a 'canton', autonomous within the political code of an ethnic community.

The causes of local differences between the various regions and cities of Greece lay mainly in changes occurring in the centuries between the fall of the Mycenaean monarchies and the time when our historical knowledge begins. This was a long interval, during which our only precise information is about the first movements of colonisation, which Greek tradition and local legend connect with the voyages of the Homeric heroes returning from the Trojan wars, and with the Argonauts.

The colonising movement probably sprang from the need to find new homes and livelihoods for peoples outgrowing the local resources. On the routes which had been well known and used for centuries, to the South of the Italian peninsula and in the North Aegean, on the Bosphoros, there were settlements cultivating the fertile land.

The founding of colonies wherever circumstances encouraged it had the result of opening up old markets for commerce and giving new impetus to trade. As the sea once again became important to the Greeks as a means of communication, so the geographical position of the various cities came to have a new significance. When the economic regression from trading to agriculture set in, men banded together to settle in places easily defensible from a hill or a castle, near to the best farming land; but when they once again took to navigation and trade, their chief interest was to find the best route between the interior and the sea, and to secure safe harbours.

This led to an increase in the political importance of ports;

they became the centres of attraction, the most powerful groups of the population settled there, and the ancient cities dwindled into tributaries to them. Only Sparta, in the Peloponnese, with her uniquely efficient military organisation, succeeded in creating for herself a broad territorial domain in Laconia, Messenia and the island of Cythaira. The development of Athens, however, owed nothing to her military power, but was simply the domination by the greater settlement, with convenient access to the sea, of the smaller agricultural settlements.

The sea and trade were the underlying features of a political development which led to the opening up of markets for the Greek industries, bases for re-stocking vessels, and control-points on trade routes, and which enabled the Greeks to come face to face with the Phoenicians and to challenge their position as the only controllers of the trade routes between the Aegean world and the East. After the Mycenaean period, the Greeks gradually recovered their skill in ship-building and navigation, taking advantage of the Ionian settlements on the coast of Asia Minor to improve their relations with Lydia and to secure, at Rhodes and Cyprus, re-stocking points on the route to Egypt, where they soon had their own base.

The demand for sea trading also arose because of the development of agriculture in Greece; increasing concentration of capital in the hands of a few landed families led to the downfall of the small-scale farmer, and so to increasing reserves of labour for industry, shipping and trade, and for agricultural labour.

In the Greek world, apart from the two communities clustered around Athens and Sparta (the first devoted to trade and sailing, the other tied to ancient concepts of civilisation), autonomous cities or cantons were developing along a wide variety of lines, each attempting to find its own solution to the problems of a communal existence.

An important group of cities in Myceanaean times, Nauplion, Tiryns and Mycenae, was drawn into the zone of influence of Argos, which was not on the sea, but sufficiently close to control a port and become the centre of an autonomous region which also included a part of Arcadia. Corinth used her position on the sea to increase her trade considerably, and the growth of her colonies in the Ionian Peninsula and Sicily put her in a very powerful, perhaps dominant, position in the competition for markets. As a great naval power, not conflicting with Sparta in her sphere of interest, unlike Argos, which was Sparta's rival in Peloponnesian politics, Corinth was Sparta's natural ally, without being in any way a dependent, and enjoyed a period of great commercial importance throughout the Mediterranean. Thanks to this alliance, and in spite of the rivalry of Argos, the Peloponnese flourished and prospered. The two cities had different, but not hostile systems of government; in Corinth the monarchy was followed by an aristocratic oligarchy of a single clan which had economic and social supremacy, and then by popular demagogues who were the champions of the mass of the population, risen to a greater importance with the growth of Corinth's trade and industry.

Thus the Peloponnese was divided into three zones of influence; in the rest of Greece, apart from Attica, Boeotia was sub-divided into the territories of various cities, each fully autonomous, Aetolia was still a primitive region without pressures to unite it; most of the other regions of Greece posed no political problems, for the self-sufficient structure of the local city-communities was all that was needed for the communal life of the inhabitants. Thessaly was organised into autonomous centres which were linked in a confederation uniting the peoples living to the north of Attica and the Gulf of Corinth in the cult of the Earth-goddess Anthele, whose shrine was near the Malian Gulf. For a time the Anthelian League had influence over the Delphic oracle – a very important period in Greek history, for this was an attempt by regions where the old military nobility still held power to subjugate by force regions socially and economically far in advance of them.

This attempt by the North at unification and conquest showed clearly the nature of the conflict in Greece as the hostility of communities that had reached different stages in their political and economic development. The various cults enabled the people to give a foundation of legitimacy to their cantonal federations, as 'oracular states' which gave precedence to one cult and one sanctuary, without denying the value of the others.

The sanctuary of Heliconian Poseidon on Mount Mycale, that of Apollo Triopes at Cnidus, of Apollo at Delos, of Poseidon at Caluaria, of Zeus at Dodona, and Mount Ida in Crete, of Athene at Athens and Lindus, were all shrines where periodic festivals were held such as those of Olympian Zeus, Apollo-Dionysos at Delphi, or Poseidon at Corinth. The old Homeric racial unity underlay the existing ethnic basis of political unity, but working against this unity were the profound differences in the situations of the various communities, so that they lacked the common interests which are the cement of inter-state solidarity. It became more and more difficult to live together under a common administration and legal system, while the different paths of development taken by different states led them still further from strengthening their links with cities or cantons under other administrations.

Within the 'oracular state' the cantonal divisions marked the divisions into political streams or parties. What looked like the opposition of Thessaly and the Anthelian League to the Amphyctionic League (the organ of the Delphic oracle's pan-Hellenic and judicial ambitions) was in fact the effort of one current in Greek political thought to impose itself on all the Greeks, by means of a pan-Hellenic organisation with its own governing class.

In the same way the pan-Hellenic movement centred on the Olympic shrine was essentially a unifying movement even though at one period it lost ground by comparison with the other great pan-Hellenic movement, centred on Delphi. But all these attempts at unification, even those which never became anything more than regional in their influence, held the seeds of a true pan-Hellenism, and failed to achieve it only because the people of that particular area lacked the force, or will, or self-interest to impose themselves on the rest of the country.

The efforts towards expansion by the Anthelian League were an attempt to impose an aristocratic and military supremacy on the Greek world. If it had succeeded, Greece would have been organised by these aristocratic clans, strengthened by a claim to legitimacy based on the will of Demeter of Anthele. The Peloponnesian supremacy of Corinth and Sparta was a joint effort of a military and agrarian aristocracy, and an economic aristocracy of sailors and merchants. Around the Peloponnesian powers and their shrine a compact, enduring group was formed, whose cohesion is shown by the importance of the Olympic Games in Greek life, by the high level of culture reached in the Peloponnese, and by the powerful position held by Sparta and Corinth at the beginning of the Persian wars.

In the period before the Persian wars, Greek unity was founded on the influence and prestige of the two sanctuaries, Olympia and Delphi, which balanced one another in authority. They were the source of legitimacy, the one derived from the God of Heaven, the other from the God of the Sun. The cult of Zeus represented the solemn seal of unity in the ancient ties with a common Achaean-Minoan past, the comman bond with a god who himself represented the sovereign will to which all the Greeks were bound to submit, and who was above all the author and teacher of the sublime principles of morality and justice which govern men's relations with one another. The Delphic oracle, however, had a more specifically legislative function, laying down rules and giving advice in particular cases, and acting, in a way, as a positive governing force, day by day, case by case. The two together were sufficiently powerful for us to recognise the existence of a form of political unity among the Greek peoples in the era after Thessaly's failure to penetrate Phocis, and before the Persian wars.

To understand this era it is important to see its political system as something quite different from medieval or modern schemes; it is comprehensible only as the synthesis of the Egyptian, Mesopotamian, Anatolian and Persian concepts of the theocratic monarchy with the customs and way of life of an Indo-European dominant caste from the north. The intervention of oracles in human activities, the sovereignty of a supreme God of Gods and men, were the solutions of a civilisation which had no idea of legitimacy apart from that deriving from the gods.

These considerations have very important results for the evaluation of the Greek Polis, a development which has aroused much interest and speculation among modern historians. Modern nationalist theory, and even the more precise ideas of recent federalist doctrine, has spread the idea that the Polis was the limit of Greek political concepts, and that by being unable to grow beyond it, they had not achieved the power that comes with unity until the Macedonian threat forced them to combine their resources.

The ineffectiveness, perceived by Thucydides, which was a feature of this period of Greek history, was thus the result of circumstances which did not have their origin in the Polis. The autonomy of the Greek states did not prevent their functioning as a unity in the oracular period, that is, from the end of the Mycenaean era to the Macedonian conquest; it was rather the deep divisions and differences, the parties, which were the reason for the tension and conflicts that disrupted Greece, for in similar circumstances even in a united state, even in those whose pattern of organisation we are most familiar with, men have struggled to impose the supremacy of a philosophy, a political ideal, the interests of one region or one class.

For a long time the Polis and the unity of Greece existed side by side, for legitimacy was founded on the transcendence of certain deities who communicated with men through the oracles. Within this system the Polis was guided in the interests of the dominant class in it. When a particular class was predominant, like the aristocrats of the Peloponnese, the whole of Greek life was regulated by its particular bias. Opposition survived, but everywhere a homogeneous ruling class was to be found, guiding the individual cantons along common lines, taking its authority from the oracles, which gave utterances conforming with the policies of the ruling classes. Greek unity is thus clearly to be seen operating within the limits of local autonomy, and no other interpretation is possible than that the Polis of the sixth century BC was only an element in a greater unity, and not a sovereign state in any absolute sense.

The Anthelian League disintegrated because of an internal war amongst its members, when Thessaly, to defend the sanctuary at Delphi, had to call on Athens and Sicyon for aid. From that moment Delphi rose to the position of pan-Hellenic importance which it held throughout the sixth century BC, a time of great importance for pan-Hellenic political development, because of this Delphic supremacy, so that there was competition for control of this essential element in legitimate sovereignty.

In the first half of the sixth century came the formation of the Spartan-dominated Peloponnesian League, as Sparta and the other local communities grew politically closer together. The Arcadian League joined the Spartan when the monarchy of Orchomenos fell and the aristocratic oligarchy took over. In the same period Elis joined the League, but Achaia, also in the Peloponnese, stayed separate from Sparta in an autonomous League. We cannot understand why some Leagues united while others preserved their independence unless we are able to examine in detail the internal problems of the individual cities. The abstract formula, autonomy, does not resolve the question, since the autonomy was in its turn affected by the situation of the particular state, and the reasons why its leaders or rulers chose to dissociate themselves from the policy of another city or League and remain isolated, or to impose their own influence and attract the others into their own orbit.

If the landowners were in power in a particular city, they would obviously not want the industrialists to obtain control, nor the sailors and traders whose aim was increased trade and who would, on an open market, have forced lower prices and therefore lower profits for the landowners. Similar elementary cases easily explain why certain cantons clung to their autonomy, but the situation could be much more complex. If a city governed by a landowning aristocracy found itself face to face with a trading and naval community, the interests of the two cities – economic as well as political – not only differed but conflicted, since every advantage to the one was a disadvantage to the other. In our own times the interests of peasants and landowner are always opposed to those of speculators and industrialists of all sorts. But in our time the growth of vast towns and cities has imposed the dominion of city-dwellers over countrymen, who have no immediate or effective means of imposing their point of view.

Greece was a country of such varying social and economic conditions that it was possible for the interests of one class to prevail in one centre, and of their opponents in another. What is more, certain communities, although quite outside the sphere of interests of these dominant groups, came to find themselves drawn into the quarrels of the most important cities, and forced into paths of development quite unrelated to their own interests.

The groups with different interests in Greek politics were similar to the factions of any period of history; their fierce competitiveness expressed the lack of common ground for co-operation between the various parties in Greece. In such a situation disagreement led to open conflict, and the local autonomy of the states was not adequately controlled by the pan-Hellenic 'oracular state', which lacked the authority to prevent differences of political interests and aspirations leading to and supporting civil war.

The idea, expressed by Thucydides, that the Greeks should have conserved their strength, and instead of quarrelling amongst themselves should have united in foreign expeditions, like the Trojan wars or the foundation of colonies, which brought profit to all, seemed to his contemporaries to be the expression of only one point of view: that of Athens, whose interests were in trading and the sea. For the Athenians the advantages of the conquest of new bases, and of territorial and commercial expansion, were obvious. They were not so obvious to the peasants and landowners of Attica, and non-existent for the areas where the economy was basically agricultural and self-supporting, where there was neither the need nor the opportunity for trade, and little industry or manufacturing. The broils between neighbouring cities, which modern historians, under the influence of nationalist theories, claim to have arisen sometimes, or even in every case, from the desire for 'independence', were in fact struggles for life, or at least for the survival of their own way of life.

'Independence' meant the need to prevent the price of cereals, the farmer's meagre revenue, collapsing under an influx of foreign grain. So it was also the desire to avoid changing the way of life that was hallowed by tradition. A city's mean jealousy of another might, instead, be seen as the defence of customary privileges, of the power of the ruling class and of the city's own religious cult; it might be the desire for that particular god's sanctuary to become the centre of a general Greek festival, and its oracle to make laws for the whole country for the benefit of all.

Underlying all this rivalry and conflict was the generally accepted idea of the unity of the Greek people and the existence of a Greek State, where men struggled for power in order to impose their particular political theories on the whole Greek world. In the regime of local autonomy which the organisation of Greece at the time allowed, differences between city and city were vigorously and stridently expressed. Each area could develop its own characteristics to the full, and the principle underlying the words of the Delphic oracle was that traditional usages should be followed. This meant that the Greek cities could develop as far as they were able along their own lines, and that each political growth could blossom for a while. But while one group or region was not likely to be able to impose its attitudes and interests on another, it was equally unlikely to obtain any co-operation on a joint project.

Greek liberty was not the same thing as the Athenian democratic liberty of the fifth century, but consisted in conceding to each city or canton the right of self-government. From one point of view this local independence was dearly bought, at the price of laying the country open to discord and conflict. But for many Greeks it was a price worth paying, since it prevented the sacrifice of the weak to the interests of the strong, and allowed each community to find the form of government that best suited its own needs.

The characteristics of the Greek oracular state were most clearly shown in its connections with the colonies. The oracles chose the locations of new colonies, for according to

Greek beliefs they knew every grain of sand and blade of grass in the whole world. The Greek who applied to an oracle for help knew that the god would direct him honestly and propitiously, and the cities too, in historical times, applied to the oracles to be directed to the land in which they should settle their colonists. Thus from its foundation every colony had to acknowledge the hand of God directing it.

After the city had consulted its god, it held a public ceremony in which the citizens participated, repeating and reaffirming the request for approval and divine sanction of its colonial venture, in order to give it the seal of legitimacy. The colonists, provided by the city with ships and arms, were led by a captain appointed by the city itself. This leader, invested by the gods with the power to carry out their will, and burdened with the task of bringing it about, bore the mark of his position upon him. It made him worthy of veneration and worship as a hero, both before and after death.

The religious character of the colony's foundation and of its founder shows that in the oracular state, as in the theocratic monarchy, any collective action was sanctioned and at the same time assured of success by the divinity. The divine approval of the choice of expedition leader gave him all the powers of a sovereign in a particular form of monarchic state. He was military commander, since he was the one to lead the colonists in battle and to reduce a conquered enemy to slavery; he apportioned the land to be reserved for the gods, recognised the privileges of certain classes of the population, when these corresponded to the political conditions existing in the mother country, and so disposed of the rest of the territory. Like a king, he was the owner of all the land, and entrusted a part of it to each man according to his due, in a system of equal partnership which was not true possession, for personal property could be sold, but what belonged to the divine ruler could be entrusted to another but not sold, for no one could sell what was only his on trust.

Even more important was the relationship existing between the colony and the motherland. The colonial settler was now a citizen of his new home, not of his city of origin, but if he wanted to return home he received his old citizenship again. However, if he settled somewhere else, he would become a 'metic', eligible for the broad, general legal protection which all Greeks extended to their countrymen, from whatever city, but not for an active part in the life of the community, with all the problems and benefits which made up citizenship of a Polis.

So the colony was to a certain extent dependent still on the city which founded it, and also on the whole of the Greek community. To have refused to take part in the Games of the mother city, to have refused help when asked, or to have aided her enemies, would have been considered as transgressions of laws recognised by all the Greeks; to break them would be to put oneself outside the pan-Hellenic community and to behave like the barbarians.

The period during which the Greeks concentrated once again on colonial expansion, after the Achaean era, was a prosperous and favourable one for them. The new colonies of the eighth to the sixth century BC were mostly established by the Ionian Greeks: the cities of the Anatolian coast set up naval bases and farming communities on the Black Sea coast, in Thrace and on the islands of the North Aegean. Expansion on the Asiatic coast of the Aegean was encouraged by the rich hinterland opened up by the new coastal cities and the success of their trading ventures inland. But power and prosperity were not limited to these cities alone, for their example was followed by the settlements on Euboeia and other islands, as well as by some of the maritime cities of central and southern Greece.

But the mainland cities, especially those like Euboeia and Corinth which had the greatest naval and financial resources, directed the mainstream of their colonisation to the west. This undertaking involved not only cities like Corinth, Megara, Chalcis and Eretria, but included people from all over central Greece and the Peloponnese, whoever wished to emigrate.

Colonisation was outstanding evidence of the unity of the Greek community even in this obscure period of its history. Dazzled and fascinated by the history of Athens, modern historians have given too little attention to the time when the alliance between Corinth and Sparta gave a strength and splendour to Greek civilisation, and forced the amazing renaissance of the pre-Achaean naval empire.

Corinth and the other leading cities ruled the sea to the benefit of the whole community, and the settlements in Sicily and Asia Minor, on Corcyra and its neighbours and on the coast of southern Italy, were the work of Greeks from all over the mainland. The colonisation movement stimulated and directed by Corinth held implications of considerable importance. When the colonists penetrated into Sicily they came into competition with Carthage for bases on the island, and eventually left only the extreme west to the Phoenicians. Sparta's share in the colonisation, and her settlement at Tarentum, showed that the movement could also include non-maritime states without fleets, and confirmed the collective quality of the undertaking.

If the Ionian colonisation was the work of individual cities with strongly independent aims, quite the opposite was true of the movement to the west. It was a concerted effort under the encouragement and guidance of the great sea powers, and lacked the resources to develop desert or semi-desert areas; Sicily was won from the indigenous population which had inhabited its town and those on the surrounding islands for thousands of years; the Greeks had been forced to fight for possession of the island with Carthage, the greatest naval power of the central and western Mediterranean. So it was not a case of an organised transfer of men exported like so many flocks of sheep, but a slow and gradual conquest.

The cities of the south-eastern coast of Italy, founded by the peoples of the northern Peloponnese, were also a part of this united movement of conquest under the political supremacy of the Peloponnese. Even the states of Locris, Rhodes and Crete shared in the victories of this age of conquest – although they themselves were not always victorious, and sometimes had to yield to Carthage or the local population; yet it seemed that there were no limits that such vitality, bravery and enterprise could not pass. The Greeks sailed west of the Pillars of Hercules, founded colonies on the coasts of France, Spain and

Africa, and maintained their own bases in Cyrenaica and inside the territories of Egypt and Carthage.

Crete under the Minoan kings had known a similar power, but now it became clear that the Greeks did not need an oriental or heroic type of theocratic monarchy in order to recover the lost empire. The oracular structure of the archaic Greek state was as effective as the monarchies could have been, and sufficiently stable and powerful to co-ordinate and stimulate Greek efforts in a single direction.

The period of alliance between the land-power of Sparta and the sea-power of Corinth was one of the great eras of human history. In the whole of the Mediterranean the Greeks could sail and trade in safety; they controlled naval bases and their hinterlands, created markets and customers for their products, could land almost anywhere and be on Greek territory. For many centuries Greece maintained a close economic control over the coastlands of Italy, Sicily and the eastern and western Mediterranean. They provided them with merchandise, spread their own civilisation, and created the political situations and problems which they later collaborated with the Romans in resolving. As a result of these conquests the Greek economy changed completely, for the whole known world became a market for Greek fabrics, pottery, metalwork, wine and olives.

Greek colonisation spread the cultivation of olives throughout the Mediterranean. Shipyards were opened up and down the peninsula, and the general increase in public and private prosperity gave an impetus to all the arts, and made possible the first great manifestation of a power of expression, a taste, a view of reality, independent of the long Oriental tradition, which still influenced Corinthian art but seemed already far removed from the great achievements of Peloponnesian sculpture.

The Greek aristocracy of the eighth to the sixth century BC laid the foundations of greatness for the Greek people. It was an aristocracy of warriors, horsemen, farmers, merchants, but above all an aristocracy of men, of individuals with a sense of their own personality and humanity which enabled them to submit to the gods without humiliation.

CHAPTER THREE

*

THE SOCIAL TRANSFORMATION

THE long and complex task of expansion and conquest, the building of an empire ruled not by a king but by a nation, was transforming Greek life and opening up new political, social and economic prospects throughout the Mediterranean.

We have already discussed the origins of this development. The days of the warriors with their armour and their chariots had passed centuries ago and now the age of cavalry too was coming to an end. The hoplite infantry and the warships had become more and more important, with cavalry as a small subsidiary, so that the manufacturing and merchant class became more and more wealthy.

The aristocracy had made Greece great and prosperous, and a result of this had been to free a great part of the citizen population from its state of economic and social inferiority: its new importance in the army and in manufacturing correspondingly increased its political influence and responsibilities.

The first stage in the decline of the oligarchic aristocracy resembled that of the theocratic kings. Written laws had limited the kings' powers to the administration of justice; new laws limited the legal privileges that the aristocracy had assumed not simply because of its powerful position, but because of the popular vision of the nobleman as someone superior to ordinary mortals, closer to the gods and under their protection.

As the conditions of the poorer classes improved, the theoretical gap between the two classes began to close, and the almost hero-like superiority of the rich was no longer accepted. Men began to challenge the traditional laws based on the idea that the rich and the poor were almost different species. They demanded written laws, justice by arbitration, and powers of legislation.

The causes of this crisis were complex, springing from the new social situation which developed from the new expansion in shipping, trade, industry, and the new contacts throughout the Mediterranean world made by Greeks as the dominant sea power.

The capital for shipbuilding and cargoes was probably put forward in the first place by landowning aristocracy itself, but the lower classes profited by it to improve their conditions, not only because they became better off, but because they acquired a greater importance in the life of the community; the labour of each man working as a sailor, trader or artisan was now an essential and irreplaceable element in the welfare of the whole society.

Together with new social doctrines came new methods of warfare, and therefore new systems of levying troops for defence and conquest. Ancient tactics made each warrior into a tower of metal moving cumbrously over the battlefield, fighting individually in a duel which was not much more than the collision of two lumps of matter. Now the Greeks had to adapt their fighting methods to accommodate enemies who used methods of attack and defence outside the scope of Greek tradition, to deal with both hand-to-hand fighting and the disposition of bodies of troops over large distances.

The larger contingents now levied precluded the use of the 'heroic' warrior with his burden of armour; the shield became small, the breastplate lighter, with leather used in place of metal in the less exposed parts. The soldier warded off attack with a long lance, and the individual weakness of the new arms was balanced by a new system of fighting which made the troops dependent upon each other, placing them shoulder to shoulder so that every man was partly covered by his neighbour's shield, and the front rank presented to the enemy a continuous metal fence of shields, bristling with lance-points. Under this new system, the job of the richer citizens was no longer to provide themselves with heavy, and now obsolete, armour, but to maintain and train cavalry troops to support the infantry attack on its flanks. The effect of the new tactics was to make the infantry the decisive element in battle, while the importance of the aristocracy's contribution diminished.

In the same period technical progress resulted in innovations in shipbuilding too, which had their political and social repercussions. The perfecting of a technique of navigation by sail allowed the cargo ships greater economy and independence, while the warships, which could not rely on sail, were built for greater speed. The hull was elongated and streamlined, the decks covered throughout their length, the number of rowers increased and set in ranks one above the other to create the classic Greek man-of-war, the trireme. The whole ship was better adapted for long voyages and greater speed and momentum. These innovations, and the greater number of ships that Greek military policy now demanded, increased the importance of the poorer citizens who provided the labour, and assisted the rise of the middle class which the new Greek economy and policies were creating.

These groups, which for the first time were gaining a place in public life, could not be satisfied with a system of government still founded exclusively on an aristocracy that no longer contained within it all the essential elements of society.

But the political consequences of the new situation could never be the same throughout a land where local autonomy and profound differences of economy, environment and social relationships prevented any sort of political uniformity. In some places the aristocracy defended its institutions and privileges, legal and religious, even using violence to oppose the middle and lower classes, who in their turn did not shrink from using revolutionary methods to assert their rights against the ancient legal codes. In such circumstances the only hope of a peaceful and legal settlement was the setting up of a new social order, using someone trusted by both sides as arbitrator, or giving him the more complex task of creating a new legislative foundation for the state, as the heroic founders of the colonies had done.

The arbitrator or legislator had to find a language which

the local population would accept as expressing not merely the product of individual initiative, but truth of an absolute validity. This meant that he had to link legislation with religion, with the gods who were the source of authority; his method depended on the religious customs of the locality.

The legislator could himself assume semi-divine, heroic powers, or could simply be appointed to his job by an oracle, or else his actions and decisions could be held to be inspired by the oracle. But the development of Greek religious thought could lead to yet other solutions: not only the soothsayer, but the wise man, the poet and the artist too could be divinely inspired, and their words could have the value of insights into the absolute truth of the mind of God.

Where the peaceful solution was possible, it was based on class relationships within the oracular state which were fluid enough to permit agreement without violence. In other regions the struggle was fiercer, and the privileged classes were attacked with a greater concentration of forces, under the guidance of a popular leader. Such conflicts were resolved not by peaceful agreement, but by the domination of the community by the middle and lower classes. Their leader did not hold the position of legislator or arbiter, but of executor of the revolutionary will of the people.

The power of a faction-leader who imposed himself on a community by force seemed to the Greeks to be an offence against the principle of the divine origins of authority. These leaders were called 'turannoi', a name which linked them with the military governors who commanded the garrisons in Asia Minor, making their headquarters inside the fortifications and surrounding themselves with armed men. The image of the 'tyrant' was that of the usurper, holding power without legitimacy based on the laws and the will of the gods, but simply as the result of intimidation by force. This was an open attack on the Greek concept of the state as an organisation under the guidance of the gods, through the oracles. The tyrant did not act in the name of all, under divine guidance, nor by virtue of his transcendent gift of the knowledge of truth and justice. He imposed himself by the use of force, and substituted the will of an individual for the supremacy of an absolute truth, or, as it has recently been defined as 'the event' for 'the form'.

The tyrant in Greek history, however, appears as someone rather different from the governors, government officials and local commandants of Asia Minor. There power was held by delegation, from God to the King, from the King to the official, and so conformed to the local idea of legality. But in Greece the name of tyrant marks the first example of power without divine authority to occur in the ancient Mediterranean world, as far as our limited evidence shows.

It cannot be said that the abnormal character of tyranny consisted in its denial of equality between members of the community. Such equality was continually being denied to men, and in a much more serious way. Any man's pre-eminence over others, or comparison of himself to the gods, is a negation of human equality. The legislator, the hero, the colonial leader, were human beings who distinguished themselves from their equals by being chosen by the gods and divinely inspired. But according to the theory of the oracular state, in which all power must derive from the gods, this superiority was legitimate, but that of the tyrant was not. Even if the tyrant enjoyed a certain amount of support, even if he represented the interests and hopes of large sectors of the population, even if his power was not founded only on arms, the reason for his superiority was not considered by the ancient world, before the fifth century BC, to be a basis of legitimate power. Authority belonged to God alone, and had done everywhere for thousands of years. To think that it could belong to any group of men, large or small, would be to imagine that the mass created by the union of a number of men could assume the nature of a transcendent being.

The tyrannies spread throughout the seventh and sixth centuries BC. It would seem as if the new crisis in class relationships in Greece had two possible solutions: that of the legislators and arbiters, within the bounds of oracular legality, and that of the tyrants, which was utterly beyond the pale.

The legislators and compilers of written codes could model themselves on the law-givers of Mesopotamia and Asia Minor; the legislators of the Siceliot cities were figures vanishing into legend. They were believed to be inspired by the oracles, and were the authors of a very varied collection of codes, although in part almost certainly contemporary. The codes aimed at safeguarding property, preventing the individual's taking justice into his own hands, establishing a scale of punishments and fines in the place of the private or family vendetta.

The codes attributed to mythical, divine or heroic persons, to some of whom temples were built, did not differ much from those of men whose historical existence is proved. Neither made pronouncements on questions of public policy, but both confined themselves to criminal law and the protection of property, regulating the position of the debtor and the rights of the creditor, safeguarding the family group, bringing into prominence a social group of increasing importance which was so far without any other legal protection than the arbitrary justice administered by the clan leaders according to the gentlemanly traditions of a privileged and all-powerful aristocracy.

The new class demanded as its first concession secure legislation on the matters that chiefly concerned it, and it is important to notice that this legislation contained no constitutional reforms for the community or the canto, that is, for the Polis. It is clear, therefore, that the new class was not interested in its political position, but only in its private, family, economic situation. So the ruling aristocracy was able to maintain its political supremacy, making concessions on matters concerning the individual. Where aristocratic resistance was more bitter and tenacious, one finds that the new classes had begun to have political aspirations; on other occasions the very resistance of the aristocracy provoked revolt, which they had to put down by using force, which led inevitably to tyranny.

Thus the difference between arbiters, legislators and tyrants was considerable. The first two remained inside a flourishing state organisation, while the third set in motion a revolution which was destined to be one of the greatest – perhaps the greatest – in human history. The fact that the whole of the ancient world condemned tyranny shows what very deep roots the state and divine authority had in its culture, and how the turmoil of revolution had never been able to shake that tradition.

A notable feature of the history of the tyrants, and one that often appears at revolutionary periods in history, is that the men who come to power in the struggle with the aristocracies nearly all come from the same class themselves. When the political situation has been settled for a long time, the men who hold effective power and public office in the state belong to the privileged and dominant group which is, therefore, synonymous with the governing caste. But at times of crisis and revolution a new class which is rising, or hoping to rise, to power is unlikely to have at its disposal men with the ability to govern in its name and interest. So it happens that the governing caste can to some extent detach itself from the dominant class, since the old dominant class, like the new, finally has to use the same men to fill public offices.

In fact, the tyrants accomplished nothing more revolutionary than did the legislators. To start with, the very enormity of the revolution that their positions represented intimidated them, and they tried in various ways to give an impression of traditional legality, although it was contradicted by the presence of the forces that had brought them to power.

In their methods of governing they were more concerned to preserve traditional forms of state organisation than to regulate their own positions to make them more permanent. Their instinct in legal matters was always to avoid open recognition of the fact that a revolution had occurred in the very sources of law and authority, and to display the trappings of traditional legitimacy in an effort to show that their own power did not contradict it.

In the interests of the classes that had raised them to power, they allowed them financial concessions and certain legal guarantees in matters affecting the individual and the family. In politics they managed to reduce the resistance of the aristocrats by dispersing or silencing the most active members of the governing caste. In economic affairs the tyrants to some extent preyed on the richest class either by heavy taxation or by legal actions followed by sequestration. With the money gained in this way the tyrants began public works which were a sort of aid to the poorest classes. Thus the policy of the tyrants at least in some places about which we have some information, succeeded in making life easier for the poor, giving them greater security and opportunities for work and production.

However, one obvious result of the tyrannies was their transformation of every aspect of the Polis; above all economically. The Polis of the aristocrats was run by a small number of families, and every military and financial burden was divided amongst the citizens on a family basis – which, in fact, long survived the aristocratic regime. There was no such thing as a communal financial policy, but the financial administration was so much a matter of personal allocations that profits as well as expenses were shared.

When the tyrants' policies in search of greater 'social justice' led to the need for public intervention in the state's economic organisation, the community was given a new function, and took an important step in the direction of greater and more positive local autonomy; independence of a genuinely political character. Even Thucydides reproached the tyrants for the excessive chauvinism of their policies. The effect they had was to make their supporters rich, themselves more secure, and to commit their cities to ambitious public works which emphasised their independence of pan-Hellenic unity and encouraged enthusiasm for the success of the one particular Polis even at the expense of the others. On the whole the policies of the tyrants tended to damage the fundamental unity of the Greek people which aristocratic solidarity had supported with the help of the oracles. The functions of the Polis as a community became more complex, local loyalties more often conflicted with loyalty to Greece as a whole, and Greek unity suffered by it.

By the end of the sixth century BC the age of the tyrants was over in mainland Greece. But the disappearance of the regime, which had been the product of political crisis, did not leave all the various Greek communities in the same condition or do away with the differences that had made independence necessary. The cities were left more active and less inclined to any co-ordination of policies; they had every encouragement to grow apart.

In particular, the Lacedaemonian situation was different from any other. Sparta was not a local community ruled by an aristocracy, but a survival of the ancient system which had grown up after the Achaean conquest. The Spartans could never merge with the landowning aristocracies of the other Hellenic states. Their system of landowning, which was linked with the governmental organisation of the Homeric-Mycenaean conquerors of the peninsula, gave total possession of the land to the conquerors, reserving a part for the kings and their households and a part for the gods; the rest was divided among the conquering warriors, who cultivated it with the labour of the Helots, the expropriated inhabitants, and lived on the produce.

The situation in the colonies was no different: the leader reserved a part of the land for the gods and for himself, and divided the rest into equal shares for the colonists. This continuation of the methods of the Achaean conquerors in Greece created a political order identical with the one which the Spartans had preserved unchanged for many centuries.

Thus the Spartan 'cosmos', whose claim to political wisdom was the limitation of the citizen body to a small proportion of the inhabitants, was not the product of exceptional political wisdom and deep thought, but the fossilisation of a very ancient system, which had been developed to deal with the conflict of power and right at the time of the conquest of the Peloponnese.

Sparta preserved her original position while the rest of Greece moved on by cultivating a deliberate isolation. In particular family and business relations between Spartans and non-Spartans were forbidden. They did not want to concern themselves with industry or trade, and indeed the use of iron coins only when everyone else used silver impeded any sort of trade and made necessary a rigidly self-sufficient economy. The permanent military service imposed on the Spartans, their consanguineous marriages and their birth-control, enclosed them in an ever-narrowing circle, led to a diminishing population, and made it increasingly difficult for them to defend their privileges. So they had to use fierce repressive measures against the Helots, and gradually transformed the typical example of the ancient, legitimate form of the Doric state into a 'police state' whose policy of oppression had no legal justification apart from centuries of tradition: tradition which now had almost no contemporary relevance.

The institutions of the Spartiates also revealed how the character of the community had developed, as the single ruler of the Homeric era gave way to the dual kingship, and the assembly of warriors grew into the 'Apella', composed of the men over thirty years of age, the 'Gerousia', a select junta of 28–30 of the elders, and as a final limitation on the kings' power, the Ephors, who gradually emerged from the Apella as the true leaders of the community, thanks to the enormous powers which were delegated to them.

So Sparta, in her artificial isolation, had undergone her own evolution, only in part in line with the rest of Greece: even in Sparta, in spite of the original, ancient equality amongst the Spartiates, there were differences between richest and poorest, more and less powerful; the kingship had first been reduced to an office held by two magistrates, then abased to become an instrument of the assembly of the privileged. In this sense Sparta's leanings towards the aristocracies in the rest of Greece are understandable, but the affinity was very limited. Sparta was the relic of an ancient past, and she tried to ally herself to those groups and movements that had most in common with her, or at least were not dangers to her internal stability.

The balance of power between Athens and Sparta is commonly taken as the pattern of Greek history of the fifth century BC, but there is no justification for thinking that everything in Greece moved between these two poles.

In the seventh century BC Attica was not yet organised into cantons under the Athenian aegis. The city was completing its transformation from an ancient monarchy dominated by the landowning aristocracy to a state in which the aristocrats succeeded in retaining their political position at the expense of their economic and legal privileges. The result of the reforms in Athens was a substantial change in the conditions of life of the poorer classes. The new Polis, no longer exclusively aristocratic in its administration, protected its agriculture by prohibiting the import of grain and encouraging the export of olive oil, which gave employment to both farm labourers and vase-makers. An 'inflated' currency of lower intrinsic value was introduced, which facilitated export, and also earned general confidence by being of the finest alloy and constant weight. Then the Athenian merchants increased their attack on an area where the power of the Hellenic cities of Asia Minor was declining, after Persian repression of their revolt, and so an unexpected prosperity came to Athens from the mercantile empire which stood open to her.

The aristocratic 'Eupatridai' of Athens survived the long parenthesis of tyranny, and by yielding to the economic pressures of the lower classes became a typical example of a governing body functioning without any attachment to the class from which its men came, or even conflict with it.

It was in fact men of the highest birth who destroyed the privileges of the great families, when this was necessary for the preservation and furtherance of the classes to whose prosperity the whole Athenian economy was now linked. The profits of the great as well as the small investors were at stake, and the aristocracy continued to rule only by putting into effect laws directed to the destruction of its own predominance and privileges. They were aristocrats who brought about the legal and economic reforms which gave protection to the lower classes, support for their financial enterprises, more humane debtors' laws, and, little by little, concession by concession, full legal parity of all members of the citizen community, with no distinctions made for wealth or birth.

All the states during the classical era preserved the system of dividing the citizens into clans based on common descent, an arrangement which survived in even the most advanced social organisation, as a means of determining and dividing amongst the citizens their duties and debts to the community as a whole, in such matters as military service, public offices and tribute. The rights of the citizen were proportionate to the value of his services; those who served in the army, or contributed more than usual to its upkeep or effectiveness, or paid larger tributes, had rights denied to the rest. The changing conditions, which allowed the poorer classes greater participation in the life of the community, made it necessary to cancel the clan-divisions based on birth or wealth, in order to put all citizens on an equal footing. New divisions were made, based on place of birth or residence.

The Athenian tyranny, destroyed, like the others, by the efforts of the aristocracy with Spartan support, left Athens in a situation that did not allow the restoration of the old oligarchy, as happened in Corinth and Megara.

During the sixth century BC Sparta became the leading light of the Greek world, because of her domination of the Peloponnese and her alliance with Corinth. Her influence extended to the Delphic oracle, and so she had a means of imposing her will on the rest of Greece through the mouth of the god, and so giving her domination the aura of legitimacy. The Spartiates had become the fighting arm of all the well-born and wealthy groups which dominated most of the Greek cities.

The arts in all their forms helped to create an atmosphere favourable to the oligarchies of birth and prestige. It was not only the ancient heroic ideals, which failed to create a favourable impression in the modern context, but useful and effective new concepts that served the purposes of the oligarchs.

Poetry had developed into one of the most important influences on popular ideas. The vitality of Homer's verse and its place as the foundation of the Greek system of education impressed its ideals of heroic virtuc, physical excellence and valour, and its code of manners on generations of Greeks. Nor did the poems of Hesiod, who wrote in Boeotia at the end of the eighth century BC, in any way conflict with the vitality of the Homeric tradition: Homer created the image of the heroic and in every way superior warrior nobility; Hesiod described the world of the poor, men without any other concept of their destiny, content with what little good came their way, resigned to the many miseries and hardships which made up their lives on earth.

Hesiod's world was not at odds with the world of Homer. It

does not have the boldness of a new people claiming a great position in the state, but describes the life of the humble, seen by a man who has observed it at close quarters, understood it and taken part in it, with the simple conviction that in the world men cannot be equal, and the destiny of the humble is as necessary as that of the strong and powerful. If anything can assure the poor and insignificant that they are not debased to the level of slaves or animals, it is the dignity of labour and the awareness of a task honestly performed according to the will of the gods.

The new commercial prosperity created a new aristocracy drawing its profits from shipbuilding and trade, which was perhaps further than the warrior nobility had been from the humble and resigned day-to-day reality of the poor peasant with only an ox and an acre of land to his name. In the cities of Asia Minor and the islands especially, the heights and depths of men's experience were expressed in poetry that exalted the individuality of man, whether it was Archilocus' pride in the valour of the soldier and lover, or Hipponax's contentment with the lazy, graceless, greedy life of a beggar.

It was still a world where men accepted wealth or poverty as something as inevitable and unchangeable as beauty or ugliness, physical perfection or deformity. Callinus and Tyrtaeus accompanied the troops to battle exulting in the might of the hoplites fighting in the serried ranks of the phalanx; Mimnermus celebrated youth and love in poems which hold echoes of a society without cares or duties in the army or government, wanting only to enjoy a life made simple by wealth. Sappho too expressed in her love songs the feelings of this new spiritual aristocracy, which felt itself linked by its perception and discrimination, and found in the arts a new way, apart from the traditional pre-eminence of the warrior or athlete, of rising above common mortals and approaching the gods.

In the social order of this society, in these centuries, nothing changed. Men preserved their fundamentally aristocratic idea of the natural domination of ordinary people by 'their betters', and their betters were, inevitably, the richest, since only they could excel in war, train for success in athletics, and get the education needed for distinction in science or poetry.

But when the political conflict reached the point of questioning the values of the aristocratic view of society, the voice of poetry reflected the change. When the upper classes, content with the privileges they felt to be eternal, just and divinely ordained, began to feel the pressure of the lower classes and the persecution of the tyrants, and saw the transformation of the world which had been organised to suit them, poetry became a cry from the heart, expressing passions and anxieties, rancour and hatred in a way that would not have been conceivable some decades before.

One poet, Solon, spoke with ancient wisdom and almost divine inspiration to invoke order and justice in a city torn apart by civil war. All men, he said, must be treated as humans, and their fury and desperation appeased. Unlike Hesiod, he recognised that the wretched man does not have to resign himself to his misery, and that the rich man does not have to accept his privileges as if they were just and due recognition of his natural superiority.

A revolution was proclaimed in this poem of the sixth century BC, a revolution which the oligarchs tried to avoid by means of legislators and arbiters, but which often, when it was under armed leadership, they could not escape. The conditions of the poor improved, their status in society rose, and with it their awareness of their own value to the state. But some who saw their own traditional privileges disappearing and wealth and prestige fall in ruins, while leaders of gangs and factions rose to power, gave expression to their sorrow, indignation and nostalgia: Theognis observed the disappearance of a world of tradition, education, noble birth and lofty sentiments, and Alcaeus abhorred the attempts to reconcile the opposing factions by arbitration, glorifying the swashbuckling traditions of the warrior élite.

For several decades of the seventh and sixth centuries BC a new world was being born, and all Greece was aware of the crisis. The political conflict was not given the same name in every city and canton, but everywhere, throughout the world whose civilisation had been made by the encounter of the

Achaeans with the monarchies of the Levant, people were working out a theory of political values which was gradually eliminating the traces of the oriental attitudes from Greek society, in both its cultural and its economic aspects.

As long as the existence of a class of demi-gods was generally admitted, men born to be heroes and leaders, entrusted with the task of guiding and defending, succouring and caring for their flock like shepherds, it was easier to keep that flock content with its destiny and convinced of its inferiority to the king and his peers. But when the differences between men were seen to be wealth and intelligence, it became clear that although success was due to divine will and inspiration, it was still open to anyone to be given that inspiration, and in any case there was no justification for oppression, injustice and exploitation.

Once it became possible for common men to rise in society by their own efforts and because of the divine element in every man, the distinction between the few elect and the common herd began to lose its significance. The Greeks were beginning their conquest of the arts and sciences, and in this intellectual revolution the upper and lower classes were on an equal footing, even though the first great sages were thought of as almost divine and surrounded with a veneration and respect which made legends of them.

Although they no longer had kings, the Greeks did not feel that they were abandoned without guidance. The gods were present among them, living in the house-temple that derived from Mycenaean constructions, and were described in verse as intervening in human affairs. Their passions and emotions made them more like men than solemn idols. As the gods were invested with the appearance of human beings, the human form became idealised and minutely studied in an effort to re-create it worthily of its divine associations. So the archaic 'kouroi' and 'korai' were created. The proximity of gods and men produced its own theocratic aristocracy, the aristocracy of the oracles and the religious Games. But this was not a closed order living on its ancestral privileges and mysterious relationships with the gods. With the passage of the centuries, the Greeks learnt the holy truth that an aristocracy like this was open to all who were worthy of it.

Athens learnt this secret and so assumed the historic mission which distinguished her from all the other Greek cities. Dominated by its aristocracies, Greece had a unity and uniformity, but Athens, for reasons inherent in her history and environment, detached herself from it to find her own solution to problems common to the whole of Greece.

In spite of Spartan domination and vigilance, the Athenians affirmed the full equality of all men in their relations with the Polis, and limited the powers of the old aristocracy until it was left in control only of the Areopagus, an organ of judicial and political character made up of those who had held the highest offices of state. Athens was becoming the ideal of the motherland to all who could not tolerate the rule of aristocratic oligarchies, and the natural enemy of all those who could not renounce the privileges of centuries. Within the Greek community the rise of a new vision of human society brought with it the beginning of a greater, graver disunion.

Modern historians show more unanimity in their enthusiasm for the Persian wars than did their Greek predecessors. The Persian ambition to rule the world seems clearer to the critic of today than it did to the political observers of the sixth century BC. But still the replacement of Lydia with Persia was a serious embarrassment to the eastern part of Greece, especially when the great Persian conquest menaced some of the Greek markets and commercial and naval bases. A nation with interests extending from Crimea to Gibraltar could not watch without alarm and hostility the rise of a power which united lands extending from the Black Sea to Cyrenaica, from the Bosphorus to the Indus. Greek trade was threatened not only by the size of the Persian empire, but by the fact that their most active rivals on the seas, the Phoenicians, who were dependants of the King of Persia, were given his support and preference. New supply routes were opened to Egypt, new possibilities of extension to the west opened to Carthage, since so many of the harbours formerly available to the Greeks were now under Persian rule, and so many markets – beginning with Asia Minor after the fall of Lydia – were no longer open as in the past.

Persia was a problem to the Greeks for other reasons as well. Already some Greek cities were under Persian control; those of Asia Minor, Macedonia, Thrace and the Chersonese had accepted Persian supremacy, and some of the Aegean islands were now part of the royal domain. In these areas Persia continued her policy of encouraging conservative tyrannies, local regimes looking for security without too much independence.

When the Greek cities of Asia Minor rebelled against Persia and their leader, Miletus, was destroyed, the mainland Greeks remained neutral, apart from a little temporary aid sent by Athens and Eretria. But after the revolt ended, it was Athens which was able to profit by the newly opened possibilities of trade with the Black Sea ports.

Fear of Persia was widespread, and when the expedition against Greece was being prepared there was a considerable movement in Greece in favour of submission and against resistance, probably led by the aristocratic oligarchies to whom Persian rule would have done no harm; they would, if anything, have gained greater security in which to enjoy their power.

Even in Athens not all the political movements were in agreement. The Persian cause had supporters everywhere, and of course the power of the Persian king and his suppression of the Miletan revolt aroused great apprehension. The people who wanted war were those who feared that Persia would put an end to the possibilities of commercial expansion, that is the people who made their living in industry, export and commerce.

Sparta's decision was necessary before a policy of resistance to Persia could be adopted. Athens adhered to her alliance with the city, but the Spartiates found themselves in a difficult position: as an agrarian aristocracy, they had nothing to fear from Persia; as a military oligarchy, controlling vast areas of the Peloponnese and its inhabitants, and as the nucleus of the strongest of the Greek armies, they could look forward to being dispersed and ruined by the Persian king, who would make Sparta a tyranny and destroy the cradle of the Spartan army.

The alliance of Athens and Sparta was the decision for war, which the two cities wanted for conflicting reasons: Athens put herself under Spartan command in order to rescue her trade and support her middle classes; Sparta declared war to preserve her supremacy in Greece, but above all to preserve the privileges of the Spartiates.

While preparations for war were being made, conflicting aims continued to divide the Greeks, even if they could not prevent armed resistance to Persia, and all military operations were accompanied by endless political intrigue. Persia promised to restore to power the tyrannies that took care to accept her supremacy, and among these were the heirs to the Athenian tyrants, who promised, on their return, to pursue policies different from those of the past, no longer working for expansion of trade for the good of the lower classes, but bound to the interests of the aristocrats.

The policies of the aristocrats and other supporters of the new tyranny split and threatened the solidarity of the Athenian army itself. It was held together and led to victory only by the ability and valour of its leaders, and even so success did not prevent internal conflict, suspicion, and accusations of corruption. Before the second phase of the war the aristocratic groups were once again active to prevent the development of trade, which strengthened the opponents of conservative policies and agrarian interests. They did not want defeat, but refused to admit that Athens must fight by sea as well as by land. A great fleet, a great naval victory, would have justified and encouraged the merchants and sailors and diminished the authority of Sparta, their chief support and hope now that they could no longer count on keeping their privileges under Persian rule.

Although the Boeotians were on Persia's side, the alliance of Attica and the Peloponnese was victorious. Victory prevented the limitation of Greek expansion and of the pre-eminent position held by the Greeks throughout the Mediterranean. But there was nothing strange in the fact that some parties had been opposed to war and favoured

Persia; in many parts of Greece the advantages of a maritime economy were not felt, or consisted only of the still uncertain and often unwanted benefit of greater safety at sea through the repression of piracy. In spite of Greece's position in the Mediterranean, piracy had not disappeared, and there were even Greek ports which drew considerable profits from it.

So naval supremacy was not by any means generally appreciated. The poorer, basically agricultural economies had everything to gain from a peaceful, orderly existence, untroubled by any too enterprising competition. The local aristocracies too felt menaced from every side. The upper classes of landowners and business men, who had carried Greek influence into every corner of the Mediterranean, had not completely disappeared or succumbed to discouragement; but many formerly naval centres had declined and given place to others, and even these had more to fear from the rise of a new power, like Athens, than from Persian control.

The idea of Greece ruled by a king seems to trouble modern historians of the romantic, nationalist school of thought, whereas it meant little to most Greeks, who would not have been in sympathy with modern attitudes to moral and political problems. Persia was for them the power that had succeeded, by triumphant conquests, to the position of all those states which had given thousands of years of civilisation and glory to the lands of the eastern Mediterranean. Also, Persia succeeded Lydia, with whom Greece had enjoyed the friendliest relations. The differences of political theory between Persia and Greece were fairly serious, but not sufficiently so to have much influence on everyday life. Persian sovereignty was based on religious principles which were utterly alien to the Greeks, and considered all those who were not Persians or Medes to be merely subjects without political rights, outside the community of free men. But the result of this was, as has been shown, absolute tolerance of the religious, social and economic activities of the subjects, so long as the king's dominion was acknowledged and the tributes regularly paid.

Persia gave to the Greek oligarchies and landowning classes

a surer guarantee of security to enjoy their way of life than did the new movements in Greek public life. Upper-class Greeks had already taken many habits and customs from the lands now ruled by Persia, and life in some parts of Asia Minor was now something worthy of imitation. Many things that contributed to the refinement of the Greek way of life were in fact learnt from Asia; many products of Greek intelligence, skill and science were destined to reach the Persian empire.

With all this in their minds, the Greeks had also to face uncertainty about Persia from the Delphic oracle, the source of divine guidance for their lives. This, together with the respect shown by Persia for its subjects' religious beliefs, fostered the idea that the gods were not hostile to Persia, and that a single, universal empire could be of general benefit. The universal empire of the King of Persia, in the conditions then existing in the Mediterranean world known to the ancients, was not the ambitious dream of political adventurers. The Greeks, of course, were not impressed by the religious aspect of the idea, but their continuous civil wars, their bitter competition with the Phoenicians, the difficulties of trade with the east, and their close cultural links with the Levant all made it easy for them to appreciate the advantages to themselves of the universal supremacy of the Persian king.

CHAPTER FOUR

*

THE ATHENIAN REVOLUTION

WHEN Greece declared war on Persia, two streams within the Greek community were fighting for control of the country. This conflict had been going on for many centuries, and followed a pattern found in every state; the conservative aristocrats, the class which in the past had held absolute power because its existence had been essential to the survival of the community, versus a reforming movement of classes with less wealth than the aristocrats, but an increasing importance, led by men who claimed that only their policies had any real relevance to the state's political and social needs.

So the war against Persia was more in the interests of the new middle classes than of the old upper class, and the victory was the success of the political movement which was changing the system of political relations with the Polis and so within the Greek community. The accidental communion of interests between Sparta and those cities where the new movement was already dominant resulted in general Greek resistance to the invasion.

The conflict which vitiated the alliance between Sparta and many of the other Greek cities that took part in the war soon came to the surface again as the tide of war retreated. This was either because the non-Lacedaemonians found it difficult to accept Spartan control, and especially the lordly attitudes adopted by some of the military leaders, or because of the character of the victory itself. The reform movements and the new classes themselves took credit for the Greek success, and this gave them a greater confidence and enterprise in the political battle.

After the victory, the aristocrats who had opposed resistance to the Persian invasion thought that once Persia had retreated across the Aegean they could come to an understanding which would guarantee peace, a new political regime, and the re-establishment of their own supremacy. Like some modern political parties, they could see no reason against forming an alliance with any foreign state that would help their own cause to victory.

Meanwhile the political conflict between the cities was becoming no less bitter than that already being fought out within the individual Polis. War had forced the two groups to declare themselves. Athens had witnessed the victory of a party that was gradually bringing about reforms in favour of a section of the population without privileges to preserve, but dependent on increasing its trade, its wealth and its political and economic opportunities.

The Greeks were victorious against Persia because they were fighting an army which had no vital interest in winning. Not all the Greeks were in favour of resistance, but the cantonal and 'oracular state' system of organisation left to each group the freedom to fight without the dead weight of allies with little or no enthusiasm for the cause. All those involved in the war, even if pursuing different aims, were at least agreed on the necessity for resistance, and were not preoccupied with the possible advantages and benefits to themselves to be gained from a Persian victory.

There were also technical reasons for the Greek military success: the distance of the battlefields and occupied areas from Persian bases, the difficulties of communication, the doubtful valour under attack of some of the Persian contingents, Greek tactical superiority and understanding of the value of surprise, and above all the naval supremacy that she gained in the course of the war.

No other factor in the Greek victory was as important as this last. Nor was it a new situation. For more than a thousand years ships and fleets from the Aegean had controlled the Mediterranean. Centuries of tradition accustomed the Greeks to looking on the sea as the road to power, independence and prosperity, and at the same time made of them experts in the arts of navigation and shipbuilding.

The Greeks and Phoenicians were the only nations which could dispute the supremacy of the Mediterranean, and the Persians had neither the fleets nor the tradition to make it even remotely possible for them to acquire naval power; moreover their religion forbad them to sail. So Persia was dependent for her requirements as an imperial power on her subjects' fleets: after the Ionian revolt and the punitive destruction of Miletus she could not rely on the Phoenicians.

The growth and technical improvement of Greek naval power was the decisive factor of the Persian wars: especially as the creation of a great Athenian fleet, built up hastily during the two phases of the war, with a hundred ships under construction at a time, shifted the balance of naval power in favour of Greece: also the new Athenian fleet was a centre of attraction for all the Greeks whose interests coincided with those of Athens in matters of trade, expansion and the development of shipping.

Thus the war did not introduce new factors into the political situation, but was an opportunity for a rearrangement of the balance of power. The conservative, agrarian interests which had dominated Greece in the sixth century BC were still strong, for Sparta and her army were on their side, but now the opposition was also strong, for Athens and her fleet was behind it.

The sense of unity which the Greeks had always preserved as an absolute political necessity did not allow them to imagine the possibility of splitting the body of the Greek community to give it a greater variety of organisation. At the end of the Persian wars Athens found herself at the head of an organisation of cantons which included all the greatest naval powers in Greece; she could have satisfied herself with an alliance leading to a pan-Hellenic hegemony.

The centre of the Greek state was always an oracle, the religious focus and source of political authority. There were many attempts to make Athene, the Goddess of the Acropolis, an oracular deity. The legend so commonly shown on Attic vases, of Heracles becoming angry with the oracle at Delphi and stealing the tripod, was a transparent allusion to the desire to make Athens the centre of the Greek oracles.

The most conspicuous result of the Persian wars was the Delian League. Not only was it the most important movement towards Greek unity in historical times, but it was also the basis of Athens' claim to succeed Sparta as commander and guide – as 'hegemon' – of all Greece. The choice of Delos as centre of the confederacy underlined the Athenian ambitions, for the island which was the birthplace of the sons of Latona was perhaps the only place in the Greek world that could possibly compete with the authority of the Pythian oracle.

So this was not a secession, but an imperialist, aggressive bid to strengthen a movement towards the conquest of the state; it was an aspiration to bring the whole country under a single popular government along lines familiar to the Greeks from several occasions in the course of their history.

Sparta was unable to hinder the aspirations of Athens and the forces in whose name she was acting, not because the traditions of political behaviour forbad her to impose her policies, to interfere and to threaten, but simply because she lacked the means of enforcing respect for her authority. Many factors added to the difficulties and dangers faced at this time by the Lacedaemonian community, and thus by the Peloponnesian League. In particular the internal situation, for the Spartiates controlled the populations of Laconia and Arcadia, and held a large number of its subjects in a state of serfdom, and so had always to be on guard against uprisings by the enslaved peoples. Also there were dissenting voices within the League which would never have allowed Sparta to use the League to attack Athens and her allies. Arcadia and Elis were incited to rebel against the Spartan hegemony by the example of Argos, when Athenian influence had encouraged the maritime and trading powers of the city to break the conservative oligarchy and substitute its own reforming regime. After the Argive revolt the two other cities followed suit, with Athenian encouragement.

The struggle was on for the leadership of Greece; the

episodes of the conflict followed one another for almost a century. Sometimes the trouble was over a wall, built against the will of Sparta who did not want the other Greek cities to be fortified, sometimes it was a plot to remove or ruin the most energetic and effective champions of Athenian reforms.

The Persian wars had scarcely ended before voices were heard denigrating the men who had contributed most to the victory; accusing them of disloyalty and greed for money; personal polemics backed up by accusations of secret agreements with the King of Persia, of thefts, personal ambitions, and duplicity rampant amongst the leaders of the two chief political movements. It cannot be denied that both sides hoped to find support from the King of Persia, now safely back in Asia Minor, which would help them to victory in Greece, since whether the movement favoured a conservative policy based on an agricultural society, or an expansionist trading policy in the Mediterranean, it was useful and logical to provide for a compromise with Persia, for neither policy was likely to harm her empire, and it would be to her advantage to be able to rely on a friendly Greece, without ambitions against Persian territory.

The forces at work within the Athenian party did not allow an unlimited choice of solution. The Delian League was not an established organisation with a fixed character, at least according to many of its members. Even if there were many reasons for linking their future development with Athens, the purpose for which the League had been founded was to finish the war against Persia and to eliminate any possibility of further danger from that quarter. If Athens had either accepted or provoked a new situation in which, all question of offensive or defensive war against Persia having disappeared, the Greeks now found themselves in close accord with the King of Persia, it would have been difficult to keep the Delian League going without coercion, on the necessary basis of spontaneity and voluntary tribute.

A federation based on force would have been against the spirit of the thousands of years of civilisation to which the Greeks were heirs. It was the threat to the freedom and autonomy of their cantonal structure that more than anything else incited the Greeks to fight against Persia, and the unity of the Greek peoples and the autonomy of the individual state were the only matters over which the Greeks could not be persuaded to come to terms. So the imposition of the bonds of federation on unwilling cities could not be generally acceptable. In Athens, many political managers, who were usually of aristocratic stock, were in favour of continuing the war with Persia, of refusing any compromise with the King, and of using Greek arms to exploit their success by carrying the war into Persian territory.

The policy of 'strateia', of prosecuting the war with Persia, was the banner around which rallied the Athenian party that supported the aristocratic ideal. These were the aristocrats who had adapted themselves to the realities of the new situation in Athens; and certainly the aristocratic party in Athens after the end of the Persian wars had nothing in common with the conservative movements of other times and other places of ancient Greece.

The Athenian aristocrats of this period were fighting to save the unity of Greece by encouraging solidarity among the privileged sects of each canton. It was often said in the propaganda of the time that a Greece solely dependent on Athens, without Sparta, was lame. It was true that peaceful relations with Sparta were the only hope and only safeguard of the Athenian aristocrats, who were aware that the might of the Spartan armies still counterbalanced the naval power of their own city, not just because of its military potential, but because of the social system which was its basis.

The only way of ensuring peaceful co-existence with Sparta, and the peaceful continuation of the Delian League side by side with the Peloponnesian League, was to direct Greek energies towards further victories against Persia. Success by land and sea along the coast of Pamphylia greatly increased Athenian popularity with the aristocratic and oligarchic parties throughout Greece. During these years Greece was acquiring a new self-awareness and self-confidence. The policy of appeasement towards Persia was condemned instead of tolerated as it had been in the past; what used to be called 'reaching an understanding with the enemy' was now called 'Medism', and caused the downfall of some of the greatest Greek politicians.

The victories won by the Athenian aristocrats against Persia coincided with Spartan victories against the Peloponnesian rebels against her hegemony, and the restoration of conservative governments in the cities of the peninsula from which they had been expelled. The Athenian armies played a chief part in the restoration of aristocratic control throughout Greece. Her policy did not aim at bringing about profound innovations in the traditional patterns of Greek political life, such as would have accompanied territorial conquests, as was later shown by the Macedonian invasions. The Greeks did not force their way into the fortresses, palaces and treasuries of the King of Persia. Athens was less ambitious. Her aim was to win control of the Aegean, which meant stripping Persia of one of her most distinctive possessions, while at the same time avoiding direct confrontation with the Persian armies on their own ground, which would have reversed the situation which had enabled the Greeks to win the wars with Persia on Greek soil. By continuing to fight at sea the Greeks used the weapons and tactics which suited them best, and Persia least, for she was still dependent on the aid of her Phoenician subjects. The reserves of naval power on which Athens counted need not have been unequal to the task. It was only necessary for all her allies to remain united for the attack to succeed. But this did not happen. The difficulties in which Athens found herself because of discord within the Delian League, financial problems, and jealousy among the cities and their factions, greatly complicated the problems of the naval commanders, and in the end brought to nothing the plans for expansion. But perhaps more important than all these obstacles to the plans for harrying Persia and expanding the Greek empire eastward was the struggle growing within Greece to prevent the aristocracies from remaining in power, especially in a city such as Athens.

In Athens, in fact, some members of the old aristocracy had been forced, in order to retain their position in the governing body of the state, to act as the representatives of middle-class interests and aspirations, and to ally themselves with the groups which had recently become wealthy, landowners and industrialists, to defend themselves from the pressures put upon them all by the poor, to whom the naval policy had given an importance out of all proportion to the attention paid to their needs in the economic policies of the city.

The classes which equipped warships for the city now knew that their importance to the state was no greater than that of the classes from which the hoplites were enlisted. Equally, all the makers of cloth or pottery or metal goods or any other merchandise providing the city with trade knew that for economic reasons the city had to take them into account. But this was not what happened. The politicians paid little or no attention to these developments, and this political inadequacy to deal with social conditions created the situation from which, inevitably, revolutions spring.

In foreign politics, the poorer classes of the population wanted the greatest possible commercial and naval expansion, and this could only be achieved by breaking down Persian control of the Levant and driving the Phoenician fleet from the eastern Mediterranean, even perhaps from Carthage. Only this policy could provide work for all, a ready market, and cheap imports. But it was precisely this which the upper- and middle-class landowners were anxious to avoid, for they were afraid that the success of the lower classes would lower their own standard of living.

So the political conflict flared up all over Greece, for internal and foreign politics were inextricably interwoven. In Athens the struggle between reform and conservatism was kept within the bounds of party politics, but in the Peloponnese it led in the end to civil war. The resistance put up by the Arcadians forced Sparta to seek help from Athens. It was the speed and enthusiasm with which the conservative politicians in Athens embraced the Spartan cause, as well as the discourtesy with which Sparta treated the auxiliaries she had solicited, which created a tense atmosphere in Athens and started the democratic revolution there.

This was the beginning of a period of vital importance in the political history of the world. The question being fought out in Athens was important enough to justify a revolution;

while the close relations of the various cantons, and the ambitions of some political groups to dominate the whole of Greece, made it inevitable that Athens and Sparta would take a close interest in what went on in the other city.

The Athenian democrats and their supporters were bound to see the Athenian expedition to help Sparta as an act of hostility and oppression towards themselves by the conservative aristocrats who governed them. To use the state's armed forces in an enterprise against the interests and principles of a class that in any case thought itself undervalued by its rulers could only strain the situation to breaking-point. Solidarity between the governing bodies of the Greek cities was something comprehensible, expected, normal; but now Athens was in the throes of a battle over the constitution of her governing body, and so gave voice to the opposition to the Spartan oligarchy felt by the opponents of the Athenian conservative regime.

The Athenian expedition to the Peloponnese mobilised several thousand hoplites, that is, it removed from Athens several thousand citizens with safe incomes who were able to offer themselves for military service in the fully-armed infantry. This was a large proportion of the landowning middle class, which had been on the side of the conservatives ever since the Persian wars. This was the chance for the popular party to be successful in the public elections.

The chance was not lost, and the elections marked the end of the Areopagus as a political power, and the downfall of the conservative oligarchy. It was the beginning of a new experience, unique in the history of the ancient world, of a governing body deriving its authority from the most numerous but poorest group of the population, the basis of the city's wealth through trade and industry.

In Athens, as in the whole of Greece and the ancient world, the legitimacy of the state gave an authority to the acts of the kings, the wealthy aristocrats, the military leaders and the exponents and adherents of religious cults, loosely referred to as 'priests'. Theocratic legitimacy was not necessarily linked to the power of a kind or an aristocracy, nor need the king, if there were one, necessarily base his power on an aristocratic group. The revolution in Pharaonic history probably consisted precisely in the ruler's reaction against the dominion of an armed aristocracy, a priesthood, and a tightly knit group of rich men. But never before had the social, economic and military relationships of the various groups in any community created a situation in which the poorest citizen class could claim political power.

The conquest of the Attic community had not yet spread to the whole of Greece. The reforming political current had swept over Athens, but the conservative domination of parts of Greece was still untouched, and the country as a whole was still represented by the Spartan oligarchy, which controlled, amongst other things, the law-making institution of the Delphic oracle.

The conflict in Athens was, all the same, of pan-Hellenic importance. Being the greatest naval power in Greece and the Levant, Athens had not yet lost the opportunity of being the leader of Greece in place of Sparta. The Athenian intervention to assist the Spartan conservatives was itself taken by some as a gesture of generosity and ostentatious military display calculated to offer a proof of superiority and, almost, of protection.

The Athenian aristocrats, in their dealings with Sparta, never lost sight of their most passionate aim of leading the Hellenic community, uniting its two factions and co-ordinating Athenian policy with the Greek political scene in general. The problem of relations with Sparta and the other Greek centres also weighed very heavily on an Athens under popular control, for new motives of internal politics were added to the usual reasons of foreign policy.

For many years the rise to power of the democrats did not mean that men of this class took over complete control of the administration. The men who had governed under the old conservative coalition continued to govern – different individuals, different policies, but the same families and social class – and the transformation of the lower orders into a dominant class came about in the only way possible, which became the pattern of later social revolutions on the Athenian model. The idea governing developments in Athens was that some way must be found to enable the men who had to work day by day for their living to take part in the assemblies and public administration. The solution found was that of paying compensation for attendance at the judicial assemblies.

Unprecedented events were taking place under the gaze of the ancient world. Before this time manual workers had been kept in a state of near-slavery, lacking even the means to clothe themselves properly, considered an inferior category of mankind worthy of no better education than the harsh school of military service on the warships. This mass now found itself, by sheer force of numbers, dominating the men who a generation before they had thought of as superhuman beings, the aristocrats whose beauty, cultivation and physical, oratorical and military gifts made them seem closer to the gods, whose occupations and attitudes they imitated, than to men who lived in filthy hovels, starving, brutish and exhausted with toil.

Once the system of payment for attendance at the judicial assemblies had been worked out, a method of levying public funds for the relief of the poorest citizens was used for the first time. No tribute was demanded of the rich to pay compensation to jurors, but the public treasury which met these expenses was no longer responsible for other public expenditure or for the usual redistribution of profits to the citizens, and this created a sort of indirect taxation of the rich to benefit the poor which could not have been carried through directly.

The compensation to the jurors of the Heliaia was, inevitably, only a beginning. Gradually all public offices came to be salaried, attendance at the political assembly was paid, and finally it became customary to distribute money at public festivals and the theatrical performances that accompanied them. The poor had gained control of public administration, and naturally encouraged the view that they should be able to leave work to carry out any public office of any sort. This led to the feeling that people taking such an important part in public life, without any adequate education to prepare them for it, should be given access to every opportunity for cultural and spiritual development. So a special form of compensation was invented, enabling the treasury to make payments for attendance at the most accessible and useful form of cultural life, the theatre.

The revolution in Athens was no easier to keep going than in any other part of the Greek world. The popular majority had to defend itself against all sorts of ambushes and obstacles. Although the power of the upper classes had been reduced by the limitations imposed on the Areopagus, it was still strong enough to organise the democracy to their advantage in some ways. In particular the men of the upper classes had the advantage of an education which enabled them to attract the attention of the masses by their oratory and eloquence, and win great prestige for themselves. In the same way their financial position aided them, for by giving work to the employees of their farms and factories they could secure their votes for themselves. Birth and family retained their importance; men of the upper classes continued to be elected to posts of command, and even when they were under the supervision of delegates of the popular party and working in its interests, their links with relations and friends in the opposition party were only too clear and dangerous.

These difficulties were dealt with by the use of a method of appointing magistrates which was without precedent and has never since been seriously imitated; appointment by lot. It was a system founded on an absolute, abstract concept of equality, denying the realities of human variation in intelligence or any other quality. Lottery was of course regarded by the ancients as being to some extent guided by divine intervention, but it is clear that in this case it was used as a defence against electoral imbroglios, and against an inexperienced people's weakness for soap-box oratory and specious arguments.

In Athens' relations with other cities, and especially in her relations with the Delian League, the effects of the revolution were very marked. The democracy suspected every conservative regime, needed more money than ever before, and more than ever wanted to lead Greece, to impose her regime and her attitudes to foreign policy, expansion with Persia and with the west.

This led to a coalition between the conservative opposition

in Athens and the conservatives of the rest of Greece. Where they were still in power they wanted to prevent the Athenian example from influencing their own people. All Greece was split into two political camps, fighting for control city by city, canton by canton. Other factors too influenced the course of the conflict. One of these was the pressure exerted by Athens on the members of the Delian League; fiscal pressure, to exact tribute in cash in place of the ships and crews covenanted for the common fleet; and political pressure to hold the League together at all costs, and to prevent the conservative elements from gaining control. In this way the naval power of the League became a police force under Athenian control.

Athens' relations with the Delphic oracle were equally complicated. Spartan influence there and the conservative tradition meant that the law-making activities of the oracle were inevitably in favour of the oligarchies and opposed to the new Athenian regime. The pan-Hellenic authority of Delphi was one of the great strengths of the opposition to Athens, since it forced the democrats to make an unwelcome display of rebellion against religious authority.

Greek culture was constantly revising accepted ideals and expressing new ones in the work of philosophers and artists. For Pindar, the Greece of the aristocrats, of religious unity, of the Games and festivals, was the true Greece, and so her greatest gifts were the superhuman perfection of her noblemen, the heroic and sacred character of her Olympian victors.

Pindar wanted peace and non-resistance to the Persian invasion, which would have safeguarded the aristocratic privileges. But later on, the Athens of the aristocratic revival and the continuation of the Persian wars was exalted by him as an illustrious and blessed city, the 'divinely-protected bulwark of Greece', whereas he expressed contempt for the foolish attempt at democratic government, since to him it was clear that the gods blessed only the government of men made wise by long tradition and divine descent.

Athens had won the praises of poets and philosophers, especially those closest to the aristocrats, when at the end of the Persian wars she returned to an aristocratic government and followed this with new victories against Persia. Simonides too gloried in the humiliation of Asia and the power of the Greek fleet led by Athens, and it was at this time that the idea took root, to the disadvantage of Sparta and her army, that the greatest responsibility for the Persian defeat belonged to Athens. At this time Athens succeeded in using the admiration and gratitude felt by all Greeks for the conquerors of Persia to give an emotional support to her supremacy over a large part of Greece and her hopes of gaining the position of 'Hegemon.'

If the testimonies of Pindar and Simonides show us that the state of mind which supported the Athenian supremacy was to be found throughout the Greek world, Aeschylus expressed the religious and spiritual problems and anxieties existing behind the Athenian façade. Aeschylus is for us the most important exponent of the political idea which corresponded with the secure sense of religious values found in the earliest tragedies; it is the idea, expressed in the 'Persae', of the peaceful co-existence of Persia and Greece within their respective confines. In religious matters Aeschylus was the exponent of aristocratic ideals, and so too on the greatest political questions. His solemn affirmation of the eternal, awe-inspiring force of oracular law, in the 'Seven against Thebes', is at one with the recognition of the rights of human reason against the tyranny of Zeus, and of the existence of a justice which, although divine, is bound by pity and reason.

Aeschylus' world had its problems, but was still linked to the aristocratic tradition of relations between gods and men, a tradition still unthreatened and unbroken. In Sophocles' work, however, it is impossible to escape his preoccupation with human arrogance and pride in relations with the gods and their intentions expressed by the oracles. Aeschylus debated the problem of reason as a limit set on the gods themselves; but for Sophocles reason was a cause of pride, 'hubris', and thus a stumbling-block to mankind. In the greatest moment of Sophocles' poetry, in the 'Oedipus Rex', the tragedy of insensate rebellion against the oracles is drawn with all the anguish of a man who has lived through a time of such human defiance.

The exaltation of man's intellectual and physical gifts had changed its emphasis, from the admiration of the qualities in man which brought him closest to the gods, to the conviction that man had within himself the elements of his own perfection, and that he was worthy of praise in his own right, not merely for the virtues which linked him with the gods. In art there was a movement away from god-like, impersonal perfection of form toward the expression of emotion and personal characteristics; the individual no longer subordinate to a pattern but portrayed as himself in all his human greatness. The Panathenaic procession was carved for the Acropolis as a series of portraits of the youths of Athens, the most representative part of the democracy, now become the subject of history.

The people of Athens had found masters, teachers, orators, who taught them things never before heard of: that they should pay no attention to the oracles, that there was no superhuman quality in men that could give them the right to pose as gods. Inevitably the nation rebelled against the exhortations of an oracle which formed the focus of this hostile tradition.

The new Athenian regime, directed by members of the same ruling class that had provided the leaders of the old oligarchy, had only one chance of winning its battle against tradition, the opposition, and religion itself. The democracy must make a success of its foreign policy, gain control of the eastern Mediterranean, and so dominate the whole Mediterranean world. Once the Greek thalassocracy was re-established, Athens could be sure of her hegemony, and the democracy of retaining control and of making great changes, political, social and economic, throughout Greece.

However, Spartan opposition forced the democratic movement to fight in Greece at the same time as it was leading a decisive attack on the Persian armies in Egypt, hoping to seize control of the country and of the seas bounding it. It was not an easy situation for Athens, and became even more difficult when the Egyptian expedition was abandoned and the attempt against Persia ended in failure. This was not simply the failure of one particular expedition, but a crisis for the regime, which had to recognise its lack of resources and agree to the return to power of conservative politicians whose military prestige and experience had proved indispensable. There was no possibility of reopening the Egyptian affair, and the Athenian government had to be content with a peace treaty with Persia which might have pleased the conservatives, but which brought little honour to the new regime or the class which supported it. The democrats had been gravely deluded by their own government of the external expansion and internal consolidation they hoped for.

A peace treaty which established with Persia, after thirty years of war, the very relationship which had been the aim of the conservative aristocracy, represented failure for the democrats. They needed to find markets, bases, trading posts, secure shipping routes, freedom from rivals or competition with their products. They had the Aegean, but it was too small a sea for the most powerful navy of the classical world of that century, and they saw the chance of a peaceful pan-Hellenic hegemony slip from their hands.

The Persian treaty which threatened the Athenian alliance encouraged the opposition. The Delian League, whose members had been humiliated by the removal of the federal treasury to Athens, was now a mere formula. The Athenians made a desperate effort to institute a common Greek fund to reconstruct the sacred buildings destroyed in the Persian wars, and in fulfilment of vows made in the course of the wars. At the same time they proposed the formulation of a common policy for the suppression of piracy. With the first of these proposals, Athens was trying to impose on the whole of Greece the tributes and controls which already existed for the Delian League. With the second, she was hoping to gain for herself the right to patrol the Mediterranean and all the Greek ports. There was no possibility of such proposals being accepted; but Sparta, by taking on herself the job of opposing them, ruined her reputation as spotless guardian of tradition and laid herself open to accusations of supporting the smaller Greek maritime cities which, having no other resources, lived by piracy.

The Athenian proposals had all the characteristics of diplomacy put to the service of propaganda. Such a move could be defended by the plea that Athens was herself the victim of intense, hostile propaganda spread by her adversaries, their allies, her exiles; propaganda based particularly on the intangible questions of the cultural inferiority of her governing class, the heresy of her attitude to the gods; and on the financial questions of the tribute she imposed on her allies for a war no longer being waged, and the damage caused to agriculture by her thalassocratic policies.

The Athenian democracy was suspect in the eyes of the ancient world not only because it was a regime based on the lower classes of the population, but because it was something every bit as uncommon at that time, a state without a secure religious foundation for its legitimacy and authority. There had been usurpers in the kingdoms of the Levant, but these had always surrounded themselves with the trappings of legitimate sovereignty, and if they governed well had found it quite easy to gain the credence of their subjects. There had been tyrants throughout the Greek world, and they still existed in Sicily, but Pindar himself reveals that they took care to invest themselves with the outward forms of legal power. The revolutionary regime in Athens could not be called illegitimate on the same grounds, and there could be no religious objection to its extension throughout Greece. If it had been successful, it would have directed Greek policy in the interests of the poor, the manual workers, the young and obscure, the sailors and traders of all Greece.

The opposition found its opportunity in matters of religion and culture. Thanks to the opposition, although Phocis was now under Athenian control the Delphic oracle still expressed conservative views, and those who disobeyed it were branded as illegitimate powers. Criticism, satire, polemic, vituperation, insinuation flourished everywhere at Athens' expense. All literature derided the Polis governed by workmen, and condemned the revolution as being against nature, common sense and the divine will.

The authority of tradition, and the weighty opinions of the country's spokesmen, writers and politicians, were united in denying recognition to the revolutionary regime, and refusing to adjust the formal, theocratic idea of legitimacy to the realities of a political system in which the importance of the various social classes was to some extent represented in the governing body.

Athens therefore had to defend her political principles with force alone. The Delian League had lost its political and military justification, and found no way of substituting other aims. In order not to submit to the forces of disintegration, Athens was compelled to use her fleet to impose fidelity to their obligations on her allies. As well as transferring the treasury to her own vaults, Athens tried to safeguard her control over the federation by abolishing the Assembly, sending out inspectors and controllers to exact the tribute, and establishing colonies to populate and garrison the territory of federal states. This meant that the League was no longer a group of cantons hoping to create a pan-Hellenic unity. It became a new political form, which the ancient world called an 'Arche', in which Athens became the ruler of a sort of broad territorial dominion whose citizens did not have the same political rights as her own.

Throughout the Greek world, as well as in Athens, this policy opened the way to the possibility of completely new political doctrines. As an autonomous Polis, Athens was part of a community of cities of equal rights, even if they acknowledged, according to circumstances, that one city or another held the position of Hegemon. Indeed the Athenian revolution had tended to secure the hegemony of Sparta over the other cities, free and equal amongst themselves. The difficulty of overcoming the resistance and opposition provoked by the situation in Athens, as well as the problems of the conservative resistance and the Delphic oracle, led the Athenians to adopt solutions which permitted them to defend themselves against the opponents of the revolution, and the Arche became a state in itself within the Greek community, but a state founded exclusively on force, a police state. The absence of a recognised foundation for authority transforms any political organisation into a police state, since force alone can replace legitimacy. The Athenian revolution was in fact founded on the presupposition of the use of force or the threat of it to gain political ends.

The great public works which adorned and glorified Athens were carried out in order to raise her so high above the other cities that her supremacy would be, at least to the eye, generally perceptible and comprehensible. They were also needed to give employment to her people and to enable them to share in the city's weath; this was also a way of gaining a greater following amongst the lower classes, that is, of increasing the effectiveness of the revolutionary regime within the city.

More important was the effect of the 'force' principle on relations between Athens and the members of the League, between Athens and Sparta, and those cities which wanted only to stay outside national politics. Force alone enabled Athens to gain acceptance or submission as both Hegemon and overlord, and to consolidate her new regime. By turning her back on the oracular state, its laws, and the principles of local autonomy, Athens affirmed her revolutionary status not solely in her relations with the Greek community. In the past the links between the cantons, cities, members of federations, colonies and their cities of origin, were all regulated by oracular law, obeyed as a religious obligation. As there were no sacred laws requiring the acceptance of Athenian rule, only the power of might could compel submission to her.

The use of force by a political body without oracular sanction was not permitted by the code of relations between Greek cities. They could use force to impose oracular law; but to found a hegemony which detached a part of the population from the Greek community, and with it to build a dominion, an Arche, was to create a new relationship which Greece had never seen before.

The democracy, as well as the Arche, was a new feature of Greek political development. Since the source of legitimacy was a religious tradition with which both the new developments were in conflict, it seemed to the Greeks that just as Athens had become the tyrant of Greece, the democracy was the tyrant of Athens; all power without legitimate foundation was in Greek political theory defined as tyranny.

In the ancient world the right of citizenship was too closely tied to ideas of birth and race to be easily reconsidered in new and different terms. The population of the Attic Polis knew that it was a part of the Greek community, and while it aspired to the hegemony it never wanted to make a life separate from the other Greeks. However, membership of a particular Polis involved the assumption of certain rights, rather like patrimonies or birth-rights, and to renounce these was, to the Greeks, an impossibility.

Thus the wealth of the city was directly, exclusively, the wealth of its component members. This was one of the essential features of the Polis which gave support – although not for the generally accepted reasons – to the theory that 'independence' was behind the difficulties of building a united Greek state organisation. Such an organisation did exist, as has been shown, and it was publicly acknowledged, although its form was as unfamiliar to the ancient world as it would be to us today; but apart from the economic and social differences which made autonomy necessary, conflicts easy, and collaboration difficult, there was also the network of interests and financial relationships which made up the Polis, and which could easily find itself at odds with the interests of the Greek community as a whole.

The Athenian democracy stood for the principle that every human being (every free citizen, that is) must be allowed equal rights and that the needs of each must be equated with his value to the community. However, this equitable principle was bounded by the concept of the Polis, as a social group something between the family and the oracular state. Just as an individual would not admit strangers into the blessings of family life, so neither did the Polis share its blessings with strangers, or the members of one Polis with the members of another. In Athens the new idea of human rights brought new ways of participating in the life of the Polis, but it did not dispense with the concept of the city, nor with the ideas governing relations between city and community, or ethnic and state groupings.

Athens claimed dominion over what had been a League in order to secure its fidelity to her, but she could never imagine that she was building a Polis, a united canton, out of all the territories she controlled, and use this as an argument for their obedience to her. The idea of forming a single Polis, with a single citizenship, which would be the logical thing in modern terms, was never suggested or proposed. At that time it would have seemed an absurd innovation. The struggle to impose Athenian hegemony and revolutionary policies on the whole of Greece seemed more likely to be successful, even if it meant the end of all the oligarchies, Athenian instead of Spartan leadership, and, in order meanwhile for the struggle to be successful, the subjugation of a part of Greece in a new form of state, the 'state empire' which the Greeks themselves aptly defined as a 'state tyranny'.

There is plenty of contemporary evidence of the character and vicissitudes of the Athenian revolution. In particular, there are two more or less openly opposing points of view expressed in the 'Athenian Constitution' of pseudo-Xenophon, a violent polemic written at a time when the nature of the revolutionary movement was becoming clear, and in the famous debate the 'Melian Dialogue', which is the culmination of Thucydides' work. The dialogue form is used to emphasise the importance of this passage as a résumé of the doctrine of the whole work.

The short polemical tract on the Athenian constitution underlines the defects, the deviations from tradition, and the illegitimate character of the revolution, founded on force and the power of the majority. The writer expresses many of the current objections to the democracy; he protests against a state of things which seem to be unchangeable because it is based on force and is therefore alterable only by equal force. He objects, on behalf of the aristocracy, to the city's total commitment to foreign trade, implying ever-increasing demands for labour and crews for the fleets, endlessly reinforcing the status of the lower classes and increasing their social importance. The pamphlet also echoes the complaints of hostile groups outside Athens; allies oppressed and deprived of the greater part of their autonomy, drained of their resources and economically at Athens' mercy; Greeks outside the League who could not tolerate either Athens' aspirations to a naval empire or the rule of the lower classes.

The Thucydidean dialogue is analytic rather than polemical, and aims at throwing light on the practical disadvantages of the revolution without considering the ideals or aims which might have justified them. As in every other part of his history, but with greater critical intensity, Thucydides paints a clear picture of the errors of the revolutionaries, without illuminating the great new doctrines that they were trying to put into practice. In his view the Athenians had broken, one after the other, all the rules of political co-existence which governed the oracular state. The colony's dependence on its city of origin, the reciprocal obligations of the two, fidelity to sworn pacts, faith in the idea of justice and in the word of the oracles, all the moral principles on which Greek traditions of legality in the oligarchies were founded were now denied, their existence disproved and ridiculed. In their place one argument was given credence and importance; the power of force. After all the argument and discussion, for Thucydides' the chief consideration was the fleet at anchor within sight of the island.

The two documents have a lot in common. In both a protest is made against a policy of force which denies the tradition of legitimacy, but there is no perception of the birth of a new civilisation quite different from that in which the traditions were formed. Those who protested that the revolutionaries consistently ignored the principles of right and wrong referred to revealed law, transcendent values, the divine, ideal world of abstract perfection in which there existed the 'form', the model to which man must refer for his concepts of right and justice. What the conservatives did not consider – could not consider, for the time was not ripe – was that the new doctrine specifically refused to accept the basis of their principles, by affirming the dignity of mankind which was capable of making its own standards of measurement, relevant to the actual occurrence and the individual case.

The democratic revolution seemed invulnerable to its critics precisely because of this appearance of realistic lack of prejudice. But in this too they lacked insight, for they ignored the fact that although Athens denied transcendent origins for its moral principles, it did not deny the axiomatic truths of the normal, human, moral and religious perceptions.

The enemies of the revolution, who thought that its precise calculations of actual forces meant that it was insensible to sentiment or idealism in any form, forgot that human beings cannot cut themselves off from these any more than they can from any other aspect of human nature.

The position of the democratic leaders was unassailable as long as the people were united, but this unity could be threatened by the very idealism that swayed the state at the expense of practical considerations. The only effective weapon the opposition had was the use of law-suits and scandals involving the political and moral leaders of the new regime.

Accusations of administrative dishonesty, impiety, and private immorality made against leading Athenian figures were the first onslaught of opposition to the revolution. Athens lost prestige in these scandals, and embarked on the inevitable civil war with Sparta with a smaller chance of victory than she would otherwise have had. The Peloponnesian war was a conservative insurrection against democracy, which had begun to lose ground with the failure of its Persian policy. This failure, coming as it did at a time when the revolutionaries believed that they had established a firmer position for themselves by refusing the offered help of members of the old regime, was the cause of the democracy's downfall. New and inexperienced military commanders and politicians could not cope with their responsibilities, the failures multiplied, and members of the old ruling caste had to be called in to deal with the crisis.

To Athens in this state of compromise between old and new, the way to salvation seemed to be a return to the fight for a naval empire. She needed a network of treaties which would neutralise the influence of Sparta, and then a supreme effort to conquer the central Mediterranean and regain the empire of the Minoan and Mycenaean sailors of old.

The vital, urgent voices of contemporary writers reflect the emotions of the time; the young men, impatient and full of dreams, who met in the streets and squares to draw maps with twigs in the dust, picking out the goals for which the world's greatest fleet was bound, Syracuse, Sicily, Carthage, Africa, the whole Mediterranean. A nation on holiday, going down to the sea in procession to watch the departure of the fleet and to salute with prayers and hymns the crews as they embarked; the triremes sliding away along the sun's path to the west. These accounts are full of the hopes of a poor and courageous nation, anxious for work and prosperity, trusting only in their own efforts to gain what nature had refused them; they are full too of sadness for the disillusion that waited at the end of the journey.

So the Athenian revolution perished at sea, surviving the Egyptian disaster only to succumb at Syracuse. But everything that the people of Athens experienced in those years of passion, vituperation, conflicts, trials and violent effort brings them closer to ourselves, a part of our own heritage.

The fall of the Athenian democracy, the return of the oligarchy and the restoration of Spartan hegemony could not destroy the record of that experience. Men had learnt that not even the gods can be allowed to support injustice. It had been proclaimed just for each man to have in proportion to what he gave. It had been possible to hope – even if that hope was not fulfilled – that birth and wealth should not by themselves be qualifications for ruling the state. Even more important steps had been taken: men had shown that it was possible to build up a code of law not by revelation, but by discussion among the people, the fruit of their reasoning and their need.

Before this it had been impossible to imagine any form of state or kingdom not of divine origin. Law, to be universal and binding, had to be in some way an expression of the divine will. The Athenian revolution was the unique attempt to base a state and its authority on human reason, and not on fear of the transcendent and unknown, respecting the individual and his rights, and acknowledging that each man had a soul and a conscience, and the right to express his ideas of rights and justice. It cannot be said that Athens chose, or wanted, to follow this path; the development was forced on it by the course of events, by conflict with the opposition and the struggle for survival. It was a product of the Athenian character and the revolutionary struggle. It was this which would survive the failure of the revolution.

CHAPTER FIVE

*

GREECE AND HELLENISM

AFTER the fall of the Athenian democracy and the bitter experiences of the Peloponnesian war, the problems confronting Greece changed. Greek thought was concentrated on elaborations of ideas which are unfamiliar to us simply because we take them for granted, evaluations of the importance of human reason as a political instrument. The Athenians of the fifth century BC had the audacity to maintain that human reason is itself the source of legitimacy and therefore of the right to govern and command, in a world in which the only recognised source of legitimacy was the gods. The philosophy of Anaxagoras had produced the political results which Thucydides expounded in his 'Melian Dialogue': the fall of the revolutionary regime could not wipe out the memory of the moral principles reached by the powers of human intelligence.

The importance given to man as the measure of things, and to his intellectual and speculative abilities to discern the nature of his existence and to make laws for his guidance, was based on his powers of understanding and thus of argument, searching for a way of knowing truth and justice as before men had searched for a way of expressing the divine will. Thus the intellectual search was a way of affirming the existence of a law-making principle, and was the essential feature of the Athenian revolution.

Recognition of the errors which had caused the downfall of the revolutionary regime led to a critical attitude toward the democracy. There was, however, a great deal of difference between the contemporary opponents of popular rule and naval expansion, and the new generation of critics, whose chief interest was the nature of the principles governing the democratic organisation.

The loudest critical voice was that of Isocrates. For him the greatest problem, both in education in the strict sense of the word, and in evaluating a political system, was the question of oratory. If the state's concepts of liberty and justice were to be built up by discussion and deliberation amongst the citizens, then men must know how to discuss and argue in valid terms, and must not see the art of persuasion as the height of wisdom, even where it was being used to unjust and unworthy ends.

Thus the criticism of a democratic government became an implicitly anti-sophist polemic. The fourth century BC developed a theme already familiar from Attic comedy – satire on the power of oratory, independent of the factual or moral truth of what it was asserting. Criticism of the sophists in the fourth century BC reaffirmed the validity of the philosophy underlying the Athenian revolution, for it was this which emphasised the need for a system of oratory which could be the real instrument of the searth for truth, and this search was an indispensable part of any non-theocratic claim to legitimacy.

The particular importance of Isocrates and his successors, whose philosophic systems were developed after the fall of the democracy, was that they finally separated the results and spiritual conquests of the revolution from the problem of the dominant class in Athens or in Greece. What happened was that the classes whose interests lay in opposing the rise of the lower orders to political prominence were those who traditionally recognised and respected a transcendent source of political authority.Thus a governing body which based its claim to legitimacy on the power of human beings to discover their own standards of truth and justice could only support the democracy.

Although the democracy had collapsed, there remained Anaxagoras' discovery of the absolute value of the truth that could be reached by human reason. This transformed the whole ideological nature of the revolution, since it meant that each man could affirm the validity of reason, and the old Athenian hegemony became the supremacy of human reason over the theocratic system of revealed law. As a result, the traditional ideas of the importance of ancestors, the 'Politeia', and the rules governing the co-existence of city and city, based on divine will, were challenged by rules of human co-existence which justified themselves, because they conformed with the concept of right based on human reason.

This spiritual development affected every class of Athenian society with a deep sense of humanity and reason. Athens became the symbol of this idea of mankind, of life and of the world, an object of pride, respect and veneration to the rest of Greece.

So the moral ascendancy of Athens was once again affirmed in Greece. At the same time, men began to recall the benefits of the thalassocracy, and also the purity of the Attic lineage, the purest of any in Greece. This entitled the Athenians to greater divine favour. Such ideas had a certain importance, as relics of the old beliefs which had limited the development of the Athenian revolution. The survival of rather archaic concepts, such as that of the particular bonds created by common descent, had grown into a social grouping somewhere between family and state; the Polis, ruled by a 'Politeia', and accepted divine intervention in human affairs as part of the natural order of things. Like other traces of past ideas, these beliefs influenced later Greek development by combining with the philosophical doctrines of the revolution to create arguments of primacy, or primogeniture, in Athens' favour.

To some extent this new philosophical and spiritual dominion compensated Athens for the disillusion of the democracy. Athens had given food to the hungry, law and order to the scattered, lawless tribes, beaten down the tyrannies and created an open market for the whole country. All Greece was her pupil in every branch of the arts, and her pattern of civilisation was a bond uniting all her citizens as closely as their common racial origins.

Even the contrast of Greek with 'barbarian' had now taken on a new significance. The 'barbarian' was no longer, like the Persians for many of the lands they conquered, the bringer of a civilisation basically similar to the Greek, and in some ways superior to it. Now the 'barbarian' was one who stood outside the concept of man which had become the hallmark of the new Greek civilisation, so that now the Greek was the man who shared this vision, the barbarian, he who did not.

Isocrates gained great influence, at the beginning of the fourth century BC, by expressing views like this which suggested a new way of looking at human relations, and at political theory in general. His philosophy was the precursor of the development to which we give the broad title of 'Hellenism', for it taught reasons for Athenian superiority which had nothing in common with the reasons put forward in the century before.

The historians of the fourth century BC, far from the passions and polemics of the preceding century, tried to pinpoint the reasons for Athenian superiority by idealising both the events and the men concerned. The leaders of the revolution became almost mythical figures, who served Greece without false pride, ruled without tyranny, leaders and not masters, saviours not despots, who won the friendship of Greece for the benefits they brought, not by the threat of force. Readers of the contemporary anti-Athenian polemics could observe the course of the transformation. Even the rivalry between Athens and Sparta had become not enmity but emulation; both fought with Persia for the common good, with no trace of reluctance to collaborate or to resist the invader.

The new political doctrine led to a review of political loyalties. Greek superiority meant that once again Greece was bound to conquer the barbarian. The struggle with Persia took on a new significance. In the past the gods had willed that there should be war, and that the Greeks should win, and the Greeks had fought and won because they were a stronger and more effective army; now, according to Isocrates' view, war and victory must be the natural result of a spiritual and moral superiority. The Greek was a man, which meant a free man, whereas the Persian was a slave; the Greek was autonomous, since he made just laws by the light of his own reason, whereas the Persian had to submit to the arbitrary rule of a king who based his authority on false gods.

Athens had, therefore, the obvious claim to direct and lead the war against the barbarian, since she was already the supreme exponent of the new philosophy. Even in the ancient polemics about the 'scandal' of the Athenian attack on Melos, Thucydides' opinion that it was the victory of brute force was refuted by men who affirmed the right of Athens to further the good of the Greek people, even by an act of oppression, since Athens did not act like a tyrant.

A new conflict of political aims appeared in Greece in the fourth century BC, as a result of the old but unsolved problem of relations with Persia. Greece was deeply aware of the damage she had suffered in the most serious war in her history: that between Athens and Sparta in the fifth century BC. No longer were any attempts at Greek unity based on the premise of gaining and holding a hegemony. War as the ultimate aim of the Hellenic state was still a Homeric-Mycenaean concept.

The Peloponnesian war and those that followed it emphasised the need for a different aim for pan-Hellenic policy: to produce a power which could guarantee peace and coexistence amongst all the Greeks, peace imposed by imperial action. The 'koiné eirené', the general Greek peace, was in every respect an expression of the old, conservative policy. Even at the time of the Persian wars, the Greek conservatives had been ready to accept Persian rule without resistance, simply because it guaranteed their position. Following this tradition, Sparta, in the name of all the Greek oligarchs, accepted a 'general peace' imposed by the King of Persia, in a gesture of imperialist authority whose real aim was to prevent a democratic revolution.

Athenian democracy, especially after its military defeats, was severely criticised for its imperialist and aggressive foreign policy, and for the power left in the untrained and inexperienced hands of the masses. The problem of the fourth century BC, as expressed by Isocrates, was the problem of how to give Athenian supremacy the cultural and artistic character it owed to the world, and how to create a directly representative democracy, even if limited to the classes with the means of acquiring a complete education. Thus education and culture became the qualifications needed both to govern the city and to control Greece. This led to a new development in Greek politics, which transformed the order of society from a ruling aristocracy of landowners to an intellectual aristocracy, and education, based on oratory, rapidly became the distinguishing factor in the new social order.

The 'king's peace' and the 'koiné eirené' were clearly the decisive elements in the growth of a new political situation. If the conservatives, led by Sparta, accepted the Persian treaty in order to keep themselves in power, they obviously refused to recognise that the Greeks, thanks to their vision of mankind and the state, were superior to the Persians. They would not believe in the myth which was the very foundation of the revolutionary view of life, that the Greek, being a free man, could not submit to the barbarian tyrant and his slaves. So once again the theme of unity against Persia in the face of conservative opposition appeared as one of the problems of the revolution.

In Demosthenes' work we find a new formulation of the political conflict. A new element was added to the traditional subjects of dispute (Athens and Sparta, conservatism and revolution, divine and human authority, Greece and Persia). The appearance of a new, strong, and imperialist power in Greece, Macedon, created the need for another decision: Persian peace or Macedonian peace? Both parties spoke of liberty, autonomy and independence, but the supporters of the Persian peace still showed a tendency to believe in Persian superiority, and to deny the significance of any revolutionary ideal or vision of life which menaced their tenure of power.

When, after a struggle of twenty years, Macedon succeeded in imposing its hegemony on the Greek world, with a 'koiné eirené' and a military alliance under its command, the idea of war and conquest justified by innate Greek superiority was a powerful weapon and disciplinary force. The 'koiné eirené' imposed by Macedon gave Greek policy in the fourth century BC a war-like flavour, and it was such policies which led to the Graeco-Macedonian conquest and the fall of the Persian empire. The Graeco-Macedonian war ended in a general transformation. Once the Persian monarchy had collapsed, the Greeks who had fought felt disillusioned and betrayed by the very beliefs which had lent them strength and enthusiasm for the fight, for they saw the pressure of ruling an empire forcing the Macedonians to reveal themselves more as successors to Persia than as builders of a new state.

The demobilisation of Greek troops which had been fighting Persia, the Macedonian dynastic policy in Persia, the preservation of the Persian administrative system and the fusion of Macedonian and Persian ruling groups all gave Greece the impression that the conquered were getting their own back on the conquerors.

It was true that the speed and vastness of the conquest created difficult problems for the Macedonians. Neither they nor the Greek states could provide a governing body capable of taking over the administration of the Persian territories. They were also faced with the problem of how to make the subject peoples accept the legitimacy of their claim to rule. The mere fact that the King of Persia, successor to the Kings of Assyria and Babylon and the Egyptian Pharaohs, had suffered defeat in war, could not alter thousands of years of local tradition and make the King of Macedon the legitimate ruler simply because he had won a victory over the ruler who was himself either a god or the delegate of the gods. Divine wrath would have struck down any man who dared to lend any support to the sacrilegious man who had laid claim to a throne dedicated to gods unknown to him.

As far as organisation and administration were concerned, the only way to make the victory properly effective without reducing the country to anarchy, was to offer the defeated, dead king's governing class the chance to keep its position at the head of the administrative structure and, most important of all, to help the conqueror to gain public recognition as the holder of divine authority.

In the attempt to win recognition the new sovereign had to preserve all the outward forms of etiquette and ancient ceremonial. The feature of Persian ritual which did most violence to Greek feeling was the 'proskynesis', the gesture of the slave to his tyrant, before whom he kneels and touches the earth with his forehead.

The conflict between the King and the Graeco-Macedonian element after the conquest showed up the fundamental difference between the Greek idea of the revolution and the oriental view of the theocratic nature of the state. For more than a thousand years the Greeks had lived under a political system which preserved important traces of oriental, theocratic ideas. Revolutions, defeats, suffering and invasions had matured their political thinking until they had freed themselves of all traces of oriental influence and consolidated their own traditions and characteristics. Centuries ago the Indo-Europeans had been a race of free men, governing themselves by discussion among equals, and by the choice of leaders. As their dominions widened they too acquired subjects, and were forced to impose on them an authority based on religious principles. The pattern of their civilisation changed, so that it was not only the warriors who wielded power. Gradually all citizens were acknowledged to have a potential value to the state, and it was admitted that whereas the gods could guide and protect mankind, it was the human mind, and not the divine will, which lent authority to the men who claimed the right to command. When the Macedonian monarchy was forced to strengthen its position by adopting the outward forms of a theocratic kingship, the act of 'proskynesis' was one of the most serious points of dispute. The Macedonian kings made concessions to Greek ideas of the dignity of free men, but these concessions had important repercussions throughout the ancient world, for if the kings did not exact from the Greeks what they exacted from the Persians or Egyptians, then they, and therefore the gods, acquiesced in the existence of two worlds, that of the Hellenic revolution and that of oriental tradition, each governed by its own code of laws.

This curious duality of the Macedonian empire was workable because of the Persian precedent: Persia had reserved for the Medes and Persians rights denied to the other subjects, and based on a different concept of their place in the state. The Macedonian empire had to take over this form of governmental relativity, with each nation within the empire keeping its own view of the nature of government.

Macedonians and Greeks settled in various parts of the conquered lands. Persians and Medes took their places beside them in the army, the administration and the law-courts; the conqueror of Asia and Egypt governed not as a foreign over-lord, but as their own sovereign, in the theocratic tradition of thousands of years. But side by side with this unchanging world were new Greek settlements of traders, speculators, soldiers and scientists, teachers and sailors, colonists and founders of cities. It was a society of revolutionaries, proudly secure in the conviction of their own superiority, convinced that their civilisation, heritage and philosophy gave an almost holy quality to their search for the nature of truth and justice, without recourse to heavenly inspiration.

This world made up of the survivors of civil wars and per-secutions, of hatred and misery, splendours and ruins, could not adapt itself at all to find a common way of life with its neighbours who believed that the king was to be adored, with one's forehead touching the earth. The Greeks were unshak-ably convinced of their superiority to an enemy so much more wealthy and powerful, simply because this prostration, this adoption of ceremonials of adoration, was a sign that the enemy had an inferior civilisation to their own. Victory must therefore be to them, in revenge for the long-distant invasion, and for generations of envy and fear.

The Macedonian conquest led to an attempt to use both Persians and Macedonians to govern the empire, but this only worked in areas which had formerly been under Persian con-trol. Oriental contingents were also used to increase the forces of the Macedonian army; without them it would have been impossible to garrison all the provinces of the empire.

First Persian impressions of Macedonian rule were soon modified, partly by Macedonian efforts not to fall out with the Greeks, and partly by the need to prevent, or repress, rebel-lions and defections by Persians left in positions of command. But it would have been impossible for the Greeks and Mace-donians to take over completely the administration of the new empire, since the subject peoples could not have adapted themselves to methods and theories of government which were so different from those they had been used to. Where Greeks were put in command of Persian territory, they had to adopt oriental methods of government which brought them into conflict with the demands of the Greek residents there.

The establishment of the Macedonian empire was bringing about profound changes in Greek society. The difficulty of making a living in Greece and the mirage of the wealth of the Orient were driving thousands of Greeks to scatter throughout the new Macedonian domains, in Asia Minor and in Egypt. But ideological, political and administrative differences with the local populations led them to found new cities, and to live there, in tightly knit communities, keeping to their own customs, traditions and methods of government.

The only common feature of the two systems was that both acknowledged the divinity of their common ruler. The Greek tradition of heroes and divine intervention in human affairs made this development possible. The philosophy which had replaced the oracles as the source of authority had not denied the existence of the gods and heroes themselves. Accusations of impiety and irreligion had been made, amidst general approval, against the most advanced section of the governing classes.

The divinity of the king, which the people of the orient had accepted for thousands of years as the foundation of his authority, became a part of Greek life again after a revolution whose principles were only apparently opposed to such a belief. Even if the king were accepted by both parties as a god present among men, their political positions remained completely different. For the Greeks, the divine king could be a guide, a benefactor, a saviour; in fact all the things that a god could be; he was also present among men to share their needs and their suffering, and able to understand and help them. For this he received honour and veneration.

But then the Greeks had always been used to bestowing honours of a religious nature. All the wreaths and statues with which they rewarded the individual for his outstanding physical or intellectual gifts had always been acknowledgements of an affinity with the gods. So there was nothing to prevent them from accepting that a god could be living among them; not even the fact that he was a physical being, since Greek religion had always given the gods a human appearance.

But the real difference between the Greek and oriental view of the ruler lay not in his divinity but in his relation to the law. For the Greeks the king, even if he were a god, was fallible. They continued to maintain that the law was the product of reason, not revelation. For the oriental subjects the king, whether he were a god or a delegate, was in himself truth and therefore justice. Law was the revelation of the divine will, and human reason had no part in it. Naturally, the king could use force to impose his will – possibly his unjust will – on his Greek subjects, but the doctrine of the king's divinity made his decrees acceptable, because as a god and a benefactor of mankind, he could claim obedience as a manifestation of their gratitude and their hopes of rewards to come.

The profound effects of the theories on which the empire of Greece, Macedon and Persia was based were felt until the time of the Roman conquests, or perhaps longer. The divinity of the king was a very important element in the unity of the empire, but it always remained something revolutionary, not firmly rooted in tradition. It was bound up with the prestige of the individual, and so, for the Greeks, it was always precariously open to dispute. The economic and social consequences of the conquest also led to considerable changes in political life. The unlimited influx of all sorts of raw materials into Greece from the East, first as booty and pillage, later through the opening of enormously profitable trade routes carrying everything from gold to manufactured goods, brought ruin to some Greek industries and the breakdown of traditional patterns of trade within the Greek sphere of influence. As a result Egypt and Asia Minor were flooded with Greeks looking for work for themselves and investments for their capital.

While Greek cities were growing up in the Orient, Greece was in proportion being drained of her wealth, her population, and her leadership of the eastern Mediterranean. The Greek spirit of enterprise was exhausted in its native land, but the Greek 'diaspora' brought them into contact with the indigenous populations of the Orient. Gradually they gained control of the economic and cultural life of the whole of the Levant, and Hellenism was born. The old relationship between the individual, the Polis and the oracular state was suddenly transformed into a relationship between individual, Polis and theocratic monarchy. But whereas the god who spoke through the mouth of the Pythian oracle supported the interests of the conservative oligarchies, the deified king of the Macedonian empire was interested chiefly in the maintenance of his royal position.

The victorious, all-conquering king possessed the attributes of the ruling warrior-god: his conquests were boundless, he was unfailingly and irresistibly victorious, and this led his subjects to ascribe to him the political ambition – or, in religious terms, the inevitable prospect – of universal conquest and the establishment of a single kingdom of all mankind. This universal monarchy corresponded to the universal influence of Hellenistic culture. The separation of Greeks and Macedonians from the indigenous populations of their empire, as a result of the Greek conviction that they were both culturally superior and of divine descent, was shown by the different legal codes drawn up for the two groups. Even in legal matters there could be no suggestion that the conquered peoples were comparable with their conquerors.

The Greek conquest was felt chiefly as a cultural conquest. The Hellenic cities became cultural centres; Greek language and education were social necessities; the vassal princes tried to make themselves respectable by acquiring a veneer of Hellenism; the Greek language became the lingua franca of the Levant, and throughout the Mediterranean, from east to west, Greek and Macedonian victories extended the bounds of Hellenic civilisation and brought new areas within the range of its commercial expansion.

In these new circumstances, Greece itself was no longer the centre of the Hellenistic world, either politically or economically. Manufacturing, shipbuilding and the design of armaments had all, in this new world, become so technically complex and expensive that they were beyond the resources of the impoverished and despoiled cities of the peninsula. This general poverty led to squabbles amongst the cities to whom Macedonian supremacy left enough autonomy to enable them to fight and destroy one another, whilst the more backward areas of the peninsula united in federations, and upset the balance of power, giving Aetolia Achaia greater strength than Sparta or Athens. They contributed in this way to the provincial, peripheral, insignificant position of Greece by dispersing what resources she still had in internal strife. The new Hellenistic civilisation, the recently founded cities and Greek communities throughout the Mediterranean, all profited by the decline of Greece, and so did the monarchies which sprang up in the wake of the Macedonian conquests, new and lively centres of Hellenistic influence.

The new middle class, which had its social and political origins in the democratic revolution of the fifth century BC, was everywhere concerned to preserve the institutions of the revolution. The old aristocratic families had lost their power, the magistrates could no longer exceed their authority, the popular assemblies functioned according to the rules laid down in the fifth century BC, and had the same powers. The word 'democracy' had acquired the significance of 'rule of the people', in contrast to the aristocratic or timocratic oligarchies; it meant an autonomous government without a monarch, based on citizenship and rational law, as opposed to monarchy and revealed law.

The new, Hellenistic meaning of the word 'democracy' was the clearest proof of the fact that in the course of the fourth century BC the revolution of a hundred years before had been accepted as an inevitable political development, in spite of the ruinous collapse of Athens, and the criticisms and polemics of the aristocracies. 'Democracy' had become synonymous with autonomy and liberty, words whose meaning was anything but clear when the aristocracies too declared themselves the representatives and preservers of political liberty – liberty for themselves and their privileged sect.

But payments were no longer made to the poor to enable them to attend the assemblies and hold public office. The emerging middle and upper classes controlled the new situation, for the decline in shipping and industry had once again reduced the political importance of the lower classes which had been the moving spirit of the fifth-century revolution.

As the importance of mainland Greece declined, and new Hellenistic cities and kingdoms grew up, with different social structures, a new dominant class was formed. Its members were the capitalists, speculators, and employers of labour, a restricted, privileged class which gained prestige and authority from the political concepts of the revolution, now emptied of their original meaning.

The Hellenistic cities and the autonomous states of Greece were very important as centres of inspiration for the development of art, philosophy, science and technology; indeed for all the distinctive marks of Hellenistic supremacy in the Mediterranean. The cities and states were gradually transformed into autonomous organisations grouped together under monarchs who were the supreme arbiters of policy. The cities were ruled by the powerful, privileged sects which had grown up as a result of the political and social changes which followed the conquest; but these sects were in turn the product of the revolution, which had given a new section of the population the chance to climb to power and then to secure to itself alone the privileges of its new position.

The new monarchies were a fairly long-lasting feature of the Hellenistic Levant. Macedonia, Syria, Egypt, later on Pergamum, the smaller principalities, Hellenised to different degrees, the attempted conquest and unification of the central Mediterranean. They all, naturally, differed from one another according to their history, the nature of the country and of the population.

To the Egyptians the Hellenistic king was, as the Persian king had been, a new Pharaoh, the successor to an eternal throne. To the Syrians the new king had all the attributes of the ancient rulers of Babylon. But to the Greeks, wherever they lived, the new king's divine character was a substitute for the law-making function yielded by the aristocracies to the oracles, with the purpose of integrating the autonomous cities in a legal and political unity. The word of the oracle expressed the will of the gods, and the King-god, or King-hero, based his authority on victory in battle, which was a clear sign of his personal or delegated divinity.

In the eyes of the Hellenistic world, above all in Syria, military success was the decisive feature of legitimacy. The Egyptian king-god was incapable of error or injustice, and only if he were guilty of either would he arouse doubts of his legitimacy. The Greek king was a king because he was victorious, and if he lost a battle he was no longer a god, or protected by the gods. Birth and lineage only gave a valid claim to power when backed up by victory. This view of the nature of kingship was bound up with another concept inherent in the Macedonian type of monarchy. The two presuppositions, unlimited conquest and irresistible victory, led to the vision common to all the political theories of the ancient world: universal political unity. The divisions within this unity were like the divisions between the communities of the faithful and the unbelievers: every faithful community was looking for the universal community which every religious faith has promised. And the Macedonian king, although the leader of a military caste, like the Homeric-Mycenaean king, held his position as a result of god-given victories, and so almost inevitably tended to look for a universal empire.

In this way the king followed Greek tradition: Homeric monarch, guiding oracle, commander of the troops: but oriental influence and the demand of his new kingdoms led him to lay emphasis on other divine aspects of his position, as 'saviour', 'benefactor', and so on. These attributes were far from having only a religious or ceremonial value; like the Pharaoh and the Persian king, the Hellenistic king was the recipient of huge quantities of treasure. Money was one of the elements of his power. It was his means of increasing justice and prosperity in his realms, of redressing wrongs, alleviating sufferings, and mitigating disasters.

To have any real force, adulation must have some basis in truth. The royal titles of the Hellenistic king alluded to functions which he really performed. As the 'living law' (nomos empsuchos), the king took his place at the centre of the free Greek community and at the head of his oriental subjects; as supreme commander, he appeared always on ceremonial occasions in Macedonian military uniform; as God present amongst men he wore no other mark of his divinity than a white (or red and white) ribbon around his head, the Persian 'diadem', a sacred symbol which was equally acceptable to the Greeks.

The ceremonials surrounding the king were not very complex. He needed ranks of administrators to assist him, and developed what might be called his own breed, taking on the sons of the most distinguished families as pages, and companions to his sons. In this way he built up a group of official 'friends' of the king, who governed side by side with the ruler. These were the 'hetaroi' or 'aulikoi' of the king, amongst whom all the most important offices of state were divided.

In this way the empire acquired a governing caste, completely distinct from the Greek element in its cities, just as the cities were not involved in the sovereignty of the empire and its king. He and his administrators were the link between two worlds, the Greeks and the subject peoples, existing side by side. Without fusing the two, the greater power and prestige of the Greek element in the empire led to a wide, though superficial, diffusion of Hellenism throughout the Levant.

The Hellenistic states had an advanced culture, a highly developed military technology, and great experience in the arts of diplomacy. But the most striking characteristic of the empire, one which sprang from the old Greek political background, was the variety, complexity and different development and structure of its component parts.

The highest offices of state were reserved for Greeks and Macedonians, lower posts were given to Orientals who had been brought up in the Greek language and customs. Greek was the official language of administration, and ensured that Greeks retained their control of the government. After the conquest the monarchy in Macedonia did not undergo many changes. In Syria, the king's power extended to the cities, the cultivated areas, and the regions served by roads, while the more remote and peripheral regions needed constant diplomatic intervention, threats, and punitive expeditions to exact recognition of the king's sovereignty, and tribute, from the local dynasties or the chief priests of the local cults. Thus in the Hellenistic state, as in classical Greece, unity was only achieved by a balance of widely differing regional and social conditions.

The Hellenistic state, with its hierarchy of officials, its professional armies, its immense royal possessions and monopolies, its Hellenic cliques firmly settled in their own cities with their own laws and privileges as conquerors, had preserved the characteristics of the oriental state, and at the same time adopted the features of Greek civilisation. In the eastern parts of the empire the Greeks had built up a powerful commercial influence, but they were completely dependent on the king who, with his tributes, reserves of precious metals, and various monopolies, was the sole arbiter of the economic life of his state. This accentuated the superhuman character of the ruling dynasty, which appeared to ordinary men as a force capable of intervening in the life of any man, bringing with it prosperity or ruin, but certain to bring about changes in the natural course of events.

Clearly, then, the situation of the king is the key to understanding the nature of the state at this period of history. He was the law, living and breathing source of right and justice, the leader of the armed forces for reasons doubly inherent in his position as king, and the lord of many nations in many different forms of subjection to him.

Even more important than his position as representative of every aspect of the state was his place at the centre of the governmental system. The link between the king's divinity and both these aspects of his position is clear, whether one is thinking of the veneration of the dead king, or of the living king and sometimes of members of his family as well. The cult could be that of the King-god, as king (or that of a queen or another member of the royal family), associated on equal terms with a god who was considered to take a particular interest in the sovereign.

Naturally, this elaboration was only possible for the Greeks For the oriental subjects worship of the king followed fixed and immutable formulae which could not be altered without endangering the very unity of the state. The variations in the Greek forms of the royal cult were due to the natural variety of elaborations on the theme of a man endowed with superhuman, heroic, semi-divine, or divine gifts, enabling him to perform acts beyond the powers of common man (victories, benefactions, public works of outstanding magnificence). So the Greeks had as many ways of expressing their gratitude for divine intervention as there were events or deeds which clearly showed the hand of the god at work.

The two aspects of the Hellenistic monarchy thus mirrored the two societies which lived side by side under its control. In the ancient world the division of society into ethnic and social groups made it impossible to create any equality of the two elements before the king.

The king's divinity, and his relationship to the other gods, reflected the religious attitudes of the Hellenistic states. Like the Persian empire, Macedon had a reputation for religious toleration which was, in fact, the result of excluding the subject peoples from participation in the rights and duties, and therefore the religious obligations, of the conquering races.

In Asia Minor, a similar situation developed, fostered by the Achaemenids along the lines of their Babylonian predecessors. The only cause of quarrels between the king and the local temples was financial, and such conflicts rarely occurred since the king and the state influenced the local cults very little. The fact that some kings were guilty of seizing temple gold, with no discrimination about the faith of the temple they attacked, and the manner in which the dynastic cult was always adjusted to suit local religion, suggest that the king, like the rest of the Greeks and Macedonians, retained his own religious beliefs. In the case of the only monotheist race in the empire, the royal cult became simply a matter of an annual festival; but in this case, as in every other, the king respected the local religion while remaining outside it.

In Egypt, however, the king's position was more closely bound up with the local religion. The whole Egyptian administrative system was dependent on the divine king's participation, and so his complete adherence to the local cult was absolutely essential if he was to follow in the footsteps of the Pharaohs.

But it was inevitable that the Greek religion should not only remain the faith of the Greeks and Macedonians, wherever they lived, but should take on the characteristics of an official religion in the eyes of the subject peoples who saw it as the faith of the king and the dominant classes. The Greek temples and oracles continued to preach pan-Hellenism, a theme whose importance increased with the dispersion of the Greeks, and the king's obvious respect for such traditions. The ceremonial Games, far from disappearing, gained in importance and number, for the exiled Greeks started new festivals and pan-Hellenic assemblies, as the old ethnic unity retained its significance in spite of the vast areas over which the Greeks were now scattered.

The character of the new empire, however, altered the nature of the old state religion. The existence of rulers, whose religious functions varied from place to place in the empire, made it more difficult for an oracle or a ceremonial to retain the unifying power which Olympia and Delphi had exerted.

The political and judicial functions of the oracles were taken over by the king. The religious festivals lost their former character to become popular feast-days, and their only significance to the Greeks was as occasions for amusement and for a sentimental reaffirmation of their ethnic unity.

Throughout the Hellenistic world, but above all in Egypt, a sort of religious syncretism was growing. The ancient Greek gods, Zeus in particular, were becoming linked in one way or another with the local deities. At the same time, new gods were being created, like Sarapis, with both Greek and regional characteristics, or philosophic and moral concepts were given the form of a god, like Tyché, the goddess of fortune.

This review of the religious situation in the empire reveals the particular character of the new Hellenic, Macedonian and oriental state. Just as the king's authority had a double foundation, so the religious life of the empire reflected the co-existence of two peoples and two civilisations in the same state. This situation was not as awkward and artificial as it might have been, because of the tradition left by earlier empires of religious and racial toleration. However, the official position of certain religious ideas in the state, and the tendency for new experiences and new needs to change the nature of the official faith without reducing the vitality of the old cults which existed alongside it, brought to light new religious problems, involving a reinterpretation of old ideas.

The same thing was true of cultural life. The Greeks could

not live in close contact with other, ancient civilisations without being influenced by them, and this affected not only their cultural and philosophical development, but also their relationships as a social group. The most important and significant effect of the Athenian revolution of the fifth century BC was the new concept of man which spread throughout Greece. The first sign of the importance of this development was the importance given in the figurative arts to man as an individual, with his emotions and his sufferings.

The new governing class was the group from which the artists emerged, and also the patron of these artists. Its interest in the world of art and learning was encouraged by the value placed on man and the new ideas on philosophy and morals put forward by the creators and interpreters of its culture.

In architecture more than in any other art oriental influences made themselves felt, but the value placed on the individual is also perceptible in the design of private houses. The development of the private house, and consequently of the town as an architectural unit, led to greater interest in comfort, privacy and proportion. It was a reflection of a predominantly middle-class society, which could not afford to live in palaces, but wanted houses designed to suit its standard of living.

The pursuit of particular characteristics and emotions is conspicuous also in the figurative arts. In sculpture, each work represents a particular emotion, person, or event. Each painting is a psychological investigation, a portrait or a caricature. It is the art of a mature, secure society, sufficiently pleased with itself not to want to emulate gods and heroes. The distant descendants of the fifth-century revolutionaries had become the preservers of their ancestors' faith in the value of the individual, and the whole world of the time was the expression of a dominant middle class.

The fundamental interests of this middle class were intellectual rather than military, like those of the aristocracy which it replaced. Of course, the Hellenistic monarchies clung to their Macedonian military nucleus, but the larger states which made up the empire depended on vast hordes of untrained and ill-disciplined mercenary troops. So even the army was in need of education and technical training, while in other fields the state needed diplomats, administrators and officials, capable of organising the complex working of a highly civilised and technically advanced empire.

All this demanded abilities which the middle class was both able and willing to supply. Amongst its innovations was a new philosophic system, and a new method of logical argument. The influence of foreign races, together with industrial and administrative problems within the empire, led to further new developments. Greek was the common language through which the Hellenistic civilisation was spread, although the Greek system of education was less concerned with the search for new truths than with the cult of physical skill and perfection. Learning was generously and with due solemnity patronised by the kings, but it was at its highest level mere erudition, and at lower levels was nothing more than the collection of undigested information. It had lost its drive for original thought and investigation, and ventured no further than the classification, collation, and scholarly exposition of the philosophy and art of a revolutionary past. The same thing happened in political life. The reforming spirit, the urge for adventure and progress, were replaced by the jealous preservation of dead forms.

In technical matters too the Hellenistic civilisation was capable of accumulating quantities of information and mobilising enormous forces, but it lacked initiative. The ruling class, satisfied with the position it had gained and convinced that it could survive indefinitely on its inheritance of knowledge and wealth, opposed every new development. Society was becoming sterile, lulled into inactivity by the comfort and prosperity of life protected by the phalanxes of royal troops. The king's very claim to power depended on his ability to defend this prosperity in battle. He was a conservative ruler at the head of a conservative empire, which owed everything it enjoyed to a few long-past years of struggle.

As with its architecture, painting, drama, and system of education, the Hellenistic world was reflected in a literature which represented it to perfection. The lofty Athenian eloquence, which had proved its value as a tool for creative thought, had served its purpose, and was replaced by rhetoric; pompous and insincere, over-emphatic and over-ornamented, it was a system of rules designed to please the listener's ear rather than to convince his reason. It was oratory adapted for the use of government officials and compilers of documents, and dressed up in the ready-made phrases of administrative jargon. The public had lost its taste for literature dealing with the nature of the world and of man, or of debating, with an audacity unique in history, problems which for thousands of years men thought they had solved, and which for the next two thousand years remained at the point where the Greeks of the fifth century BC left them. Literature consisted of romances full of bizarre, erotic, or sentimental adventures; flights from the tedium and corruption of a prosperous and secure daily life.

The classical style of poetry was now the repository of stale mythological learning. The Hellenistic civilisation found for itself a new means of expression: in refined, elaborate, circumlocutory verse. It expressed the longings of people bound up in the daily monotony of an office or a shop, in a city too clean and decent to have anything unexpected and exciting left in it. It painted fantastic pictures of rural life, unknown to most of the audience, and indulged in a tasteful impressionism, drawing caricatures and sketches of a world without problems and without urgency.

There had never been so widespread and uninterrupted a diffusion of prosperity and culture as this society achieved. The revolution that Athens brought about, in spite of the scorn and incomprehension of the rest of the world, led to the social order of a century later, in which the characteristics of the classical world distinguished it clearly from the oriental world.

The nature of the Hellenistic civilisation was clearly revealed in its arts, but was fundamentally an economic matter. The Greek peninsula had produced this world, but in the process destroyed itself. War, competition from oriental raw materials and manufactures, the emigration of labour and capital to the East, changing sea trade routes and the opening up of new supply depots and anchorages, all led to the decline of Greece. She was reduced to relying on her mercenary troops and her schools and universities as her chief means of support.

The wealth of the great cities was dispersed, and with it most of the families who made up the landowning, city-dwelling middle class typical of the previous century. As well as these, there was a lower class of labourers who owned no land, who in the new circumstances lost any social importance they had ever had, since there were more manual labourers than there were jobs for them. Their value was debased by the ready supply of slaves, whose condition in the end was often materially better than that of the free workmen. A few local revolts occurred, but they had little political significance and no chance of success. The power of the middle class was impregnable. For generations it had built up and preserved its position as the greatest power in an unchanging society created by its efforts and abilities.

The solid immobility of Hellenistic social life, with its roots in a rich and active economy, was only superficially disturbed by wars. These were fought by mercenary armies, and concerned only the military and diplomatic castes, while the economy was largely compensated in booty for the damage caused.

It was in its spiritual life that Hellenistic society felt the consequences of this immobility. Fantasy went out of life, and with it energy and imagination.

Side by side with this Hellenistic society, which defended itself so effectively from outside influences that it caused its own decline, there existed an indigenous, Asiatic, Egyptian society, which was kept in a state of near-slavery and political impotence, apart from a small Hellenised minority.

As soon as the great Greek monarchies came face to face with a new, energetic nation, it was clear that Roman dynamism would find no obstacle in the desiccated, conservative immobility of the old regime.

CHAPTER SIX

*

ROME AND ITALY

THE Roman state did not grow up from nothing, in an uninhabited peninsula. The islands of the Tyrrhenian sea had for centuries been linked with the Orient by Cretan and Phoenician trade routes. The races which had inhabited the islands since the end of the neolithic period were related both to the earliest settlers in the peninsula and to the races of the western Mediterranean. In the complex of relationships between the peoples settled around the Mediterranean, the inhabitants were already linked to the Orient and the Greeks by trading interests, even before the Greek colonisation of Sicily and southern Italy. Of course, the strength of such ties varied from region to region within the peninsula, and whereas the Etruscans were deeply influenced by these more advanced cultures, other groups like the Latins, who had no contact with the sea, were hardly affected.

The Etruscans had a highly developed feudal system, and the Latins a simple pastoral community, so it is not surprising that the situation was soon transformed into an Etruscan domination. We have little direct information about the details of this political organisation. It appears that the Etruscans had a sort of federation of cities rather like the early Greek system, with each city enjoying a broad autonomy in a federation held together by religious bonds. The ancient world called it the 'League of the Twelve Etruscan Cities', by analogy with the Ionian League.

The similarity of some of its institutions suggests that the Etruscan state organisation was like that of the Mycenaean-

Homeric state; a racial union of autonomous cantons controlled by a dominant princely caste with cultural, legal and military functions. As in archaic Greece, the central power had no power to direct the daily affairs of the cantons, but it is clear that the source of authority, even in the individual cantons, was the same as for the federation itself, so that the federal bond was effective only at times of political or military crisis, while in times of peace unity was encouraged by a common religious cult. Greek experience had already shown that this was sufficient to give a community of autonomous cantons the character of a state.

In the Etruscan language, the cantonal community was called the 'spur', translated into Latin as 'populus', but the Etruscans also had a word for the ethnic community as a religious or judicial concept: the 'methlum', as well as for the generic concept of the state, the 'tudthi', which differed from both the others. In classical Rome there was a 'praetor Etruriae', an office of which there are traces in the Etruscan language. This suggests that at one stage of Etruscan history there was a regular state administration, possibly of the kind found in Greece at the same stage of its political development.

The Etruscan political organisation of a League of autonomous cities ruled by overlords who held power for reasons we may guess at, but cannot prove, was one of the most characteristic forms of government in pre-Roman Italy. Its similarity to the contemporary Hellenistic civilisation helped it to assimilate Greek ideas. Many of the rituals connected with the 'Laukhume' or King of one of the cities of the League show that Etruscan society recognised the divine origin of the power of command: the golden crown, the quilted toga with its border of palms, the sceptre, the throne, which was the origin of the Roman 'sella curalis', the ceremonial triumph, and the lictors with their 'fasces', which included the axe, the Mediterannean symbol of legitimate sovereignty. Latin used the word 'auctoritas' for this power of command, and derived from it the term for coercive military power: 'imperium'.

Etruria changed from a monarchy to an oligarchy in the same way as all the Mediterranean peoples known to us, and probably for similar reasons or by example. The king's power waned as the importance of the upper classes increased through their control of land which had probably been held in the first place as collective property. This gave them the means of arming themselves and maintaining the horses they needed. The Etruscan monarchy was similar in its organisation to the monarchies of all the Mediterranean peoples, Indo-European or not. A class which held power by right of conquest possessed the means of production, land and animals, in common. The subject peoples worked the land and tended the animals on behalf of the rulers. In return they expected to be protected from human and animal attacks, and to benefit to some extent from the more elaborate quests for wealth and booty undertaken by the nobles.

At the southern limit of Etruria's zone of influence was a region of great importance, in the lowest range of hills on the lower course of the Tiber, before the river becomes navigable on its way to the Tyrrhenian sea. These heights were inhabited by Latin and Sabine shepherds who settled around the valley of the Forum, at the foot of the Campidoglio. The Etruscans succeeded in imposing their rule on the area and transforming it into a city, and it became an essential possession, equally important for their control of the newly opened route to the sea and for the maintenance of their line of communication with southern Italy. Here they introduced their customs, their religion and their political system. Whilst their aristocracy was ruling the city, a small local class of artisans, manufacturers and merchants was growing up as a result of Etruscan economic policy and the outlet to the sea which the city had gained.

When the Etruscans had to withdraw west of the Tiber, their monarchy at Rome fell, and with the passing of the 'laukhume' the most influential local class came to power. They retained the administrative and cultural structure of the Etruscan 'spur', as well as the exterior forms of the legitimate Etruscan sovereignty. The Ruler's power passed to two magistrates chosen annually from an assembly of nobles. This assembly, which was similar to many others in lands bordering the Mediterranean, believed that it was invested with the same divinely sanctioned authority as the monarchy had been. The senate composed of the clan leaders, who were the military commanders, under the supreme Roman deity, Jupiter Capitolinus, became the repository of the 'augurium' from which 'auctoritas' was derived.

Independent Rome inevitably resembled Etruscan society very closely. In common with most Mediterranean peoples, they believed that the right to rule was given by the gods to those who fought for their country. The division of the city's inhabitants into two groups occurred for reasons which were not necessarily financial, but the result was that one group had all the religious and political rights, while the other group were merely inhabitants of the city, linked to the ruling class by neither religion nor family. They had no military obligations and so no political rights. They were excluded from the ancient and noble ranks of the 'patres', and there was no possibility of business relations or intermarriage between them, for the two groups did not belong to the same community. The patriciate was a 'nomen', a closed sect, with its own religious observances, 'sacra'; it governed the state and defended it. To belong to the 'populus' which possessed these sacred rights was the gift of the gods, and dependent on doing military service.

But the patricians needed, and could not avoid, the participation of the 'plebs' in the life of the community. Some modification of the total separation between the two groups was inevitable. The first of these occurred when some of the patrician families offered legal protection to certain plebian families, with a mutual exchange of support and aid. This was the beginning of the institution of 'clientela,' which brought no change in the legal position or political rights of the plebs.

After the Etruscan domination ended, Rome once again became an agricultural and pastoral community, in contrast to the neighbouring Latin federation. The Latins, in alliance with Cumae, had united to defeat the Etruscans in Campania, and then had tried to destroy the wealth and independence of Rome by forcing her to join their confederacy, which centred around the shrine of Diana Nemorensis. In order not to lose her freedom, Rome had to face war. The struggle gained her parity with the Latins, and this was later turned into a Roman supremacy. The Roman army was more compact than the federal Latin army, and this, together with the political rivalry between members of the League, enabled the Romans to get the upper hand and to take over the command of the combined forces. This was the basis of the armed community which was to play so important a part in the political and military development of the Roman state.

Relations between the Romans and the Latins were to some extent a reflection of those between patricians and plebs: the Latins and the plebs both formed 'nomina' outside the patritiate which inherited the dominant rôle of the Etruscans. When the plebs began to take a more important part in the life of the state, the relationship between the two groups began to change. As the financial distinctions grew less marked, so did the political division caused by the inheritance of Etruscan power by the class which already held a part of it, at the expense of those who by tradition had always been deprived of it.

The defence problems created by events following the fall of the Etruscans and the victory over the Latin confederacy imposed a very heavy burden on the patricians eligible for military service. Each of the ancient patrician tribes was divided into ten sections, called 'curiae', which were divisions of the citizen population, and areas marked out for the levying of troops, given the connection between political rights and military obligations. As a result the assembly was composed of men eligible for military service, and the recruiting body was the assembly itself.

When the patrician contingents were no longer enough, they had to recruit plebians, and later allies, 'auxilia', and detachments of foreigners. Greater and greater military demands were made on the plebs, and so the question of the law in relation to the two groups came up. The plebs had to be inscribed on levy lists, and so the Romans attributed to the ancient monarchy the creation, side by side with the racial tribes, of twenty territorial tribes. Those who belonged to the 'gentes', and so to the 'curiae', the original levy lists, citizens and patricians, formed the 'classis', the basic contingent to be levied. The plebs, who entered the levy lists by way of the territorial tribes, formed a contingent described as 'infra classem'. Although there were differences in the levies made on the two groups, the road was open to a fusion of the two nomina, and so to the admission of the plebs to the state assembly. The oldest Roman constitution was founded on the institution of the monarchy. The king was the source of power, but under the direction of the patrician assembly. It was believed that the divine forces giving the king his authority acted also in the assembly: the laws made by the assembly in collaboration with the deity had the same authority as those made by the king under divine guidance. When the monarchy disappeared, its religious functions passed to a person invested with the power to make sacrifices on behalf of the community, the 'rex sacrificulus'. The executive, judicial and military powers passed to two annual magistrates called praetors. The same powers were given to two lieutenants of the praetors, known as consuls, while the praetors remained the titular holders of authority in legal matters.

When the consulate became the highest office of the Roman magistrature, the evolution of the state from the Etruscan model reached a significant point. Now the very idea of the 'people' was identified with that of the 'army'. Military service was the single basis of any claim to citizenship, and now the military magistrates took precedence over those with religious or legal functions. Even the development of the public assemblies shows the increasing importance of military forces in their ranks as the basic element of collective life.

Gradually the consulate assumed all the attributes of royal power. The year took its name from the consuls, and either one had the right to veto the action of his colleague and subordinates. Around the city was drawn an imaginary line, the 'pomerium'. The territory of the state, in which the powers of the 'numina', the Roman gods, were felt, and the laws inspired by them were effective, came to an end at this point, and foreign territory began. Here Rome held power by virtue of her military control of the area. But within the city no one was allowed to carry arms, the power of open violence was restricted, and the greatest care was taken to maintain good relations with the gods, for only in this way could the prosperity and happiness of the citizens be assured.

In order to preserve the 'pax deorum', the citizens had to take care not to offend the gods by acts of sacrilege or violation of divinely inspired laws. The will of the gods was revealed not by oracles, in the Greek manner, but by the Etruscan method of interpreting signs visible in the sky or in the intestines of animals. The most important consideration, for the Roman magistrates concerned with the legitimacy of the power they held, was to ensure that the gods approved of the decisions taken by the councils and magistrates, before they were put into practice. It was generally accepted that in the right conditions the gods would grant their approval, help and inspiration to the assemblies, who then could not be wrong or unsuccessful.

Within the pomerium the magistrates also lost the absolute military power which they had inherited from the early kings. They did not have absolute powers of life and death over the other citizens, their authority extended over only a limited field, and, most important of all, their superiority to the rest of the community was the result not of inherent right but of a temporarily held office. Elected by the 'populus', that is by the men who held full citizenship because of their service in the state army, the magistrates were an expression of the collective sovereignty of the assembly, guided and assisted by the gods, as the celestial signs confirmed. The original assembly consisted of the thirty curiae into which the tribes were divided. When the plebs were admitted, in archaic times, they were given the right to vote but not to be elected to office. The curiae also had religious functions, when they were united in their assembly, the 'comitia'. There they invested the magistrate with the authority to command; the legitimate authority without which his position was invalid and his 'imperium' meaningless. This was a religious ceremony, and only citizens in full right, who belonged to the racial, and so to the religious community of Rome, could take part as priests in the sacrament in which the 'imperium', uniting human and divine power, was transmitted to the magistrate. Thus only full citizens could transmit legitimate sovereignty. When the Comitia Curiata lost much of its political importance because of the increased influence of classes which could not become members of it, it still retained the function of transmitting the right to command, for this was a religious function, in which the formal act was of supreme importance, and any variation of it would diminish the potency of the concept of legitimacy.

For a long time the Senate remained another exclusive stronghold of the patrician class. Apart from the consuls, members of the Senate held the same consultative and executive offices as had existed under the monarchy. When the supreme magistracy of the Senate became an annual office, and the aristocracy took over complete control of the state, the powers and importance of the Senate increased. The assembly itself represented the continuity of power, while the magistrates came to office for a year, and then took their places as former holders of the highest office of state. Thus Rome had a simple, constitutional distinction between the governing class, consisting of all rightful citizens participating in the assemblies and under an obligation to do military service, and the men whose chief occupation was state administration or military command. These were the real governing caste, whose numbers were limited to the members of a few families. With the growth of the republic the importance of the Senate grew as well. The opinions which it had originally offered to the king gained more and more weight when offered to the elected magistrates. Eventually the 'Senatus Consultum' gained the value of an absolute decree, binding upon the whole community, including the magistrates.

The development of the Roman state shows many characteristics in common with other Mediterranean countries, although the time sequence is sometimes different. The parallel with some Greek cities is particularly close. Similar social, economic and cultural traditions, as well as the exchange of ideas which affected especially the development of the Roman religion, help to explain the affinity of Greece and Rome as something like the affinity of the various Greek cities. But in both cases it is not always possible to trace exactly parallel courses of development, because of the different geographical, political and social conditions of the various centres.

The political conflicts resulting from changing social conditions in Rome reflected those that had occurred in Attica. Archaic laws on the protection of property and the individual contributed to poisoning the relations between the patrician and the plebian classes. When precious metals became scarce, and shortages of raw materials led to frequent famines, following the collapse of the prosperous Etruscan domination, the situation worsened. The defaulting debtor was liable to personal enslavement or even death. Such laws as this were evidence of the political supremacy of the wealthy classes. They were incompatible with the increasing importance of the formerly poorer classes who no longer tolerated the existence of privileges which no longer had any justification.

The introduction of compulsory military service for the plebs made it perfectly clear that active participation in the life of the state no longer depended on birth into families of a certain inherited position in the state, but on the possession of a certain income. The revolution in Roman politics closely resembled what happened in Athens, substituting the armed infantry for the cavalry and chariots of the warrior lords, so that the less wealthy classes could afford to equip themselves.

In Rome the situation was complicated by religious questions. Certain cults were open only to the descendants of the families through whom the cult was transmitted from one generation to the next. To admit strangers would be an act of sacrilegious impurity which would arouse the wrath of the gods. This was why the plebs could not enter the assembly, and was also the reason why the plebs began their struggle for equality by attacking the legal situation, concentrating on specific laws governing the rights of the individual. Absolute legal equality was not even thinkable when the two factions were not part of the same 'nomen', and so on matters of great importance had no common ground.

The Romans' first attempt to solve this problem was to recognise certain political rights of either of the two groups which emphasised their particular characters. At this point we cannot compare the political history of Rome with developments in any other country, because of the religious and racial basis of her political ideas. The Romans found it more acceptable to reform their political system by recognising the official leaders of the plebian community as officers of state. Thus within the territory of Rome there existed two political communities, federated after a fashion, with reciprocal rights and guarantees. The plebs had their assembly, the 'Concilium Plebis'; their own leaders, called tribunes, who superintended the civil and military activities of the plebs; and administrators of their own temples and cults, which were particularly the three gods of the Aventine, Ceres, Liber and Libera.

The greatest problem was one which had only recently become important: the reciprocal validity of the laws and decisions made by the two communities. This problem was as difficult to resolve as it was urgent, because of the old subordination of plebian interests to those of the patrician class. In fact the political superiority of the patricians to the plebs was generally admitted, but it was only when the plebian community officially recognised it that the two communities acted in unison, and thus the problem of legal guarantees was posed. One of the first requests made by the plebs was for the inviolability of their tribunes, and for their right to represent and defend plebian interests ('ius auxilii ferendi plebi').

From the first it was decided that nothing should upset the functioning of the plebian 'concilia'. The patricians recognised the sacrosanct character of decisions reached by the plebs, because of the sacred oath by which they bound themselves to respect these decisions. Every concession in this direction led to further concessions; the right of 'auxilium' had to be given a concrete form. At a fairly early date the right of 'veto' was introduced. This gave the plebs power of a sort over the patricians, since by interposing their veto the tribunes could prevent the carrying out of decisions made by any magistrate, the Senate, or the committees, and could impose penalties on anyone who challenged them.

Later on another transformation of the political scene occurred when the size of the army was increased to keep pace with the rising population. The need to take income as the criterion of liability for service in the army made it difficult to preserve the distinction between the patrician and plebian communities. All those eligible for service were grouped into 'centuries' according to five predetermined levels of income. The richest were bound to serve in the cavalry, and the rest were drafted according to income. The relationship between income and military service was based on the ability of the family to survive without its paterfamilias or one of his servants, and to bear the cost of his arms, which varied according to the 'classis'. The lowest carried only slings.

There were ten tribunes who led the contingents, two for each 'classis'. To ascertain incomes there was a single magistrate with power over both patricians and plebians in matters of establishing incomes and drawing up lists of the population. So already the two groups had reached the point of having magistrates in common, and also a single list of citizens under military obligation to the state. The censors appointed to this office were nominated every five years and remained in office for eighteen months. Their job was to draw up the census which imposed a state control on the private lives of individual citizens. The successful creation of a mixed patrician-plebian citizen body brought to life again the old identity between the population and the army, and this created the need for a new popular assembly, divided into classes and subdivided into centuries, which was called the 'Comitia Centuriata', and represented a new form of military organisation of the citizen body.

The new political situation made the power of wealth very clear; in this matter the richest members of society, both plebs and patricians, found themselves in agreement. The division between patrician and plebian lost any practical significance, and membership of the upper class, formerly dependent on family and military service as well as wealth, was now simply a financial matter. In fact the biggest contribution to the state army was no longer made by the hereditary aristocracy, but by the new moneyed aristocracy. Since they were now so important to the defence and prosperity of the state, they wanted the political position which they felt was their due. The subdivision of the voting population into 'classes' and centuries gave this to them. The century was the voting unit, and the number of centuries varied in each 'classis', the two upper ones containing ninety-eight centuries, out of a total of 193, which gave them an absolute majority.

Thus the most important aspect of Roman political development at this period was the gradual resolution of the problems causing the division between patricians and plebians, even before a state of legal equality was reached. Once the system which kept them apart disappeared, the two communities became simply two sections of the same citizen body. But still they had a different civil and legal status, because of the religious tradition behind the split between them. In spite of the new regulations, the plebs still could not be elected to public offices, nor could they intermarry or trade with the patricians; although they were now citizens, in some respects they remained foreigners.

There is evidence of great agitation and unrest resulting from this state of affairs; troubles which led up to the great Roman revolution of the fifth century BC, the affair of the 'Decemviri'. The plebs had threatened many times to abandon Rome and withdraw their support of the patricians, and now they carried out their threat by retreating to the Mons Sacer. Having gained economic and political parity, they claimed legal equality next, demanding a written code of civil and criminal law, as the Greek lower classes had before them. In this way they hoped to free themselves from the arbitrary judgments of patrician justice. It was the resistance to this demand that led to the revolutionary development in which the power of the state was vested in a group of ten patricians. Under their rule the patricians successfully secured the preservation of their privileges, and all the plebians got was a written code of laws, the Twelve Tables, which embodied the principles of ancient Roman law.

Much later on, the plebians were at last admitted to office as magistrates, and the transformation of the state reached a point at which the 'Concilium Plebis', called by the tribunes, could issue decrees which were binding on all citizens, including the patricians, on the lines of the Comitia Centuriata.

Recognition of the validity of the plebiscites led to another revolution. The timocratic system of the Comitia Centuriata, which gave the wealthiest citizens the greatest voting power, came into conflict with the system of the tribunal assembly, which revived the old Greek idea of one man, one vote, without reference to his birth or wealth. Even in the tribal meetings and the Concilium Plebis, the citizen voted as a member of his tribe, and the influence of the individual vote was limited, since it affected only the majority within one particular tribe, which was the voting unit. The Romans never came to the point of admitting the political function of the individual, for the citizen was seen simply as a soldier, subject to jurisdiction solely on the basis of where he lived and what tactical unit he belonged to.

Once the validity of the plebiscites had been recognised, the deliberations of an assembly where men's votes did not depend on their incomes were often given greater weight than those of the Comitia Centuriata. The will of the plebs sometimes counted for more than the will of the patricians, and the poor sometimes prevailed over the rich. But in spite of these apparent innovations, Roman public life had nothing in common with Athenian democracy. The institution of the Clientela, and the rules which subdivided citizens into voting units according to tribe and place of residence, ensured that the patricians would always have a prevailing influence over public ballots and so retain effective and exclusive power in the state. They could influence the course of the elections, securing magistratures and seats in the Senate for the supporters of the richest and most powerful families, whether patrician or plebian.

When the importance of the old patrician-plebian division, reflecting the archaic Roman state, had finally dwindled away, a powerful sector of Roman society took over complete control. Its power came from its wealth and its control of the means of production: land and capital. This new ruling class of patricians and plebians reached the Senate by being born into the right families, or by making a career in public life, and made this assembly into the instrument of its power. No magistrate could ignore its decisions. Its policies were decisive in foreign affairs and financial matters. It was the most influential organ of a state whose unity was based on giving the greatest power to the men who, having the greatest wealth at their disposal, carried the most weight in the life of the community.

The privileges conceded to wealth did not weaken the unity of the state, chiefly because wealth brought with it a sufficiently wide range of duties and opportunities to justify the political importance of its possessors. Then the close connection between the human and the divine elements in Roman public life bound the members of the nomen, the community of Roman citizens, with more powerful ties than any alliance with the outside world. The force of law and tradition was very strong in Rome, because every law and custom had been developed by collaboration between men and gods, so that any infraction of them was considered a sacrilege which could (or should) bring misery to all and ruin to the state.

While the plebians were winning their long, revolutionary struggle with the patricians for political unity, using military service as their weapon, the Roman empire was extending to the lands of the Latin League, to southern Etruria and the rest of Latium. Rome was fighting the Samnites, and her armies were moving south to Capua and beyond, until they made their first contacts with the Greek populations of southern Italy. With this territorial expansion came political developments which reflected those between plebs and patricians. In Rome the two nomina were fused and the unity of the state preserved. In Italy, the peoples bound in various ways to Rome, or accepting her supremacy, gradually obtained a form of parity. Their relations with Rome did not prevent their keeping their own political individuality or interfere with their autonomy and aspirations. United to Rome by statutes or pacts which varied from town to town, they were all bound to help in the defence of the city against outside attack, but they shared equally in the benefits of victory, because of the security of the state and the increase of its power and influence.

The great political difference between Rome and the rest of the ancient world was her attitude to races outside her own ethnic group and citizen body, but linked to her by conquest or surrender. Like all the Mediterranean states of that time, Rome was governed according to a legal code of divine origins, for even the Romans could not believe that a law or decree not based on divine will was possible. Again, like all the other peoples of the ancient world, they believed that the validity of their laws was connected with their being formulated for a particular ethnic group, whose members worshipped the deities who belonged to them alone, or who were disposed to favour them particularly. The bonds of faith were the nationalist sentiments of the ancient world; men were linked by the same religion rather than by the same place of birth. In many places this resulted in serious exclusiveness; on the one hand were the elect, faithful to the one true God, and on the other hand, reprobates and infidels. Every war was a religious war, and those who did not belong to the community of the elect could never hope to become members, but were always excluded from the position achieved by the rest.

Rome's relation with other races was unique in the ancient world. Her emergence as a city from foreign domination, of higher civilisation, but differing in religion, culture and political ideas from the surrounding population, she was from the beginning a city-state of quite a different kind from other Greek or oriental organisations. From the beginning Romans had had close links with foreigners, and Etruscan beliefs had been imposed on the crude religious ideas of the primitive peoples of the lower Tiber valley. If the people of the hills surrounding the Tiber, and the valley where the Forum later grew, had their own customs, faith and laws, the Etruscan conquerors substituted for them religious, political and military institutions which had no relationship to what went before, but were more advanced and capable of removing all traces of the past. A legend which was very popular among the enemies of Rome in ancient times spoke of the 'asylum of Romulus', referring to the variegated and turbid origins of the population of Rome. Whatever the historical value of the legend may be, it certainly underlines a fact which the ancient world considered very important: that the 'populus' of Rome was without the common origins and other characteristics on which communities of that time normally prided themselves. The more uncertain the common racial origin, the less exclusive were relations between men and gods, so that the Romans must have given the impression, implicit in the 'asylum of Romulus', of a mongrel race without purity of lineage and therefore without nobility.

What appeared to other nations to be a grave fault, making Rome a very inferior state, gave the Roman state much greater elasticity than the others in dealing with peoples outside its own community, first of all in solving the problem of plebians and patricians, and then in relations with the rest of Italy. The great tolerance shown by the Romans in defining these relationships was clearly the result of the heterodox, anomalous composition of the community and of its political system.

The 'asylum of Romulus' was more important to Rome's development than it might at first appear. Even the Romans had their gods, their rites and traditions. But these were borrowed, picked up, invented to meet the spiritual needs of the community but without deep roots in national traditions. The proud Roman patricians, so jealous of their traditions, could not look far back to its origins, or trace its nobility from mythological ancestors, except where genealogies were dreamed up by imaginative mythographers and historians from Sicily and Alexandria. When the Etruscans left Rome, there was an upper class there which assumed a position of power it could not have held any earlier in history. So it is clear that the patriciate from which the founders of the old republic were descended was composed of the wealthy group surrounding the 'lauchume' or 'porsenna' in Rome.

An aristocracy created by chance, the bond holding them together was one of necessity. They were not the descendants of generations of warrior nobles, united by military exploits and conquests shared, or by a reputation for being in constant contact with the gods or for being heroes, half way between gods and men. They were not the sun-scorched conquerors who had carried their arms and their prestige through the Homeric monarchies and then gained supreme power with the fall of the kings. When the city created by the Etruscan overlords found itself alone and undefended in the midst of enemy races and immanent dangers, in an impossible economic position because of its dependence on the protection of a power which had suddenly declined, it was the important citizens of the past era who united to face the threat hanging over the city. For other peoples the bond uniting them was a common descent from times clouded in legend; for the Roman patricians necessity was the only reason for the survival of the unity created by their vanished masters. The men who gathered in Romulus' refuge were made into a nation by being made into an army. The common military bond was the origin of the political community: they were an army before they were a nation, soldiers before citizens; whereas the Greeks formed an army and became soldiers because of the racial bond and traditions they shared.

From the confusion of races meeting on the Capitoline Hill and the surrounding heights, and in the market-place in the valley of the Forum, there grew up a unity based on the need to defend the settlement from its enemies and to bring it prosperity. The City of the Seven Hills was a federation of villages, the 'Septimontium', long before it was a unified city. Such precedents made it possible for Rome to achieve what would have been impossible for other states.

The situation which arose in Sparta, when one ethnic group established its supremacy and maintained its privileged posi tion for century after century, living as an army of occupation in Lacedaemonia, could never have occurred in Rome, where no one could boast of rights and traditions like those of the Dorian conquerors. The patricians defended their privileges tenaciously, as any conservative group defends itself before succumbing to the aspirations of new classes bent on social and political supremacy. The revolution was long and bitter, but they were never forced to accept the sort of shattering transformations that the Athenian revolution caused. In Rome, the law and the state were essentially the result of ceaseless contact between men and gods. The gods shared the life of a nation under arms, and presided over the assembly of the defenders of the state.

The Roman gods had never fathered heroes to live among men; they were unknowable forces, who assisted those who had earned their help by their piety, scrupulousness in carrying out their religious obligations, and care in rendering the gods their due. In this community birth could mean little. Every man who did his duty could rely on the gods to give him the power to command and to make decisions. Thus in Rome it was possible to claim, and obtain, equal rights for equal services.

Among the states which rose to historic importance in ancient times, Rome was unique in her concept of the relations between men and gods, which were the basis of every theory of political legitimacy. From this concept sprang possibilities of legal developments unknown to other nations. Since Rome could not impose the sort of racial segregation which had limited even the Athenian revolution, it was much easier for her to assimilate other states by extending to them the rights implicit in membership of her community. For other ethnic groups the belief in a close connection between religion and racial descent was an obstacle, but for Rome a different sort of relationship had to be recognised. The Romans held that the deities were more closely attached to places than to men, for they had accepted foreign gods from the earliest days of the state. Each new group arriving to join the Roman community introduced its own gods, who claimed shrines in the neighbourhood of Rome and became local divinities, and joined the gods of the state.

The archaic form of Roman religion attributed every phenomenon or collection of phenomena to unknowable forces. This meant that there were beings foreign to man on whom depended the outcome of every action and natural process, for good or ill. As the Roman religion developed, individual gods with traditional attributes already well known to the rest of the Mediterranean world came to populate the Roman world with Etruscan, Latin and Greek gods. Although none of the archaic forms of animistic religion and magic could be said to be exclusive to one particular ethnic group, the ready acceptance of foreign gods in Rome corresponded to the unique Roman willingness to extend the membership of the political community wherever it seemed possible and suitable, without considering racial origins.

This Roman practice, separating citizenship from race, and divine protection from the direct link between the gods and one particular community, was an innovation as revolutionary as the Athenian political and philosophical revolution of the fifth century BC. The fact that Rome was such a medley of races made it impossible for any dominant party to claim power on racial grounds, and this was in itself revolutionary. But the conflicts between Rome and her neighbours, their collaboration in alliances or under political and military protection, and above all the long struggle leading to the fusion of plebs and patriciate in a single nomen, were no less important as spurs to Rome's political development. A transformation was being made in the causes of political conflict. The battle was being fought over issues unknown in earlier times.

In the Mediterranean world, so far as archaeological research enables us to say, every form of political organisation had a closed, impenetrable group of men who governed the community, and whose only relations with other men were those of enmity, domination, or simply tolerance. When Rome was beginning to develop her own form of civilisation, the example of the Persian empire was still alive and impressive, with its governing class which held complete power and tolerated the religions and customs of its subjects simply because it could not imagine having anything in common with them. The Persian monarchy aimed at universality because of its faith in its divine mission to rule the world. It believed in a community of the 'elect', called by the gods to the task of guiding the human race, not in order to convert it or raise it to the level of the elect, but simply to unite it in one flock, obeying the rules and laws laid down for it by its leaders.

The wars against the Samnites, the building of the trunk roads south from Rome and the definitive Roman victories over the Etruscans, all brought Rome into contact with the Greek colonies of southern Italy and Sicily. From this time Rome gained a new position in the balance of powers in the Mediterranean world. The very fact of the adoption of the denarius, a silver coin of a good alloy and of a weight which made it a healthy competitor with other popular currencies, shows that Rome realised the need to make for herself a position which would bring her wider contacts than she could find in the peninsula.

In one or two areas of the peninsula, and only for reasons of security, the Romans had imposed direct control, often by establishing a permanent garrison in the area. Soldiers from Rome or one of the allied Latin towns would be transferred, with their families, and given a grant of land on which to maintain themselves, while building up a new settlement and guaranteeing the security of the region under occupation. In other places, the wars of expansion ended in agreements and treaties imposed by Rome, and aimed at one thing: a secure and permanent political and military relationship between the conqueror and the conquered.

Roman policy was based on a single political aim, which rose above the usual racial and theocratic prejudices. In common with the Athenians and their 'archè', but without their preoccupation with preserving the sacred rights of the Greek citizen, the Romans aimed at securing the collaboration or the neutrality of neighbouring states, and of those which, as the empire expanded, became one after another their neighbours. For the Romans, collaboration between men and gods, in the correct form and on the right occasions, was a guarantee of the validity of the 'imperium', a concept which included both the principle of command and of the rightness of decisions reached by the collective will of the community. Roman foreign policy was based on the concept of 'iustitia', in the sense that any political action is just so long as there is clear evidence of divine collaboration with man in the action. In such a case the outcome will inevitably be successful, and the gods are always ready to assist the people among whom they dwell. The absence of their co-operation was both a portent of failure and an intimation that the Roman people and their ruling class were failing to realise their common needs and interests.

The need for security is the mainspring of all policies of expansion, and their justification. Rome had already waged war in the peninsula to control the lines of communication, gain land on which to settle her own population, secure outlets to the sea for herself, and ward off attacks on these assets. In each case she secured the safety of her conquest by treaties in which the conquered peoples were forbidden to hinder Rome in the achievement of her aims. Persia and Sparta imposed garrisons on the lands they conquered, and sent officials to supervise them. Athens imposed tributes and used repressive measures to intimidate her subjects. Rome imposed treaties of alliance, insisted on guarantees, settled colonies at strategic points, and awarded partial or full rights putting the inhabitants on a par with her own citizens. In each case the agreement was designed to solve the problem of a resurgence of hostility to Rome.

The variety of the solutions found and the elasticity of the imperial bond prevented the Roman supremacy from ever being considered a tyranny. Roman arms reached many areas because their aid was requested, and almost everywhere Roman interests were interpreted to suit the local population, or at least a part of it. Rome entered southern Italy at the request of Thurii, but immediately came into conflict with Tarentum, who objected to any Roman influence in the sphere of the Greek colonies. This conflict led to the intervention of a Greek military power, and was Rome's first opportunity to establish political relations with a state outside the peninsula and her own local interests.

CHAPTER SEVEN

*

ROME AND THE MEDITERRANEAN

FROM the time when the Greeks first began to colonise the western Mediterranean, the growth of their influence there had been seriously restricted by Carthage. At that time any far-reaching policy of expansion inevitably involved the use of a navy; the thalassocracy was not just one of the forms of imperialist expansion, but the only possible way of escaping from parochial politics and pursuing wealth and power. There were very few good roads from city to city, and those there were could not take large vehicles, which made the cost of transporting goods by land so high as to be competitive. No state could hope to build up trade or improve its economic position by exporting its manufactures unless it had a fleet strong enough to keep the ports and trade routes under control.

The successive naval empires built up by the Greeks, from the Cretans onwards, resulted from the possession, by a central Greek state, of the naval power which enabled it to patrol the sea, suppress piracy, acquire anchorages throughout its sphere of influence, and so create the conditions necessary for the growth of a trading empire. Obstacles to the Greek thalassocracy, such as the Etruscan fleet, might perhaps be thought to be no more than trivial annoyances, were it not for the close links between Etruria and Carthage. Not even Athens, in spite of her great fleet, succeeded in imposing her influence outside the eastern Mediterranean and the Aegean. The road to the West was closed by Carthage. The most ambitious project of Athens' policy of expansion was in fact her attempt to make

Sicily into a base from which she could attack the Carthaginians on their own ground.

Rome had a navy at the time of the Etruscan domination, and it was from this period that her contact with Carthage dated. Carthage controlled the expeditions of the seafaring towns of the peninsula when they came within the stretch of waters from the Tyrrhenian sea to the Atlantic. The conflict between Rome and Tarentum was due not only to Roman interference in the affairs of the towns on the Ionian coast, but also to Rome's need to secure safe sea routes to the regions on the Adriatic side of the Appennines which had recently come under her control. When Tarentum invited Epirus to intervene, the peninsula had its first experience of the broader political perspectives, superior technical skills and better equipment which were the heritage of the Graeco-Macedonian conquest of Persia and Egypt.

Until this date the great military and naval powers of the eastern Mediterranean had taken no interest in the Italian peninsula, or at least the area behind the coastal strip, any more than they were interested in the interior of France or Spain. Their only concern, in this part of the world, was to find anchorages, depots, and sites for colonies on the coast. They had neither the means nor the need to extend their sphere of influence into the interior. The well-equipped Hellenistic armies, the foundation of that widespread naval empire, enabled their leaders to covet larger areas of the peninsula and the Tyrrhenian islands. Their final aim was to defeat Carthage and seize the trading empire she had built up in such a large area of the Mediterranean.

When Epirus intervened in Italy against Rome, she was leading a new Greek assault on Carthage. Rome was not her real target, but was part of a plan to create a bridgehead in Italy and Sicily for the attack on the African coast. The Carthaginians were well aware of the threat to their empire of plans laid on such a broad scale. When the Greeks attacked Rome, she found an ally in Carthage, who was not merely anxious to help her, but to make sure that Pyrrhus' armies continued to be engaged in battle in the peninsula, when

Rome would have been ready to withdraw and give up her efforts to keep Greek influence out of Italy.

The destiny of Rome as a political power was decided in the war with Epirus. Pyrrhus had tried to rouse the southern Italians against Rome, had summoned help and reinforcements from as far away as Egypt, had even entered into an offensive alliance with the Etruscans, and finally had to attack the Carthaginians in Sicily. The failure of his expedition, and the treaties of alliance made by Rome in the course of the war, gave her a new importance in Mediterranean politics. By the end of the war she no longer confined her interests to the peninsula, for she had measured her strength against that of one of the Hellenistic military powers. Suddenly the Romans found themselves to be a new and significant factor in the contest for control of the Mediterranean.

Immediately after these events, Egypt asked for a treaty of friendship with Rome. In Alexandria the poet Licophron was already celebrating the rise of new land and sea power. With Carthaginian help, the Romans imposed a treaty of protection on Tarentum which obliged her to supply military and naval aid to Rome. Roman control of ports and naval bases, and of her own and allied fleets, made the city the leader of an Italian confederacy. A third power had come between the Hellenistic empire and Carthage in the struggle for the Mediterranean.

Of the four belligerents in this war, Epirus against the Italians and Carthage against Rome, only Rome emerged a victor. Epirus was defeated, Tarentum and the Italiots lost their independence, and Carthage only succeeded in escaping defeat at Greek hands by helping to create a new, unforeseen power in the Italian peninsula. Rome, on the other hand, succeeded in uniting Italy under her command, and took the first steps to becoming a naval power, which meant, in the context of the ancient world, a world power.

Once Roman supremacy was firmly established in Magna Graeca, the Italiot cities began to come into the Roman political scheme. Their motives varied, but the terms of their treaties were generally more favourable to Rome than to themselves. The nature of this collective bond was to some extent new to the ancient world. Rome was faithful to her constitution as a city-state, governed by members of a timocracy drawn from the wealthiest members of both the patrician and plebian groups. The composite nature of the ruling class in Rome, and the limited number of troops at its disposal, made it essential to avoid as far as possible the occupation or acquisition of new territory. Instead the chains binding the subject state to the Roman state organisation did not affect its internal politics, but only imposed a common discipline and co-ordination of military matters and foreign politics. This system ensured Roman supremacy in Italy without affecting local autonomy. However, this was more than simply an agreement between free and sovereign states, for nearly always the agreement imposed a loss of sovereignty and the inclusion in a political organisation under Roman guidance and domination.

Before the war, Rome had controlled only one large port, Naples, and her interest in the sea was limited to regulating and policing the traffic between her coastal dependencies, and to trying without much success to suppress the piracy carried on by her own allies, especially Anxur. After the war with Epirus, Rome could no longer continue on these lines. As the leader of a group of countries whose safety and prosperity depended on the sea, without a policy suitable to the situation Rome would have caused great hardship amongst her allies, and this would soon have reacted against her own peace and safety.

One of the most important and distinctive effects of the Roman political situation was the increasingly close identification of Roman interests with those of her subject states. This is the fundamental explanation of the growth of Rome's power. The way her allies supported her at difficult times in her history, in a manner that belied the forecasts of contemporary critics, was the result of this community of interests.

Rome's victory over the cities of Magna Graeca brought her face to face with the Greek settlements in Sicily, and precipitated the crisis over freedom of navigation in the Straits of Messina. By intervening beyond the straits to preserve this freedom, Rome found herself in conflict with the Carthaginians, as the champion of peoples of Magna Graeca, and so of the whole Greek world, against the Punic naval supremacy.

The long struggle – its three phases lasted for more than a generation – demonstrated clearly the characteristics of Roman policy. In the Greek world, any action taken to further the interests of one city was the cause of conflict, because of the absence of a common policy and the variations of local conditions from city to city. In the Roman world the result of the fusion of the patrician and plebian groups, and the partial fusion of Romans and Latins, was a governing class without any particular vested interests. In spite of its conservatism and its reliance on land as its source of income, it was still fairly flexible and ready to accept innovations. The dominant classes in Rome wanted to take part in the trading activities that had already begun to develop under the rule of the Etruscans, and the farming and landowning sector of the community did not hinder the rise of a class which drew its wealth from trade.

In this way Rome identified her interests with those of Magna Graeca; she became a 'Greek power' in the sense that she assumed the burden of the fight with Carthage. The first stage of the battle was for Rome to establish her position as a naval power. In the next few years the ancient world saw a new phenomenon: the transformation of an old agrarian society into a seafaring power.

The second phase of the battle was of vital importance in testing the value of the Roman system of hegemony. Since Rome, with the aid of her allies, was assured of naval supremacy, Carthage had to abandon naval tactics and to confront her enemy on land. The Carthaginians could not land on the coast of Italy, and so they hoped to take advantage of their larger army and attack through Italy from the north. They counted on Rome's allies defecting, especially when they saw the first victories going to Carthage.

In the course of the third century the situation in the peninsula had been completely transformed. There had been changes in the ruling parties, and many Italian cities were governed by groups with strong ties with Rome. A network of interests bound the whole of the peninsula to Rome, whose control of all the surrounding seas, as well as the Tyrrhenian islands and bases on the coast of southern Illyria, brought great benefits to the sea-going and trading classes throughout Italy.

Once the Po valley was open to Italian expansion, the bond of loyalty and common interests uniting Italy became even tighter. The spirit of independence which had caused conflicts amongst the heterogeneous races of the peninsula submitted to Roman discipline. By conceding a certain amount of local autonomy in exchange for a large measure of political subjection, the Roman system succeeded in keeping the different races united.

In spite of a succession of defeats on the field, Rome was able to seize the initiative and defeat Carthage in Africa. She also took possession of the rich province of Spain, thanks to the basic solidarity of her Italian organisation. Under the stress of invasion, the Roman system proved itself to be the only really solid political construction of the classical world, apart from those that either relied on violence or remained on the scale of the city-state.

The defeat of Carthage did not solve all the problems of the peninsula; in fact it created new ones. The lands seized from Carthage were of use to the merchants, sailors, investors, business men and contractors who simply replaced the Carthaginians in the same occupations. The lands under Punic control had met the needs of a small nation without any desires for expansion. However, certain areas of the peninsula were in need of land to colonise, which would provide work and greater resources for the inhabitants. The Tyrrhenian islands continued to pay to Rome the tribute they had paid to Carthage, and the cereals imported as a part of this tribute competed with Italian products only because the wholesalers could not buy more grain than what was necessary to cover the deficit without causing prices to fall. If this system did not bring agriculture to the verge of ruin, it did not make life any easier for those whose precarious existence depended on the market for their supplies.

Rome's new situation in Mediterranean affairs after the defeat of Carthage led the Hellenistic powers to revise their foreign policy. Any power in the central Mediterranean whose political influence increased became immediately the object of

Greek suspicions and rivalry. Oriental enmity had been directed at Carthage while she was the controller of the area; now that her place had been taken by Rome, the whole of the Hellenistic world began to fear that its own interests would be threatened by the new power. The Romans, on the other hand, looked forward to extending their domains and so eliminating the competition and threats of rival states, while at the same time new developments in the political situation forced them to undertake new wars in order to gain possession of the greatest source of wealth of the classical world: the industrial lands of the Hellenistic empire.

The oligarchy of rich patrician and plebian families had retained its grip on Roman politics, and guided the city safely through the difficult years of the great wars of conquest. The magistratures and seats in the Senate were held by a small circle of families. Only the very rich could afford the hordes of clients which surrounded powerful men, or the largesse expected of magistrates, and the expense of reaching their ranks. When anyone outside the nucleus of the 'nobilitas' did succeed in becoming the first member of his family to gain office, it was thought so remarkable that he was described as 'homo novus'.

The effects of the wars of conquest also brought about a gradual change in the relations of the rest of the Italians with Rome. In the past they had seen the results of the Roman unification. Ever since the Punic wars, regions not always favourable to Rome, like some of the Etruscan cities, had exerted all their efforts against Carthage in a manner that showed their firm support of Rome. The state built up by these alliances was not a hegemony of vassal states but a federation of towns with the fullest local autonomy compatible with the security of the group. Its aim was to reconcile the aims of the individual town with the interests of the whole.

The emergence of Rome as a world power brought with it profound changes in the political system and class relationships in the city. In particular, the oligarchy lost the firm hold that it had kept throughout the years of war. Before the war the attitude of the soldiers to their leaders had not created any problems, since under the political system then operating the men who held power were in fact the most important and influential members of society. But the long wars, the longer periods of military service demanded of the contingents, the increasing importance of the commanders' personal influence with their armies, and of booty as an incentive to the troops, were all bringing about changes in the citizen-soldier's attitude to his commanders and his fellow citizens.

In the past, the power to command the army and defeat the enemy was seen as the result of collaboration between men and the gods, who guaranteed the powers invested in the elected magistrate. In the course of the long wars, the commanders came to rely more and more on their personal prestige, as if it were their own heroic qualities which made them worthy of divine aid. This new development was accompanied by a change in the citizen's attitude to military service.

The relationship between the soldier and his leader had always been the normal relationship between citizen and magistrate. The power and indestructibility of the Roman oligarchy had changed all this. Soldiers who had fought for long years together, who had brought their country rich new dominions and allies, who knew that their efforts had defeated the greatest power of the classical world, now realised that their value to the state was greater than their political leaders would acknowledge. The first effect of this new political awareness was the new relationship between the troops and their commanders. The leaders, with the tacit consent of their troops, gained for themselves power and prestige far exceeding the bounds of tradition and law. In return, the soldiers attached themselves to their leaders in rather the same way as clients to their patron.

The economic developments which followed the wars increased the distance between the classes. Many small landowners lost their farms and joined the ranks of the proletarians. This started the process of the concentration of capital in the hands of a few families in the form either of vast estates or of money earned by trade and investment. Any such large inheritance naturally became the focus of a group of smaller fortunes. This situation had its parallel in the world of politics, as the control of the Senate and the magistratures was concentrated in the hands of a few families.

The oligarchic political system created a governing class which had no links with the rest of the population. As the importance of economic and foreign affairs increased, the Comitia Curiata, which was responsible for them, became the principal organ of government, and this increased the power of the oligarchy. The key to the political and constitutional developments of the next decades was the relationship between the Senate and the holders of the highest offices of state. The commanders, with the support of their armies, tended to dominate the Senate, and to break up the unity of the upper classes and the governing body by giving the members of the latter powers exceeding the limits set by the Senate. The Senate did everything in its power to halt this process, which gave individual members of the 'nobilitas' great personal power, based on the support of the masses, who up to then had been excluded from politics in spite of their growing importance in the state.

Although the distinction between plebians and patricians was no longer of any importance, a new distinction was appearing, between the men whose wealth was based on land and those who had made their money in business; between the senatorial caste and the 'equites'. The latter took no part in political life, but still exercised a considerable influence on the ruling class. They moved in different social circles from the 'nobilitas', and derived their importance to the state from their control of trade throughout the empire, and from the enormous liquid assets at their disposal.

As business men, the 'equites' were in close touch with the trading sections of Italian society. Trade and investment assisted the cohesion of the new Roman acquisitions into an empire. Once Rome had defeated Carthage and replaced Macedon in the Hellenistic countries of the Levant, and thus acquired the means of imposing her supremacy on the whole of the Mediterranean, the way was open to an increase in trade from which the Romans and Italians were certainly not the only ones to profit. Until this time Carthaginian control of the western Mediterranean had hindered the growth of trade on this scale. The political and social effects of the new situation brought about fundamental changes in the state. At the same time, the whole military organisation was being transformed. Military service was a tribute owed by the citizen to the state, in proportion to his means; a system which Rome shared with the Greek world. When the length and complexity of military undertakings made it necessary to keep armies in the field for longer and longer periods, the old system became unworkable, and payments were introduced for the troops. Gradually the army became a profession – and quite a profitable one – and constituted a separate social group.

There were large Italian contingents in the Roman army, and they, like the Roman citizens, began to have new political aspirations. Even the Romans who were not members of the privileged sector of society began to see the advantages their citizenship gave them, at the centre of a great empire. Thus the old equality between Italian and Roman, each one a citizen of the town where he was born, was no longer more advantageous to the former than to the latter, but was being used as a legal excuse for denying to the Italians the old equality of comrades in arms.

The Roman concept of sovereignty had always been based on the continuous interaction of gods and men, so that the validity of every law and political action was demonstrated by observing the manifestations of the divine will. As long as this view was accepted, it was clear that only by enlarging the religious and political concept of the nomen could other people be admitted to membership of the Roman 'populus'. The fusion of the plebian and patrician groups had already increased its numbers; the closed, exclusive character which religion had given to the Roman community had even by the time of the Punic wars been removed by changes in the religion itself. One source of influence in this matter was the culture which had made a deep impression on Rome when her incursions into Magna Graeca brought her into contact with Greek civilisation. When the Romans first came to grips with the Greek world, they had already been indirectly influenced by it through their contacts with the Etruscans and with the populations of Sicily and southern Italy.

Increased contact with Greek ideas caused the Romans to adopt many of the external forms of Greek culture, without making any fundamental change in their own cultural and religious patterns. They were much more deeply affected by the higher standard of living attained by the Hellenistic world, and which had spread from the wealthiest members of society to the middle classes. This was the first channel through which Greek civilisation penetrated the Roman world. It was followed by a genuine desire for a closer understanding of Greek art and philosophy, and this strengthened and deepened the Greek influence. Young men of the highest Roman families were sent to Greece to complete their education, and Greek elements appeared in many aspects of Roman life. Another result was the growth of religious syncretism; the Roman and Etruscan gods were assimilated to the Greek gods whose traditional attributes they shared. The identification of the idols led to a synthesis of the rituals, and this had a revitalising effect on the religion.

Roman interest in Greece put great value on the men and achievements of countries under her own dominion, and so created the impression of a single community in which every member was of equal importance for the life of the whole. It was difficult for the Romans to maintain a position apart, in the belief that their actions alone had the support of the gods, when they could see that their gods were not exclusive to Rome, but shared many characteristics with the gods of the subject races.

When other nations saw that they had gods in common with the Romans, the sacred, mysterious, inevitable character of the Roman domination disappeared, and it now had to rely on the more dubious concept that Rome ruled the world because she was divinely predestined to do so by those same gods who had desired the Macedonian victories over Persia. For many of the subject races the acceptability of Roman sovereignty was dependent on the same doctrine of unlimited conquest and unending victories as Hellenistic sovereignty had been. But this sort of doctrine not only affects the sources of legitimacy and authority, but gradually modifies political relations within the state itself.

In the early days of Rome, as in every other country at the same stage of development, political rights and importance in the state depended on military service. Later on, wealth became more important than military service, but there came a time, with the increasing emphasis placed on victory and conquest and the ever-growing size of the army needed to control the empire, when the military element regained its importance in the Roman state.

A political and social unit as large as the Roman empire inevitably brought many varied interests and influences to bear on the city that was its focus. Roman tradition and Greek culture could not always live side by side without conflicting, even though the influence of Greece was never much more than superficial. The tendency to submit to the influence of Greece and to imitate its cultural patterns, and Rome's relations with the Hellenistic civilisation, were one of the issues dividing the conservative and radical parties in Roman politics. According to the conservatives, the political situation in Rome ought to preserve the privileges of the leading citizens. This meant that the subject races must not be allowed too much influence in Rome, or it would soon be impossible to treat their countries simply as dominions to be exploited. The Roman cultural renaissance might bring with it modifications to the social pattern on oriental lines, and they were anxious to avoid the transformation of society from a basically rural, aristocratic organisation into something resembling a Hellenistic state, for they knew that this would lead eventually to the disappearance of the privileged oligarchy.

In spite of the fact that Greek society was now ruled by kings or military dictators, the effects of the 'philosophical revolution' of the fifth century BC were still felt. The rights of the individual, the value of human reason as the means of acquiring knowledge and establishing justice – principles such as these could not sink with the Athenian triremes in the Bay of Syracuse. The defeat of Athens had destroyed her chances of ruling the Greek world, but it could not destroy her right to guide and inspire it; and not only the Greek world, but everywhere that shared the same culture.

The military monarchies which sprang from the Macedonian conquest created conditions in which this new concept of the value and rights of the individual could flourish. The religious basis of political legitimacy was once again accepted doctrine, and the state was seen as a community of believers; but individual rights were not lost or suppressed, and a civilisation grew up in which the free man lived, and believed in his right to live, a life whose conditions, surroundings, culture and habits had all been changed by the Athenian revolution.

The conservative party in Rome wanted to avoid any changes in customs or human relationships which might lead to changes in the balance of power between the social classes. But whichever way they turned they faced pressure groups claiming that the situation had in fact already changed; it was they who were refusing to acknowledge and legalise the new developments.

The equestrian order continued to grow in importance. The number of slaves increased, and so did the number of freedmen who had made fortunes; they were beginning to be a considerable feature of social and economic life. The small-scale landowner, unable to face ever-rising prices and the loss involved in his long stretch of military service, was selling out to the great landed proprietors, who were growing richer every day on the profits of huge estates run by armies of slaves.

These changes in the pattern of economic life were inevitable, and attempts to restore the position of the small farmer by legislation were doomed to failure. It was an attempt by the political authorities to do this that caused the most serious crisis in the history of the ancient world, a crisis that exposed as an illusion the peace and security spread by the rule of Rome over an area reaching as far as Pergamum.

The 'Lex Agraria' was designed to redistribute the public lands, taking them back from the landed proprietors who used them for pasturing their flocks, and restoring them to farmers for cultivation. The landowning capitalists reacted vigorously to the threat, and attempts to put the law into operation met with violent responses from both parties, and unleashed political hopes and grievances which until then had lacked a cause which would give them the strength of unity.

The general disturbance caused by the government's

attempt to introduce economic reforms revealed the inadequacy of the senatorial oligarchy to the task of reorganising Roman political life. In particular the disturbances brought to light the mutinous state of the men who were forced to serve in the armies which had given Rome her power and wealth, and who claimed that their influence in the state bore no relation to their services to it.

The Latin and Italian allies felt that they were excluded from any effective participation in the rights of citizenship, and that their importance in the life of the community was not sufficiently recognised. Even the Roman citizens of the lower classes realised that although in theory they enjoyed full legal rights, in fact this applied only to their rights as private persons, for their position in the census lists prevented them from having an effective part to play in the government of the state. The oligarchs kept all the power in their own hands, and made use of the lower classes as soldiers and labourers while denying them the political representation that their labour had earned them.

The Roman state was exposed to political conflict by its very nature and origins: it had been created by forces pressing for the extension of the right to share in the government of the community. The struggles between patricians and plebians, and Romans and Latins, were repeated on a wider scale when the Italian allies rose against Rome, demanding a revision of their position in the state. In Rome, too, there had been a battle within the wealthiest class of citizens. The 'equites' demanded, and obtained, an effective part in the administration of the state, so that they could help to direct the affairs of the 'provinciae', the territories under the direct control of Rome, for the greatest proportion of their trade and investments were concentrated in these areas.

The influence of the equites was inevitably unfavourable to the nations dependent on Rome. The internal struggles of the Roman upper classes created an extremely dangerous situation for the Senate, and suggested that this was an opportunity to replace the ruling sect with men who would undertake a complete reorganisation of the system of government. An attempt to extend full political rights to all the Italian allies by bringing in legislation that would alter the balance of power in favour of the masses, could not be implemented, and provoked a war with the Italians, whose aim was to destroy the power of Rome, her dominion over Italy, and possibly even her independence.

Rome defeated the Italians, ruthlessley suppressing the revolutionary movement. The military effort and legislative innovations demanded by the war made the relations of the Roman orders even worse, and revealed the inability of the present system to deal with the new situation. The rural and aristocratic republic was no longer capable of adapting its men, its methods and its laws to suit the Mediterranean empire it had created. The war of the allies had shown that populations long deprived of political autonomy, even as individual cities, were still capable of united political and military action. It also showed that although the Romans had won the war and taken bloody reprisals, they had been forced to make concessions which changed the political situation in the peninsula in a way that seemed to damage the sovereignty of their city-state.

Italy had suffered devastations which had altered the distribution of population in the peninsula. But the Italians had won their place on the roll of citizens, and the towns that survived became 'municipia', under Roman administration. After the Italian war, Roman citizenship was extended to all the Italian allies, producing a revolutionary change in the social basis of the political community. Such a revolutionary step was conceivable only in a state whose racial origins were as confused as Rome's. The old jibe about the 'asylum of Romulus' was fully justified. The heterogeneous, disparate, multi-racial character of the original civic community, with its political groups composed of members of different tribes and clans, gave the political structure an elasticity unknown in any other state, where the religious and legal codes were so rigid that they shattered before they could be bent to meet new needs. In Rome, expansion and reform were possible, although limited by the bitter resistance of the privileged classes to the loss of those privileges, even when they were clearly without any social justification.

If the new status of the Italians brought the whole question of the scale of political representation into the open, the more pressing problem was still the political position of the army. There were two groups involved in the matter: the Roman proletariat, who had held Roman citizenship for centuries, and the new citizens from the Italian cities. Both groups had suffered for a long time from the grievance that was at the root of all the political disturbances: the difference between the importance of their services to the state and the importance of their influence on the state's policies.

The conservatives signed their own death warrant when they first made use of the army to influence the course of internal politics. The troops realised the possibilities offered to them by their own strength, and the way was open to the revolutionary change that threatened the survival of the Roman empire and disrupted its traditions; the transformation of the army into a political party, outside the ranks of ordinary citizens, with its own policies and the means to see that they were carried out. A new factor had to be considered in the organisation of the state: the army, used as a political force by commanders who continued the tendency first noticed in the Punic wars of turning themselves into the leaders of political factions, and offering to lead their men to the realisation of their hopes, and give them the position in the state which their services to the new empire deserved. The introduction of the army into Roman politics prepared the way for the great change that came over the state, when political power was concentrated in the hands of a single man, who represented the interests and longings of all the various groups which made up the mass of the Roman political community, but were excluded from the rights and benefits which they considered to be their due.

CHAPTER EIGHT

*

THE ROMAN EMPIRE

THE direction to be taken by the revolutionary movement was clear from the first hints of the changes occurring in the relations between the different classes and social groups in the state. Since the revolt was predominantly a military affair, the army commanders stood out as the natural leaders of the new ruling class. From the moment when the legions were first used to settle a political dispute, and a commander had temporarily taken over complete control of the state, the outcome of the revolt was settled, although it may not have been the one anticipated or hoped for by those involved in the struggle.

Not only the outcome of the struggle was settled, but also the religious and legal ideas on which the revolution would base its concept of legitimacy. The Athenian 'philosophical revolution' which resulted from the teachings of Anaxagoras, had not been able to impress permanently on the ancient world the idea that human reason, and the will of the people under the guidance of reason, are the source of all theoretical knowledge and moral judgments, and so of the concepts of truth and justice which in those days men looked for in various ways in revelations of the divine will.

After the fall of the Athenian democracy; that is, after the immediate, manifest failure of the Anaxagorean revolution, the rationalist, humanist theory of political authority was forgotten. The Hellenistic world saw the rebirth of the cult of the heroic, divinely inspired leader, strengthened by contact with the Persian concept of 'fravashi', which gave divine sanction, and therefore legitimacy, to the principle of royal sovereignty.

The close links of civilisation and descent between the Greeks and the Romans, and the direct and indirect influence of Greece on Roman culture, created a similar situation in Rome. The Romans felt the presence of their gods all around them, watching every action, and beside them every moment of their lives. Their conviction that no decision, no command, no undertaking could be successful without the support and consent of the gods, led them to believe that the gods did not only work impersonally in their relations with the state and its magistrates, who were the bridge between the citizens and their gods: the anthropomorphism which had been superimposed on their primitive animistic religion led them to ascribe human emotions as well as human features to their deities.

At this point in the development of their religious ideas the Romans came into contact with the idea that the gods might have a predilection for certain individuals, and that some man might be endowed with the gift of making himself the instrument with which the gods shaped the future of the state. On the day when the 'imperium', the power of political and military command, was seen to belong not to the office of the magistrate but to a man, perhaps not even a magistrate, whom the gods had endowed with the gift of shaping the course of events and the wills of men; at the moment when for the first time, on the field of battle, the enemy scattered and the ground strewn with their dead, the troops acclaimed their leader with the title 'imperator', the new, Roman concept of legitimacy was born.

The man with an innate capacity for command had gifts and opportunities which he could not fulfil within the traditional oligarchy. Tradition and sacred law could not bind the man whom the gods had chosen and to whom they had given powers equal to those bestowed by the Roman people in all the solemnity of their assemblies. The gods had given him the power of 'imperium' as his personal gift; he could do without investiture by the committees of the state. When the troops began to feel that the state had not treated them justly, but made use of their indispensable services without acknowledging their importance, it was to him that they turned to obtain restitution.

The Roman state organisation was incapable of giving the legions the recognition they claimed; it was scarcely capable of tolerating the men whose power and personal authority were too great to be contained within the normal procedures for conferring authority on the officers of state. So in the end the soldiers and all the rest of the poor and dissatisfied turned to the 'war lords' as to forces beyond the law and the constitution, who would realise their hopes in spite of conservative opposition.

The fate of the ruling class of landowners and aristocrats was sealed the moment they chose revolution, the denial of the discipline of law, and had recourse to violence rather than make financial concessions which would have meant a personal sacrifice but which would have enabled the valuable class of small farmers to be reconstituted after its destruction by the economic vicissitudes of the long wars. The whole incident was apparently of no great importance, but in fact it proved that the ruling class was not prepared to make any concessions to reality, and was interested only in preserving the privileges that it clung to all the more tenaciously for the knowledge that it no longer had any right to them. The upper classes found themselves in the situation which always precedes political revolution: they had lost the adaptability and sensitivity needed to grapple with the task of government, and so had to entrench themselves in defensive positions which ensured their decline and downfall.

The actual form that the revolution would take was determined by the conservative movement and by the governing caste, who actually sparked it off. One of their generals, fighting to preserve the political situation, revealed the perilous 'arcanum imperii', the existence in the army of a political will, and showed that the legions could be the decisive element in precipitating a political situation. From that moment, Rome lived in fear of new blows, aware that what had once been attempted with success would be tried again. It was clear that no force of law or authority of tradition could stand up to the equivocations of armed gangs in the committees and the Senate. The traditional view of the divine source of authority had been valid for centuries, and Rome could not admit any other interpretation. On the other hand, the political power of the ruling caste was backed up by enormous economic influence, armies of clients, networks of relations and kinsmen, and the prestige of a glorious history, all of which reinforced the conservative resistance and gave it the strength to stand up to the violence that menaced it when the troops and their leaders intervened in the political conflict.

The troops were a great deal more than just a military movement to conquer the state. When we speak of 'the troops', at a period of Roman history like the one beginning with the end of the Punic wars, we are referring to a great mass of humanity, and impoverished class looking for a way of providing itself with a minimum of economic security for the time when it would be demobilised. The hundreds of thousands of veterans who had returned to civilian life in extreme poverty joined the other army whose feelings and hopes they shared: the army of men whom the vicissitudes of life had deprived of the means to support themselves. This mass of poor, unemployed men and their families thronged the capital, living on public assistance, in the belief that merely to have been born Roman citizens and to live in Rome entitled them to live without working and without the means to support themselves, provided for by the empire which they, the conquering legions, had won for Rome.

Hellenism had given a political application to the concept of man it had inherited from the Athenian revolution, giving the Greek elements in the Levantine states a dominant position of power and privilege only justified by their membership of the Graeco-Macedonian conquering races which had destroyed the Persian empire. The high standard of living, the culture and civilisation of the Greeks living in the Hellenistic empire, secured for them the privileges and legal rights that enabled them to live in isolated cities with their own customs and institutions.

In Rome, the decline of the republic brought with it political chaos and serious social injustice, which was felt all the more deeply for the glaring contrast with the organisation of the Hellenistic world. Traditional Roman law imposed equal participation in the life of the community on every citizen with full legal rights. In fact, after the Punic wars, the situation was quite different. The old equality between patricians and plebians, achieved after a struggle which had broken the bonds of the old genetic system of political control, had been invalidated by the formation of an oligarchy of wealth. These men gained complete control of the state at a time when the ownership of land gave real social pre-eminence as well as serious social responsibilities. When the state urgently needed the collaboration and military services of other sectors of the population, a group made up of citizens and non-citizens had appeared, claiming a just reward for its services to the state. In earlier times war had brought with it booty and land, and it had been generally accepted that all the combatants had the right to a share in the spoils of victory. Now that wars were on a much larger scale, the spoils took the form of kingdoms and regular sources of income for the state, and only very rarely did anyone profit apart from the men who meanwhile had seized absolute control of the empire.

The revolution that put an end to the Roman republic was to some extent caused by the need for a new evaluation of the meaning of being a citizen or an ally of the Roman state. In Rome, the theocratic concept of the origins of authority and legitimacy had for a long time detached itself from any genetic criteria; the history of the city excluded any possibility that racial considerations and their connection with religion could prevent the spread of Roman citizenship. Now the demands of the revolutionaries were reinforced by those who had been admitted to Roman citizenship, and now claimed their share in the benefits that the state could bring them.

The Greek idea of the rights inherent in membership of the Greek community was taken up in Rome in a more precise form in the demand for the personal and economic rights inherent in Roman citizenship. It was more a matter of economics than of personal rights, and as in the Hellenistic world the lower classes were not claiming a share in the actual government of the state, as they had in fifth-century Athens, but simply in the distribution of wealth and in the legal safeguards protecting the individual.

The long civil war of the second century BC was basically the struggle of two groups in the state, one pressing for a broader concept of citizenship, the other defending its privileges. Both sides had to call on an ever-widening group of allies to help them; groups until then excluded from any form of participation in the public life of the Roman state, and this led to new demands for a reform of the legal and political system. The most urgent demands came from the Greeks of Levant, whose dominant position in their own countries was not reflected in their rights as members of the Roman empire. The declining republic was defended to the bitter end by the conservatives who refused to admit their own decadence or the transformation of the political scene. They were assisted by the widespread hostility to any form of monarchical government, which was considered to deprive the citizens of their legal guarantees, replacing them with a purely personal and arbitrary rule.

It is important to distinguish between two groups who were at this time fighting over the body of the Roman republic: the holders of executive power in the state, and the men who were fighting to win themselves a position as leaders of the popular movement. There were strong ranks of interests drawn up against the old 'nobilitas', but equally powerful interests were fighting on their side, and the new organisation of the state, after a century of revolution, conflict and civil war, involving the whole of the Mediterranean world, was implicit in the aims of the parties engaged in the struggle.

In fact the parties had been forced to put themselves in the hands of the military leaders who controlled the armies and the fleets. Both sides found that this was their only course, and this meant that in spite of their dislike of monarchies, neither side could do without an individual leader, the focus of the interests and loyalties of the masses. These individuals, with the armies under their command, decided the fate of the old oligarchy and of the newly vocal masses.

The beginning of the movement towards a popular monarchy was the return to an old principle: the power of the tribunes to advise and assist the common people, which had resolved the conflict between plebians and patricians. The power 'auxilii ferendi populo' was given to the tribunes at their election, together with powers equal to those conceded by the committees; but the authority of the tribunes was not circumscribed by the guarantees and protective measures that hedged in the magistrates, for it did not derive from the decision of a committee, and so was not the result of collaboration between men and gods. It was legalised and consecrated by a solemn oath. The gods were called on to recognise the authority of the tribune, and by this means it became 'sacrosancta', that is, its force was equal to that of the magistrates elected by the committees. The power to act for the good of the people, which was a recognised right of the 'princeps' during the time when the state was turning from a republic into a monarchy, was not derived from investiture by a committee, and so did not have the same character as the power of the magistrate. Its foundation was the official recognition that the characteristics qualifying a man for public office existed only in the personality of the 'princeps'; that he possessed the 'auctoritas' that gives power the seal of legitimacy.

This 'auctoritas' was the very foundation of the new sovereignty. This was because it sprang from the recognition that the force that determined divine collaboration with man could reside in some measure in a single individual, and not just in the assemblies of state or in the man who had already been endowed by the state with the power to rule. From this 'auctoritas' arose the recognition afforded to some men who were given the title of 'imperator', and the power and prestige assumed, often arbitrarily, by individuals in the civil war.

Thus the collaboration between men and gods was thought of more and more as a matter of personalities. This led to the concept of legitimacy founded on the 'comitatus' between a man and the gods; a concept that was given a concrete form when statues of the man were erected within the temples of the gods. The Romans revived their ancient national beliefs and added to them the heroic myth which they shared with the Greeks, to create a doctrine of direct co-operation between individuals chosen by the gods, and the gods themselves. This co-operation was the source of 'auctoritas', the origin of the power of the 'princeps'.

The power 'auxilii ferendi populo' became the personal endowment of the holder of 'auctoritas', like the power to command the army. The possession at the same time of religious, civil and military powers, which was strictly illegal, was possible in the case of the 'princeps' because his superiority to other men meant that he was responsible to no one for his actions. The situation was not, however, merely the effect of one man's personality or of a random display of force, but the result of a long revolution.

The principate that the Romans accepted as their governing organ did not seem to them to have anything to do with the 'monarchy' that they feared and hated so deeply, any more than the Hellenistic monarchy can have appeared to the Greeks to be a tyranny. In both cases the monarchy had been able to avoid presenting itself to the people as the triumph of brute force, without the justification of legitimacy, but had stuck to the traditional explanation of the origins of power: the incomprehensible will of the gods. On the level of philosophical explanations, even a man like Cicero, steeped in Greek culture and by nature a conservative, could not avoid postulating the necessity of a man who would stand at the helm of the ship of state, a man who would be above the political factions and their quarrels.

Once again the special characteristic of the Roman state that distinguished it from all the other states of the ancient world was demonstrated: its ability to renew itself with the changing realities of political and social conditions, thanks to its original freedom from the concept of a closed genetic aristocracy that characterised the other political organisations of Indo-European stock in the classical world. As before in Rome, the long struggle against conservative resistance ended not in a subversive revolution, but simply in the renewal of the political organisation, restoring the relevance of the legislative forms to the exigencies of daily life.

This 'return to first principles' was not the result of any particular foresight on the part of the Roman conservatives, warning them to renounce a fraction of their privileges at the right moment, and so reach a compromise with the demands of the reformer. The conservatives were saved by the fact that, in spite of their bitter defence of their privileges, and their readiness to go to any lengths to preserve them, the structure of the Roman political system itself gave them the opportunity to come to a compromise; to bow to the inevitable without provoking, by their surrender, the collapse of the state that would have been inevitable in other places and nations. .

There were, of course, proscriptions and massacres, but it was not only the revolutionaries who could not do without terrorism and murder; the conservatives were the first to have recourse to these methods. The revolutionary movement had legitimate, realistic objectives, reconcilable with tradition, and important enough to encourage it not to break the continuity of the state organisation, but to adapt itself to the religious and legal precedents.

The principate arose from the collaboration of the ruling class of the old 'nobilitas' and the leader, or leaders, of the proletariat which was claiming recognition and greater justice from the state. This collaboration was nothing new; for a century the distinction between the two sides had been far from clear. Both sides had armed the same troops, the same legions and fleets were torn between them, they had both wooed with promises and cajolery the same veterans, offering them rewards that they would only be able to produce by raiding other people's property. Neither the newly awakened masses, whose power was their indispensability to the state, nor the old, irreplaceable ranks of rulers and organisers, could do anything about their dependence on their opponents.

The final conflict that transformed the state into a monarchy carried within it the seeds of new conflicts, and also the terms of the political struggles of the principate. The conservative leaders of the Senate had been forced, in order to prevent an absolutely centralised monarchy based on military and popular support, which would mean the end of the Senate's power and privileges, to come to an agreement with one of the contenders for the monarchy, and to provide him with arms and support. This was to sink to the level of the masses in their use of force as a political weapon. After he had won his victory, the winning commander could no longer remain simply the leader of an armed band of marauders, heaping up wealth and power without any concern for justice and legality. He had to find a new regime that would meet the demands on which the revolution was based: to admit a greater number of citizens to the enjoyment of the benefits and privileges formerly the preserve of the few, to find a workable compromise with the nobles, which would allow them an acknowledged superiority while giving to the masses the rights and privileges for which they had been fighting.

The millions of ordinary people, who had become the rulers of the state because of their numerical importance, wanted to benefit from the Roman dominion over the territories of the empire in a way that would ensure them the means of life at the end of their long term of military service. The old governing class had only one ambition: to keep its position in the administration of the empire; a position for which no other sector of the population was qualified. These were the motives behind the next phase of the conflict, and they gave the political history of the empire its particular character. The dominant masses did their best to strip the old ruling class of its wealth and power, while the old 'nobilitas' tried to collaborate with the 'princeps' in order to defend itself and all the wealthy members of the state against the demands of the soldiers, the proletariat, the mass of the new 'rerum domini'.

The principate offered, above all, peace and the opportunity of enrichment to friends and enemies alike, making an instrument for itself of the weariness, poverty and misfortunes brought by a century of civil war. To the old oligarchs, the principate offered the protection of its armed forces for their lives and their possessions, and promised them jobs, the opportunity to make money, and a certain share in the executive power of the ruler. To the newly powerful masses, it offered land and employment, food and money. This was not a matter of minor bribery, but introduced the concept first appearing in the fifth-century Athens, that the rulers of the state had a duty to help to support the citizens. Faced with this new concept of citizenship, giving all citizens the right to a share in the wealth of the state, the 'princeps' fulfilled the function of a central power for the collection and redistribution of money and property.

Thus the state was restored and refounded on a new basis. For decades past it had failed to carry out its essential job of securing law and order, and safeguarding the vigour of the legal system and the amenities of public and private life. The absence of guarantees that the state will be able to protect the fundamentals of civil life is inevitable in a state where the position of supreme authority is a matter for dispute. The principate restored the effective authority of the state, and performed the task of mediator in a way that enabled the revolutionary class to keep its predominant position without provoking the irreconcilable opposition of the conservatives, and so working towards the reconciliation of the two factions, and the restoration of equilibrium and order.

The conflict between the popular, military class and the conservatives was not resolved, but continued to be the justification of the imperial system of government. Against the permanent background of this struggle, the citizen body had to face a new problem, one which had been implicit in the causes of the civil war: relations between the citizens and the subjects of the western and eastern provinces.

Ever since the conquest of Gaul regular detachments of provincial recruits had been part of the Roman army. The distinction between the 'iusta legio' of Roman citizens serving their term in the army, and the 'legio vernacula' made up of volunteers from the provinces, led to a new imperial policy that was destined to become one of the most important features of the empire. The enlistment of troops from the western provinces was not the only contribution that the state demanded of its provincial subjects: as well as the taxes imposed on them, the eastern provinces had to provide ships and crews for the Roman fleet. These were an essential part of the empire's defences, and it is significant that the power and efficient functioning of the Roman state, even in so vital and delicate a matter as its armed potential, depended on the co-operation of the subject states. History had shown that every act of co-operation sooner or later had to be rewarded.

The way was open to a new crisis in which the state would have once again to adapt itself to meet the demands of its members.

The solution of the problem of relations between the Roman state and the Hellenistic provinces was to leave the legal and administrative systems to function, on the whole, as they had before the invasion. This was made a great deal easier when Rome acquired a single individual, in place of a set of abstract concepts, as the personification of the sovereignty of the state, and the object of the cults which the Hellenistic Greeks saw as the characteristic of legitimate authority.

In Greece and Asia Minor the Greeks lived apart from the indigenous population, but both accepted the rule of a sovereign in whom they saw the image of a god present among men. The idea of the superhuman ruler was made more acceptable by being expressed in the language of the philosophy on which the culture of the time was based, but it was simply an extension of the old Greek idea of the heroic ruler, and the oriental belief in the king who mediates between men and gods, or the god who dwells with men to govern them in peace and justice. The Hellenistic cities and the indigenous peoples accepted the new overlord, and saw in him the bringer of peace and security, the benefactor, the saviour from all the perils that threatened their society, and almost the promise that their vague, mystical hopes would be realised, hopes that had grown up in the hearts of races which had suffered for generations from endless wars, devastation, piracy and despotism.

The traditional Roman culture had been heavily influenced by the example of Greece and Hellenism. The problem that the evolution of political ideas posed for the artists was that of gaining Roman intellectual life recognition in the world of Hellenistic culture. From the earliest days Roman artists had shown their dependence on Greece, and their admiring devotion to her, and this became in the end an important factor in the political situation itself. Ennius, Plautus, Terence, Lucretius, Catullus; each with greater experience and delicacy of touch wrestled with the problem of making Roman art and the Latin language capable of expressing the emotions and sentiments of Greek art and philosophy.

Virgil, too, faced the same problem. His great triumph was surely that he gave the language a dignity which equalled that of the great works of the Greek heritage. With Horace, Roman art for the first time sought to find for itself an independent place in the front rank of Mediterranean culture. But throughout the development of Roman civilisation, the superiority and independence of the Greek cultural tradition ensured that Greek autonomy was respected, and was an important element in relations between the eastern and western sectors of the empire.

From its earliest days, the Roman monarchy faced some of the most complex and absorbing problems to come within the experience of any state in the ancient world. They interest us not only because we have more information about this period of history, but because of the influence that they have had, and continue to have, on our own civilisation. The Roman state could only call on a limited number of troops, both for financial reasons and because it could not enlist too many provincial contingents or impose too heavy a burden on the Roman citizens. This put a brake on expansion since the state had to be careful not to commit itself militarily beyond the limit imposed by its financial situation and the reliance that it could place on the provincial troops.

One of the chief responsibilities of the empire was defence, and it had to transform its army from a manoeuvrable force into one whose main duty was to patrol the frontiers. There were to be more exploits designed to increase the security of the domains and win greater prestige and power for the state. Thus it was impossible for Rome to maintain its hold on Germany as far as the Elbe, so that this vast area of modern Europe was put outside the effective influence of Rome and the diffusion of classical culture and civilisation until the Christian missions penetrated it. It was equally difficult to find an immediate and radical solution to the problem of relations with the kingdom of Parthia. The Roman world was to see the revival of the power of Persia after its destruction by Macedon.

The immediate effects of this policy were perceptible in both the political and in the cultural and philosophical field.

The Roman monarchy had been given the opportunity to prove itself in the Orient as the inheritor of the ideal of unending and invincible victory which had been the foundation of the Hellenistic, and especially of the Syrian monarchies. It was precisely for this reason that Rome's failure to prevent the revival of activity and political power in Persia added nothing to her prestige in Syria or Asia Minor, but contributed to the view, widely held throughout the Hellenistic world, that the cultural superiority of the Greeks made the Roman occupation unjust and insupportable. The injustice was felt all the more keenly because Greek thought after the fourth century BC had formed and spread the doctrine that every hegemony should be, above all, a school with its own 'paideia'.

In western Europe as well, Rome's failure to contain more than a small section of the Germanic population within the bounds of the empire, and the long drawn out uncertainty of the situation on the Danube, kept the inhabitants of those areas in a permanent state of alarm. The importance of certain provinces to the general welfare of the empire was fully realised by Rome, and regions like Gaul, which was only protected from the German tribes by a narrow strip of land beyond the Rhine, were protected, placated, and given favourable treatment at the expense even of Italy itself. The Romans were anxious that the prosperity and strength of these lands should bind them securely to the empire, and that the problem of the security of the Rhine, recurrent ever since Rome had first intervened in that region, should not get out of control and even threaten the safety of a province which was essential to the empire's survival.

Relations between the army and the lower classes in the cities, and the old governing class became one of the chief problems of the principate, especially as the power of the 'princeps' was only based on a purely personal claim to legitimacy, represented by the 'auctoritas'. The problem of maintaining a balance between the different groups within the empire became even more serious when it spread to include the provinces, and in particular when the Hellenistic orient came under Roman jurisdiction. The western provinces were easily dealt with, for their backwardness made it possible for

Rome to offer citizenship and education to the influential sectors of society in Gaul, Spain or Britain, which were soon assimilated into the Roman 'nobilitas', as the upper classes of the Italian states had been before them.

It was much more difficult to deal with the problem of the Greek and Hellenistic lands, for here was a world with its own pattern of civilisation, its own political theories, a standard of living that was the envy of Rome, and a culture which had been the foundation of the education of the Roman leaders themselves. If Greek power and influence were to be extended, it would not be long before the Roman state were transformed into a Hellenistic, or Romano-Hellenistic, empire. This had been the idea behind allowing Egypt, the last Hellenistic kingdom of the Macedonian conquests, to survive and to link Roman and Hellenistic traditions in a new type of Mediterranean state.

All the problems that we have touched on had an enormous influence on imperial policies, not least on the very position and status of the emperor. For many of the conservatives the principate was at best a temporary expedient, and any attempt to transform it into a permanent monarchy would have been contrary to the Roman tradition that precluded the establishment of any form of kingdom. The difference between the philosophical and theological justification of the Hellenistic monarchy, and the actual powers of personal jurisdiction which the Romans permitted their emperor to exercise, may seem slight at two thousand years' distance, but it was a serious matter to those who saw that a Hellenistic type of monarchy in Rome would inevitably seek support from the proletariat which was accustomed to these concepts of monarchy. In the oriental monarchies the masses had found the answer to their needs, and a similar type of government in Rome would not take long to abolish the remnants of the aristocratic privileges.

The political conflict of the first period of the principate, until the renewal of civil war and the rise to power of a family of modest origins, by way of a political career, was based on problems of this kind. In some areas the Hellenistic idea of monarchy helped to make Roman sovereignty comprehensible and acceptable to the subject races, who found it much easier to accept a Roman sovereign who could appear in the guise of successor to the earlier monarchs. In Egypt the Romans had to make use of this fact, and indeed the transfer of power was made much more smoothly there than in other countries once the Roman conqueror, like the Hellenistic rulers before him, assumed the insignia of the Pharaoh. The same policy was not so easily carried out in Greece and Asia Minor, for whereas Egypt was not a Roman province but a kingdom of the Roman emperor, the lack of this direct link in the provinces made it difficult to find a compromise between Roman rule and Hellenistic protocol.

The order of the state was menaced by the absence of any systematic legislation about the principate. Every time an emperor died, the choice of his successor caused a crisis that rekindled the debates and conflicts over the monarchy itself. It was always seen as something transitory, and not as the only means of securing a fair balance of power between the various factions of the Roman world. People who could see no other formula for monarchy than that of the Hellenistic kingdoms assumed that a monarchy in Rome could only be an adaptation of this; a dangerous situation, in their eyes, as it would have given the orientals a privileged, or at least equal, status in the empire. From the end of the civil wars, the biggest problem facing the emperor was the question of the value to be placed on the oriental regions of the Mediterranean, together with the practical problems which this evaluation involved.

In the day-to-day politics of the first phase of the empire, there were endless conflicts arising out of the policies of the individual emperors, who had no chance to develop a proper system of government, and only feebly supported the interests that had made their position necessary. They were convinced and resolute supporters of Roman tradition against oriental influences, but intolerant of the attempts of the old ruling class to act in the name of tradition against the interests of the revolutionary masses, whom they supported. Their only strength lay in their contact and friendly relations with the troops and the provinces, but they laid themselves open to criticism, suspicion and conspiracy if they gave the slightest hint of wanting to avail themselves of the support and friendship of the most advanced elements of the Hellenistic world.

This see-saw of conflicting interests was itself the reason why the principate had appeared and the justification for its continued existence, at least in the first century AD. Every attempt to dispense with the principate as the mediator between the various parties and movements within the empire was bound to do as much harm to the state as to the principate, for it destroyed the stabilising element that the state needed, and that the principate had arisen to provide. The emperor could not be the leader of one faction or revolutionary movement; the character of the state, the fruit of its political experience, and the bitter lessons of the civil wars, all determined the position of the emperor as the mediating, conciliating influence on every aspect of political life.

The emperor, in fact, could not set himself free from the tradition of Roman constitutional development. The broader interpretation of the meaning of state and citizenship, the evolution of legal theory which had been possible in Rome, in spite of bitter opposition, and which had made Rome the first state of the ancient world to distinguish between kinship and citizenship, now depended on the emperor for their realisation. The reluctance, uncertainty and lack of judgment that the emperors brought to their task led in the end to their own downfall and imperilled their empire.

As a result of these crises the monarchy was transformed from a principate based on personal power, legitimacy and 'auctoritas', to an office that was more than anything a magistracy regulated by institutional legislation defining its powers and its functions. The principate became by this means a stable organ of government, recognised by the legal tradition of the state, supported both by the revolutionary factions and by those who could give the religious sanction without which nothing but temporary and limited power was legitimate. Roman law had, as usual, evolved and adapted itself, and now accepted a monarchy as being within the scope of divine approval.

The innovation which made the principate into an organ of state and reconciled it to the legislative tradition gave great stability to the Roman state and, for a while, to the principate.

Apart from the usual friction between the oriental and Romano-Italian interests in the state, and arguments provoked by attempts to give a more precise political and administrative form to the office of emperor, the principate gave to the Roman empire the longest period of security, constructive achievement, good administration, and prosperity, that has ever occurred in ancient or modern times. During this period a great effort was made to resolve two of the problems of foreign policy that had been left unresolved since the beginning of the empire. The Danube frontier was consolidated, by the use of large consignments of troops and money, and an attempt was made to overcome the Parthians, who had succeeded to the Persian empire, and had never given up their hopes of restoring the fortunes and position of the empire in the Levant.

The war with the Parthians was the decisive factor in Rome's dominion over Asia Minor and the rest of the eastern Mediterranean. There were two sides to the problem, although of course the two were closely connected: the security of the frontier, and the loss of prestige that would result if the Romans failed to secure the frontiers. The transformation of Mesopotamia, eastern Anatolia, and parts of the Iranian plateau into a Roman province was more than the imperial forces could manage, but this was the only way of making sure that the caravan routes would not be cut by the Parthians, and the Asian province constantly bedevilled by Parthian raiders.

An emperor can only give his people good government, political equilibrium, and justice, if his position is accepted without question, and if he has enough prestige to be able to govern the state without dissipating all his energies in the struggle to silence his enemies and win the recognition due to his dignity as legitimate leader of the state. In the Roman empire questions of foreign policy were of decisive importance, especially those referring to the western Mediterranean, where the rule of Rome was less readily accepted, and less beneficial, at least to some categories of citizen. The organisation of the empire, founded on the upper classes in the provinces, on the balance between rich and poor in Italy, and on uneasy relations with the Graeco-Macedonian groups and the indigenous populations in Asia, was capable of working very well, when the emperor himself had sufficient prestige to give support and significance to his office.

The imperial forces won a series of victories in the orient, beginning with the destruction of the autonomous kingdom of Judea, the only point on the Mediterranean coast in which forces hostile to the unity of the empire could work. These victories gave the empire, and the emperors, prestige enough to govern without being preoccupied with the maintenance of its power in the teeth of its hostile subjects, who could not have accepted a sovereign who was incapable of winning a battle as their divinely appointed leader.

At the summit of its prestige and power, the Roman empire was closely identified with the longings of its subjects for peace. One of the first duties of the principate was always to put an end to the constant wars and to give the people tranquillity and security. Later on the provinces too looked to the empire as their guarantee of defence against any threat to their lands, and of efficient patrolling of the lines of communication.

While the Macedonian monarchy had made victory by conquest its policy, the Roman monarchy relied on victory by security. This meant that victories that would free the empire from the danger of Parthian or German invasions were enough to secure acceptance of Roman government and imperial rule. This was made clear when the Roman armies were victorious on the Danube and Euphrates frontiers, and built fortifications and strengthened their lines of communication beyond the Rhine, to guarantee the security of the imperial frontiers.

Rivalry between the different social and racial groups in the empire was bound to play a part in every political question. Up to the first century BC there was practically no middle class in Roman society. Not only was there no such thing as a well-off, educated, but not capitalist class, but there were no real functions for such a class to fulfil. The principate itself was the result of long struggles between rival families of nobles which ended in the political, economic and military supremacy of one of them. Under the influence of the Hellenistic world, but even more under the pressure of developments in the Mediterranean world, the principate was gradually transformed from a personal dominion into a magisterial office, and at the same time a new class was coming into existence, made up of men with regular employment in the army or in civil life.

Certain institutions, like the Senate, the army and the greater part of the magistrature, preserved the names that they had been given under the republic. But now only the name was the same; the character of all the offices had changed completely. Senators and magistrates had become state employees with fixed salaries; the salaries were generous, and allowed plenty of scope for saving and investment, but the education, the economic status, the way of life and style of house occupied by these men all bore witness to the appearance of a new class, a middle class, with all the characteristics that we associate with the term.

The factors that determined the total transformation of Roman society between the first and second centuries AD were the number of provincials who became Roman citizens, either by manumission or by other means; the number of families of Roman citizens now returning to the capital after generations spent in the provinces, to become leaders in the state; and the social and political importance won by the equestrian order by their almost exclusive control of the state administration.

The principate had pursued a policy of reducing his armed forces as far as possible, even to the extent of basing his army on troops levied in Italy and the western provinces, which were more 'Romanised', so that it was easier to concede Roman citizenship to them. Once service in the army had become voluntary, and was no worse paid than many other jobs, the limitation of conscription to the peninsula, where the standard of living was high, meant that most of the conscripts came from the lowest strata of the population. It also meant that the emperor had difficulty in recruiting enough troops for the permanent garrisons needed in the provinces, because in Rome and Italy there was no lack of work that was better paid, more attractive and more respectable than an army career.

This led to the conscription of volunteers from the western provinces in ever-increasing numbers, which introduced a new element not only into the army, but into the citizen body.

The legions were now usually stationed in one place for a long time. The fortified encampments, where they lived and kept their supplies, became the centres of attraction of the indigenous population and spread the influence of Rome through intermarriage and the diffusion of Roman culture. Villages and colonies sprang up around the camps and became the established settlements of a mixed racial group, whose children provided new contingents for the imperial armies. Eventually the army was made up almost entirely of 'barbarians' from the provinces, while positions in the civil administration and the highest ranks of the army were usually reserved for Italians and Romans.

In the west the upper classes were the first to be influenced by Roman culture. Nobles from Cisalpine and Transalpine Gaul and from Spain were admitted to senatorial rank. This development did not affect the masses, however, but was confined to the aristocracy. Increasing importance was given to officers of the emperor's private household. In the first decades of the empire its administration had been entrusted to freedmen of the imperial household who were mostly of oriental or Greek origin. As the emperor assumed the functions of a magistrate, his administrators became public servants and formed on their own a class made up for the most part of 'equites'. Clearly the emperors were tending to increase the powers of the governing class while extending its privileges and prerogatives beyond the senatorial body to the wealthy merchant class.

The extension of recruitment to the barbarians changed the character of the Roman army, making it a mercenary force like the Punic or Hellenistic armies. Ever-increasing numbers of barbarians gained Roman citizenship by this means, although their assimilation into Roman civilisation was superficial. This fact, which at first seemed unimportant, gained significance when the new citizens became sufficiently numerous to affect the racial balance within the Roman state.

Now it was not just the aristocracy who had to be assimilated, but also the masses.

The solutions found by the principate to the political and administrative problems of the early empire no longer applied, since the character of the Roman and Italian citizen body had altered, creating a commercial and industrial middle class like that of the Hellenistic world. The powers and privileges of the landowning oligarchy were diminished, while those of the new middle class increased. The provinces gained in social and political importance, although they were not fully Romanised, because of their military and naval rôle in the empire, which might have become dangerous if the emperor had needed to deploy all his forces in a defensive war, thus making the army essential to the survival of the state.

When the emperor's prestige was high, as the result of his military victories, the authority this gave made it fairly easy for him to carry out his task of mediation and arbitration among the various racial and social groups of the empire. His sovereign will was unquestioned, and his position unresistingly accepted, even when he assumed attitudes and titles which accentuated the monarchical nature of his power, and its theocratic implications. The intransigence and intolerance of the conservative oligarchy increased in proportion to the weakness of the ruler, who felt the need to reinforce his precarious dignity by claiming divine honours. This situation led to the conflict which has traditionally been regarded as the most important feature of the history of the empire. The emperors, in the face of a hostile nobility, succumbed to the necessity of using force, or the threat of force, and therefore of relying above all on their armies. Every time this happened, from the time of the decline of the republic, a dangerous imbalance of forces within the empire put the state at the mercy of one particular section of the population, and made the principate incapable of carrying out its chief function.

The decline of the empire began when the principate came to rely above all on its troops to impose order and unity on the provinces. The army was becoming more and more the concern of the provinces; the levies were exclusively provincial, and the officers who had real, political influence over the troops came from the ranks, whereas the staff officers were usually Romans, and had very little real contact with their men.

The legions, settled permanently far from the centre of the empire, often in the areas from which their troops were drawn, formed closed worlds, with their own ideals and interests, bound by their formal oath of loyalty to the emperor, but often far more closely bound to a commander who had managed to win their trust and respect. Thus, from the first century of the empire, the ruler who relied to more than a very limited extent on the loyalty of his troops risked being imposed upon and defied by the legions and their officers. When the central power was weak, insurrections occurred among the border troops which were due less to the desire for independence than to hopes of winning supreme and absolute control of the empire. As soon as the legions made the fatal discovery that it was possible for a man to be acclaimed as emperor outside the confines of Rome, there were constant attempts of this sort made by the armies on the imperial frontiers.

The nature of the empire made it at the same time intolerable and essential to its subjects. Nations with enormous racial, geographical and social differences from each other were forced to co-exist, and resented the imposed peace as much as they appreciated its advantages.

For more than two centuries, a very long time for such a vast empire, Rome ruled her united dominions in growing security and tranquillity. She preserved for the oriental states the advantages they had gained from the Hellenistic monarchies, which had enriched their culture with the products of Greek civilisation. But this period came to an end, and the forces of dissolution already at work within the empire gradually sapped the vitality of the state. However, it continued for a long time to exist as a concrete political organisation, and for even longer as an imaginary ideal.

The relationship between the power of the emperor and the armed strength of the legions was the fundamental cause of the empire's weakness. The Praetorian guard, the emperor's personal detachment of troops, interfered constantly in the politics of the capital and the policies of the emperor. The commanders of legions on the frontiers often took advantage of the loyalty of their troops to further their own ambitions and make a bid for supreme power. This led to long civil wars, involving troops whose race, language and customs gave them nothing in common with their Roman ruler. This army, without any connection with the old Roman ruling classes, or, indeed, with the other more civilised races and classes of the empire, came to be responsible not only for the defence of the frontiers, but for the election of the emperor.

The races bordering the empire were invading its territories on every side and threatening its major cities; the state had failed to perform its chief function, the very reason for its existence in the ancient world, and could no longer guarantee internal peace and security from external enemies. The demands of the defence policies brought changes in the organisation of the state which separated the civil and military administrations even further, and gave the army even greater independence under the control of the emperor. The army itself underwent changes: its numbers were increased, and the functions of the cavalry were modified, while new detachments of auxiliaries were added. Strategy and tactics changed to suit the new form of army and to make use of its different possibilities.

The empire was threatened by attempts to split it up, and to make other cities than Rome the centre of its power, but its natural strength and powers of recovery were equal to these assaults. It found new vitality in the final revolution which placed absolute authority firmly in the hands of the head of state, whose position was based on the divinity of the emperor and the might of his armies.

This revolution, which gave complete power to the emperor, led to the complete eclipse of the social group from which for centuries Rome had drawn her administrators and commanders. Gradually, the senatorial caste was displaced from the dominant position that it had still retained at the beginning of the imperial era, and was replaced by a more docile and less exclusive governing class, formed from the 'equites,' who still controlled most of the wealth of the empire. This was the end of the tradition of the civil and military administration's independence in its relations with the emperor.

The new monarchy reaffirmed the religious basis of its legitimacy at a moment when a new period of history was beginning. Now that the god whose will legalised the ruler's authority was no longer the god of the pagans, a new imperial unity began to grow up from the communion of believers in the Gospel.

In the course of centuries of revolution men had come to affirm the value of the individual and the importance of the fight to uphold justice in the political life of the community. In the place of the old Indo-European state based on racial unity, a new concept of citizenship had appeared, which gave to the groups making up the state a value which depended on their services to the community. These were the political discoveries of the ancient world, and they have made possible the modern forms of state organisation and the prospect of humanity united by a common faith in law and justice, liberty and respect for the individual, irrespective of his race and condition.

INDEX

Accad, 12
Achaeans, *see* Mycenaean-Achaean States
administration, *see* Athens, Babylon, Crete, Egypt, Greece, Mesopotamia, Mycenaean-Achaia, Persia, Rome
Aeschylus, 94
Aetolia Achaia, 117
Amum, 2
Anaxagoras, 105–6, 165
anti-sophist, 106
Anthelian League, 50
  disintegration of, 53
'Apella', 70
Appollo, cult of, 41
Accadian League, 54
'Arche', 98–9
Argos, 49, 50
aristocratic government, *see* Athens, Corinth, Egypt, Greece, Mycenaean-Achaia, Persia, Rome, Sparta: *see also* theocratic aristocracy
arts, influence, 72, 93–5
Athens, 49, 70 *et seq.*
  aristocracy, downfall of, 71, 89
  authority of State, 104
  comparison with Sparta, 70–1
  effects of revolution, 92, 104
  expedition to Peloponnese, 89
  leadership of, 101
  moral ascendancy, 107
  peace with Persia, 96
  political institutions, 90–2
  political loyalties, 108
  relations with Delphi, 93
  social organisation, 71, 87–8
  war with Sparta, 103
'Athenian Constitution', 101
Athenian democracy, 100
  crtics of, 97–104, 106, 109
  fall of, 104
Assyria, 16
'autogeneration', 2
'auctoritas', 129, 131, 171, 181

Babylon, 12–13
  administration, 12
  codification, 12

Carthage, 149–54
Chaldeans, 17
citizenship, *see* Rome
clans, *see* tribal association
'classis', 133, 138
codes, written,
  Babylonian, 12
  Egyptian, 6
  Greek, 61, 65–6
  Roman, 139
co-existence, 107
'Comitia Centuriata', 138
'Concilium Plebis', 139
consuls, 133
Corinth, 50
Crete, 27–31
  administration, 29
  collapse of, 33–5
  concept of law, 30
  influence on mainland, 31
  Minoan monarchy compared, 29, 30, 32
  religion, 28
  ruling class, 28

Decemvirs, 139
Delian League, 84, 85–6, 92, 96, 98
Delphi, 41–2, 50–1, 54, 56, 72, 84, 97, 123
  and Athens, 93
  legislative functions of, 52
  Pan-Hellenic importance of, 54, 93
demi-gods, 75
democrats, Athenian, 89–90

democracy
Athenian, 100
critics of, 97–104, 106, 109
fall of, 104
Hellenistic, 117
Demosthenes, 110
divine ruler
Crete, 30
Greece, 42, 52, 57
Hellenistic, 118–19
Mycenaean-Achaiac, 36
Persia, 115
Rome, 142, 158, 181

Egypt, 1–8
administration of, 3, 7
aristocracy, 4, 7
comparisons with Mesopotamia, 8–9
with Persia, 23–6
king of, 1–8
political reforms, 6
religion, 2, 123
reforms, 5, 8
Ephors, 70
'equites', 157, 161, 188
Etruria, 128–9
monarchy, 130
political organisation, 129

federation, 85–6
freedman, 161

'Gerousia', 70
God-gods, *see* religion
Graeco-Persian wars, 23, 76–87
Greece,
aristocracy of, 60–3, 72–6
decline of, 61,
evolution of, 46
attitude to Persia, 76–87
colonial government, 47–8, 56–60
culture, 93–5
comparison with 'barbarian', 107
development of autonomous cities, 49–60
economic organisation, 54, 62
effect of Macedonian Empire, 114
Games, 44, 93
influence on Rome, 158–60
struggle for leadership, 85
political loyalties, 108
religion, 38–44, *see also* Oracle
social changes, 61–8
see also Athens, Hellenism, Macedon, Mycaean-Achaea, Pan-Hellenism, tyrant

Hellenism, 108, 115–27
Hellenistic,
civilisation compared, 129
culture, 120, 124–7, 159, 176
democracy, 117
foreign policy, 154
governing class, 120, 124
influence on Rome, 168–9, 176, 179
monarchies, 118–25
religion, 122
Helots, 69, 70
Hesiod, 31, 72
Hittites, 13–15
influence on Greeks, 27
oligarchy, 15
religion, 15
ruler, 14
sovereign assembly, 15
Homer, 72

Indo-Europeans, 14
Isocrates, 106, 108, 109
Italiot-cities, 151, 162–3

Jurors, payment of, 91
justice,
in Athens, 104, 106
in Babylon, 13
in Crete, 30
in Egypt, 2
in Greece, 104, 108
Hittite, 15
in Mesopotamia, 10
in Rome, 137, 147, 158

king, *see* monarchy
king-god, 121

Latins, 128, 131, 162
relations with Rome, 132
Lacedaemonia, *see* Sparta
Law,
divine origin of, 3, 142
and tradition, 141–2, 166
see also justice, code

legislator,
Greece, 64, 66, *see also* Delphi
Rome, 138–9, *see also* Senate
see also divine ruler and monarchy
'Lex Agraria', 161
Linear 'A', 28
'B', 30, 31
Lydia, 17, 24
fall of, 76, 79
influence on Greeks, 27

'Ma' at', 2
Macedon, 110
conquest of Persia, 110–14
effect of Empire, 114
monarchy, 111 *et seq.*
Medes, 17, 24, 112
'Melian Dialogue', 101
Mesopotamia, 8
administration, 11
influence on Greeks, 27
monarchy, 9–13
compared with Egypt, 8
Minos, 29
monarchy,
in Assyria, 16
in Crete, 29–30
in Egypt, 1–8
in Etruria, 129–30
in Greece, 42–3, 79, 114–15
Hellenistic, 118 et seq., 160, 179
Hittite, 14
in Lydia, 17
in Mesopotamia, 9–13
in Macedon, 111 *et seq.*
Mycenaean-Achaean, 34, 36
in Persia, 18–19, 110, 114–15, 146
in Rome, 133, 172–8, 181, 182–3,
in Sparta, 70
infallibility of, 3–6
see also divine ruler, theocratic monarchy
monotheism, 5
Mycenae, 29, 30, 49
Mycenaean-Achaean States, 30–40
aristocracy of, 37
decline of, 37
economic organisation, 31, 37
monarchy, 34–6
political organisation, 31, 34, 35
social organisation, 38–40
warrior-caste, 32, 34, 35

Nauplion, 49
Naval supremacy of Rome, 151

oligarchy, *see* aristocracy
Olympia, prestige of sanctuary, 52, 123
Olympic games, 45
Oracle, 40–5, 47, 50–2, 57, 60, 64, 68, 83, 116, 118, 123
political functions, 42
'Oracular-states', 51, 53
oracular law, 99
oratory, 106
Osiris cult, 5

Pan-Hellenic cults, 43
'oracular state', 54
unity, 44–6, 51, 53, 54, 56, 58, 59, 68, 83, 84, 90, 109, 122
'patres', 131, 155, 157, 171
patrician-plebian struggle, 136–40
patrician assembly, 133
Persia,
administration, 18–19
aristocracy, 20, 24–5
monarchy, 18, 146
defeat of, 111–13
weakness of, 22, 25
Peace Treaty, 96
compared with Egypt, 23–6
Persian Wars, 76–7, 87
Peloponnese, division of, 50
Peloponnesian League, 54
Peloponnesian War, 103, 109
Pharaoh, 2–8, 26
Pindar, 93
'plebs', 131, 133, 155, 157, 171, *see also* patrician-plebian struggle
Polis, 46–8, 53, 66, 76, 81, 97, 99, 100, 166
transformation of, 68
political institutions, *see* Athens, Babylon, Crete, Egypt, Etruria, Greece, Mesopotamia, Mycenaean-Achaea, Persia, Rome
political loyalties, *see* Athens
political power, concepts of, 25
'praetors', 133
'Proskynesis', 111, 112
Punic Wars, effects of, 155-64, 169
Pyrrhus, 151

INDEX

Ra, 1
Reason, 104–6, 115
Religion,
  in Crete, 28
  in Egypt, 2, 123
  in Greece, 38–44, 57, 64, 75
  Hellenistic, 122–3
  Hittite, 15
  Mycaean-Achaean, 35
  Persian, 108
  Roman, 133, 135–6, 142, 144–5, 147, 158–9, 166, 171, 181, 189
revolution,
  Athenian, 88
  Greek, 66–7, 74, 112
  in Egypt, 5
  in Rome, 139, 165
'rex sacrificulus', 133
Rome,
  aristocracy, 140, 143–4, 162, 167, 179
  citizenship, 162, 169
  civil war, 170
  comparison with Etruria, 131
  economic changes, 161
  defeat of Carthage, 154
  foreign policy, 147
  imperial policy, 179
  law and tradition, 141–2, 166
  military organisation, 132, 133, 136, 138, 158, 160, 164–8, 175, 177, 178, 184–7
  establishment as naval power, 151, 153
  political organisation, 132–40, 164–9
  Punic Wars, 155–64, 169
  religion, 133, 135–6, 142, 144–5, 147, 158–9, 166, 171, 181, 189
  revolution, 165–75
  war with Parthia, 182
  see also 'Comitia Centuriata', consuls, 'patres', 'plebs', tribunes, Senate

Sanctuaries, 51, *see also* Delphi, oracle
Sartraps, 20–2
Senate, 135, 140, 155, 157, 173, 184
shipbuilding, 63
slaves, 161
Sicily, 152
Simonides, 94
Solon, 74
Sophists, 106
Sophocles, 94
sovereignty, 25, 52
  in Egypt, 2
  in Persia, 79
  in Rome, 134, 158, 171, 179
Sparta, 49–50, 69, 81, 84, 86–7
  and Athens, 95, 96, 99, 103
  and Colonies, 69
  and Corinth, 60
  and Delphi, 93
  and Greek States, 81–2
  and Peloponnesian League, 54
  and Persia, 77
  compared with Athens, 71, 72, 76
  compared with Rome, 144
  oligarchy, 90
  political life, 46
Sun-god, 41–3

Tarentum, 151
thalassocracy, 79, 83, 95, 149
theocratic aristocracy, 75
  legitimacy, 89
  monarchy, 44, 52, 57, 60, 116
theocracy,
  in Achaean Greece, 36
  in Egypt, 4, 26
  comparisons, 61
theology, Egyptian, 5
Theseus, 31
Thucydides, 53, 55, 68, 101, 109
Tiryns, 49
tribal associations, 71
tribunes, 137, 171
tyrant,
  in Athens, 72
  in Greece, 64–7, 74

warrior caste, 32, 34, 35, 62

D1082949

SCHOOL IS DEAD

SCHOOL IS DEAD:

Alternatives in Education

EVERETT REIMER

DOUBLEDAY & COMPANY, INC.

GARDEN CITY, NEW YORK

Library of Congress Catalog Card Number 78–157619

Printed in the United States of America

My grandmother wanted me to have an education, so she kept me out of school.

Margaret Mead

CONTENTS

Foreword 9
1. The Case Against Schools 19
2. What Schools Do 31
3. What Schools Are 49
4. How Schools Work 59
5. Where Schools Came From 71
6. Institutional Props for Privilege 87
7. Are Democratic Institutions Possible? 101
8. Networks of Things 113
9. Networks of People 125
10. Financing Universal Education 141
11. The Revolutionary Role of Education 159
12. Strategy for a Peaceful Revolution 173
13. What Each of Us Can Do 185
Notes and References 201

FOREWORD

This book is the result of a conversation with Ivan Illich that has continued for fifteen years. We have talked of many things, but increasingly about education and school and, eventually, about alternatives to schools.

Illich and I met in Puerto Rico, where I had come in 1954 as secretary of the Committee on Human Resources of the commonwealth government, charged with assessing the manpower needs of the island and recommending an educational program to meet them. Puerto Rico was then in the course of rapid industrialization, and my calculations showed that dropout rates would have to decline throughout the school system if the estimated manpower needs of the economy were to be met. Everything was done to reduce these rates and they actually declined for a while, but it soon became apparent that the decline was at the expense of grade standards and, therefore, meaningless.

Illich came to Puerto Rico in 1956, at the request of the late Cardinal Spellman, to organize a training program for New York priests from parishes overrun by

Puerto Rican migrants. We soon found common interests and many parallels in the problems of church and school. In 1960 Illich left Puerto Rico for Mexico,[1] and shortly afterward I joined the Alliance for Progress. We began to study the problems of Latin American education at about the same time, and these turned out to be similar to the problems of Puerto Rico but on a vastly larger scale. It was soon clear to both of us that the countries of Latin America could not, for many years, afford schools for all their children. At the same time, education seemed to be the basic need of these countries, not only to us but also to their political parties and leaders. In 1968 we began a systematic study of this dilemma and of possible ways out of it.

Our analysis of schools was soon extended to other institutions and to the structure of the society schools serve. At first we felt that school was a lagging institution in an increasingly efficient technological society. We later came to see schools as providing indispensable support for a technological society that is itself not viable. The simplest way to expose the contradictions of this society is to point out that it promises unlimited progress to unlimited numbers of people. The absurdity of this claim is conceded by the recognition of the need for birth control, but birth control itself turns out to depend on progress. Women have fewer children if they have been to school for at least four years, but by the time children can be kept in school long enough for this to have a significant impact on birth rates, the population of the world will have increased threefold. And this is using conservative projections. If modern medical techniques were made generally available, the rate of population increase would double or triple.[2] We retain breathing space only

by letting poor babies die at ten times the rate of privileged babies.

During the past decade the actual rate at which living standards have improved among the underprivileged peoples of the world is scarcely greater than the rate of population growth. On a per-capita basis, individuals have benefited marginally, if at all.

Part of the problem lies in the inefficiency of modern institutions, including schools. The greater part lies in the open-ended nature of the promise of progress. As the world is now organized, the standard of living in India can rise consistently only if the standard of living in the United States also rises. Because of its effects on the demand for Indian exports and upon the supply of American capital abroad, stagnation of the American economy tends to depress the economic growth of India. Yet, a normal rise in the United States average income is twice the total income of the average Indian. Raising world consumption standards to U.S. levels would multiply the combustion of fossil fuels by fifty times, the use of iron a hundred times, the use of other metals over two hundred times. By the time these levels were reached, consumption levels in the United States would again have tripled and the population of the world would also have tripled. Such projections lead to results as absurd as the premises from which they start. There can be no open-ended progress. Yet this is what modern institutions promise. This is the promise of science and technology unrestrained by reason. This is the promise that has promoted the growth of schools and other modern institutions and that they in turn propagate. Schools produce the subjects of a world in which technology is king.

The contradictions of such a world are becoming apparent. They are best illustrated in the school and best corrected by freeing education from the school so that people may learn the truth about the society in which they live.

In the course of this analysis, an interpretation of human history has developed that, although sketchy and incomplete, must be shared with the reader. When techniques, institutions, and ideologies were primitive, men lived in relative equality and freedom, because there were no adequate means of domination. As techniques, institutions, and ideologies developed, they were used to establish and maintain relations of domination and privilege. From that time on, the societies that succeeded in dominating others, and thus world history, were also characterized by interclass and interpersonal domination in tension with efforts to establish equality. As techniques increased in efficiency and ideologies in scope, they repeatedly threatened to upset the privilege structure of society. Institutions were used to counter these threats by controlling the use of the techniques and by perverting the ideologies. When revolutionary breakthroughs occurred, institutions were re-established on a broader base, extending privilege to more people, but always at the same time maintaining the structure of privilege. This view does not necessarily lead to a Jeffersonian suspicion of institutions as such. Despite the historical record, the possibility of democratic institutions remains—if men determine to use institutions for democratic purposes.

I would like to be able to say that the previous paragraph contains the last oversimplification in this book. Regrettably, I cannot. I have tried to qualify my asser-

tions, to provide evidence for them, to give supporting references, and to justify my value judgments, but I do not expect to satisfy the norms of academic scholarship. To do that I would have to write not this book now but a completely different book twenty years from now. I chose to write this book now because I would like to live to see it become a self-fulfilling prophecy. Twenty years from now I might not be alive.

My view of history does not result in an unbiased appraisal of schools nor of the society to which schools belong but rather in an indictment of both. Schools are admittedly treated in stereotype rather than in terms of concrete human behavior. Schools are simply too big to treat concretely. Alternatives to school, as opposed to mere reform, require going beyond the experience of individuals to an analysis of the essential characteristics of schools. Nevertheless, in an abstract treatment people will not quite recognize themselves as students, teachers, or parents, or in other concrete roles related to schools. A few may feel themselves cast as the villains in a conspiracy of injustice. But this would be a misreading of the book.

There are unjust men in the world and it is an unjust world, but it is not the unjust men, as such, who make it so. It is an unjust world largely because it is composed of faulty institutions. These institutions, in turn, are merely the collective habits of individuals, but individuals can have bad habits without being bad people. In general, people are unconscious of their habits, particularly their institutional habits. One thesis of this book is that people can become aware of their bad habits and can change them. The world would then be a better world, made up of still-imperfect people. There are, of course, some

people who know that they have bad habits but do not want to change them. There are others who are afraid to examine their habits for fear that their consciences would then be troubled. This is the worst that can be said of most people. It is enough, however, to explain how the world can be worse than the people who live in it.

The realities of school are both better and worse than they are here described. Others have made more of an attempt at concrete portrayal, and their work is an indispensable supplement to the present analysis. Tom Brown, Charlie Brown, Miss Peach, and the children and teachers from George Dennison's[3] and Jonathan Kozol's[4] accounts are a few examples of the reality of school. A model for general description and analysis of institutional behavior is to be found in Floyd Allport's book by that name.[5]

This book owes far more debts than I can remember, let alone acknowledge. Several, however, I cannot forget. Except for the insistence of Ralph Bohrson it might never have been written. The Ford Foundation travel and study grant that he administered allowed me to spend time writing it that might otherwise have been spent on other work. Cooperation from CIDOC, which has permitted me to work intensively with Illich and to publish earlier drafts and discuss them with students and associates, has been even more vital. Many educators, economists, administrators, and political leaders from Latin America, the United States, and Europe have by this time participated in the analysis that Illich and I have conducted. Most of them are referred to in the text and in the appended notes. I want especially to recognize the invaluable editorial assistance of Jordan Bishop,

George Dennison, John Holt, Monica Raymond, Joan Remple, Michael Samlowski, Dennis Sullivan, and of many students at CIDOC with whom I have discussed earlier drafts. Not least is the debt I owe my wife and sons and daughters for years of critical conversation about education and the rest of life. None of my collaborators is directly responsible for anything in the book. Even Illich may disagree with parts of it. By the time it is published it is quite likely that I will too.

SCHOOL IS DEAD

1. THE CASE AGAINST SCHOOLS

"If sharks were people," his landlady's little daughter asked Mr. K, "would they be nicer to the little fish?" "Of course," he said, "if sharks were people, they would have strong boxes built in the sea for little fish. There they would put in all sorts of food, plants and little animals, too. They would see to it that the boxes always had fresh water, and they would take absolutely every sort of sanitary measure. When, for example, a little fish would injure his fin, it would be immediately bandaged so that he would not die on the sharks before his time had come. In order that the little fish would never be sad, there would be big water parties from time to time; for happy fish taste better than sad ones. Of course, there would be schools in the big boxes as well. There the little fish would learn how to swim into the mouths of the sharks. They would need, for example, geography so that they could find the sharks, lazing around somewhere. The main subject would naturally be the moral education of the little fish. They would be taught that the grandest, most beautiful thing is for a little fish to offer himself happily, and that they must all believe in the sharks, above all when they say that they will provide for a beautiful future. One would let the little fish know that this

future is only assured when they learn obedience. They must shy away from all lowly, materialistic and Marxist inclinations, and inform the sharks immediately if any one of them betrayed such tendencies. . . . If sharks were people, there would of course be art as well. There would be beautiful pictures of sharks' teeth, all in magnificent colors, of their mouths and throats as pure playgrounds where one can tumble and play. The theaters on the bottom of the sea would offer plays showing heroic little fish swimming enthusiastically down the throats of the sharks, and the music would be so beautiful that its sounds would lead the little fish dreamily to the chapels and, filled with the most pleasant thoughts, they would stream down the sharks' throats. There would certainly be religion. . . . It would teach that true life really begins in the sharks' bellies. And if sharks were people, the little fish would stop being, as they are now, equals. Some would be given offices and be put over the others. Those a little bigger would even be allowed to eat the smaller ones. That would only be delightful for the sharks, for then they would more often have bigger crumbs to gobble up. And the most important of the little fish, those with offices, would look to the ordering of the little fish. And they would become teachers, officers, box-building engineers, etc. In short, there could only be culture in the sea if the sharks were people."

Bertolt Brecht, Kalendergeschichten

Most of the children of the world are not in school. Most of those who enter drop out after a very few years. Most of those who succeed in school still become dropouts at a higher level. UNESCO data show that only in a small minority of nations do even half the children complete the first six grades.[1] No child, however, fails to learn from school. Those who never get in, learn that the good things of life are not for them. Those who drop out early, learn that they do not deserve the good things of life. The later dropouts learn that the system can be beat, but not by them. All of them learn that school is the path to secular salvation, and resolve that their children shall climb higher on the ladder than they did.[2]

For most members of the present generation this hope, that their children will benefit more from school than they, is doomed to disappointment. Schools are too expensive for this hope to be realized. For many, it may appear to be realized, but the appearance will be a delusion fostered by inflationary debasement of the academic currency. More college and high school degrees will be granted, but they will mean less, both in terms of amount

and kind of learning and in terms of job qualification and real income.

In all countries, school costs are rising faster than enrollments and faster than national income. While the school's share of national income can afford to grow slowly as this income increases, it cannot continue to grow at present rates. In Puerto Rico, for example, the national income was ten times greater in 1965 than in 1940. School enrollment more than doubled during this period, while school costs multiplied twenty-five times.[3] Yet, even in 1965, less than half of all Puerto Rican students finished nine years of school,[4] and the proportion who reached the higher grades without learning to read was higher than it had been twenty-five years earlier. Puerto Rico is atypical in its absolute rates of growth, but not in the vital relationships among them. Monographs on the cost of schooling in African and Asian countries, sponsored by the International Institute for Educational Planning, paint a similar picture, as do studies in Britain and most of the countries of western Europe.[5,6] Recent studies in the United States suggest that it would cost eighty billion additional dollars to meet educators' estimates of what is needed to provide adequate schooling.[7] Even the settlement of the war in Indochina would provide only a small fraction of this amount.

The conclusion is inescapable: No country in the world can afford the education its people want in the form of schools. Except for a few rich nations and some not yet exposed to the development virus, no country in the world can afford the schools its people are now demanding from their political leaders. Continued attempts to supply the demand for college study in the United States will condemn the black and rural minorities to an indefinite wait for an adequate education. In India, Nigeria,

and Brazil the majority must, for generations, be denied all but marginal educational resources if a tiny minority is to enjoy the luxury of schooling that would still be regarded as pitifully inadequate by United States standards.

School is the world's largest enterprise; larger than agriculture, industry, or warfare. School's rivals for the educational dollar are demonstrably small by comparison. The mass media are the most prominent, the easiest to define, and the smallest. Large as the press and television are, along with movies, radio, and all other forms of publishing, broadcasting, and public entertainment, they account for less than half the time and money involved in schooling. This might not be true for the United States in terms of man-hours of exposure, but the rural masses of the rest of the world, as yet largely untouched by mass media, have all begun to send their children to school. On-the-job training, while harder to estimate, may be a little closer but still a losing rival to schools. There are a few more people at work throughout the world than in school, but not many more.[8] Not enough more to offset the smaller proportion of their work time devoted to learning.[9]

There are still people who believe that we could finance the education we need by means of schooling, if only we were willing to give it priority, but this belief ignores the dynamics of schooling. No sooner is universal high school attendance approached than the competition shifts to colleges, at higher costs. There is already agitation for degrees above the Ph.D. on the grounds that the doctorate has become common and degraded. There can be no end to schooling in a world that puts no limits on consumption—where degrees determine people's position at the trough.

Schools are an almost perfectly regressive form of taxation, paid for by the poor to benefit the rich. Schools are supported, largely, by general taxes that ultimately fall more upon the poor than their direct incidence suggests. Property taxes, for example, are paid by those who occupy dwellings rather than by those who own them, excise taxes by consumers rather than producers. Meanwhile, the benefits of even public expenditures for schooling are distributed in direct proportion to present economic privilege.

The children of the poorest tenth of the United States population attend school for an average of less than five years. The schools they attend, at this grade level, spend no more than five hundred dollars per pupil per year. These children cost the public, in schooling, less than twenty-five hundred dollars each over a lifetime. The children of the richest tenth of the population finish college and a year of graduate school, which costs about thirty-five thousand dollars. Assuming that one third of this is private expenditure, the richest tenth still get ten times as much of public funds for education as the poorest tenth.[10]

Schools make it impossible to equalize educational opportunity, even in terms of the allocation of public resources. Unless they abandon scholastic standards altogether, they can never keep poor children in school as long as rich ones, and unless they reverse the cost ratios that have always characterized schooling, they will always spend more at higher than at lower levels. Even compensating programs specifically designed to help poor children cannot achieve their purpose within the present structure of the school. Of three billion dollars earmarked by the federal government of the United States for supplementary services to poor children, less

than a third was actually spent on eligible children; these children showed no measurable improvement, while the non-eligible children with whom they were mixed and who also benefited from the money, did make a measurable gain.[11] Many of the school administrators responsible for these programs had good intentions. Short of segregating the poor children or giving them privileges that their classmates could not share, they found it difficult to help them selectively.

Compared to the rest of the world, the schools of the United States are relatively fair. In Bolivia, for example, one half of all public allocations for schools are spent on 1% of the population. The ratio of educational expenditures on the upper and lower tenths of the population, respectively, are about three hundred to one.[12] Most parts of the world are nearer to the Bolivian than to the United States ratio.

Schools constitute a regressive tax because the privleged go to school longer and because costs increase with the level of schooling. Graduate schools, for example, provide by far the highest student subsidies not only in relative but also in absolute terms. Graduate students come largely from the upper income levels of the society. Nevertheless, students pay almost nothing at this level, in fact are frequently paid, while graduate-school support, even in private universities, comes largely from public funds. Costs in the sciences, for example, run up to several hundred thousand dollars per student per year. An argument is sometimes made that graduate students are exploited as underpaid teachers and research assistants. In a narrow sense this is true, but in the longer view, graduate-school exploitation is merely an initiation fee paid for larger lifetime earnings. At undergraduate levels there is a higher proportion of private expenditure, but

even here public subsidies average thousands of dollars per student per year, as compared with hundreds of dollars at the elementary level, where most of the poor children are.[13]

Development economists argue that peasants in India, sharecroppers in Alabama, and dishwashers from Harlem do not need more education until the world is ready to absorb them into better jobs and that these better jobs can be created only by others, who must therefore be given educational priority.[14] But this argument ignores many of the economic, demographic, and political facts of life. Economic growth, where it is occurring, principally bolsters the level of living of the already better off, fattens military and security-police budgets, and supports the markets of more-developed nations. Population is growing so much faster than the rate at which real educational opportunities can be expanded, by means of schools, that deferring the education of the masses merely leaves a more difficult task for the future. On the other hand, few people have voluntarily curtailed birthrates without a minimum of education and social mobility.[15] If there were a monopoly of power in the world, population growth might be curtailed arbitrarily. In the world as it is, to ignore popular demands for education is not only morally indefensible, it is politically impossible except for military governments. For most people, forcing others not to have children would be a completely unacceptable policy in any case.

While children who never go to school are most deprived economically and politically, they probably suffer the least psychological pain. Andean Indians, tribal Africans, and Asian peasants belong to communities that have no schools or have them only for the children of the elite. Their parents and grandparents have never

known schools as places they expected their children to attend. They do know, however, what schools imply. Going to school means leaving the traditional life, moving to a different place, laying aside physical burdens for the work of the tongue and the mind, exchanging traditional food, clothing, and customs for those of the larger town or distant city. Parents often prefer to keep the child in the traditional community, bearing the familiar burdens, confined to the enjoyments that primitive means can provide. They know, however, that this implies continuing domination by others, continuing dependence in times of hunger, war, and sickness, increasing distance from those who enjoy wealth, power, and respect. When the choice becomes a real one, most unschooled parents all over the world decide to send their children to school.

These first attenders have a harder time than their older brothers and sisters, for whom the school came too late. They do not last long in school. In 1960, half the children who entered school in Latin America never started the second grade, and half the second-graders never started the third.[16] Three fourths dropped out before they learned to read. They did learn, however, how unsuited they were to school, how poor their clothing was, how bad their manners, how stupid they were in comparison with those who went on to higher grades. This helped them accept the greater privilege and power of the deserving minority and their own relative poverty and political impotence. Yet they were not as ready as their older brothers and sisters to accept the limitations of their traditional lot. A little schooling can induce a lot of dissatisfaction. The more schooling a dropout has, the more it hurts him to drop out. The child who never learns to read can still accept his inferiority as a fact of life. The child who goes on to higher grades may learn

that he is really no different from the sons of the mayor, the merchant, or the schoolteacher, except that they have the money or the influence needed to go on to secondary school or college, while he must stay behind for lack of it. For him, it is much harder to accept their getting the better jobs, enjoying the higher offices, winning the more beautiful girls, all because they were able to stay in school longer than he.

A winners' world? If this were all, schools might still be defended; but the winners of the school game are a strange lot. The Ottomans used to geld their candidates for managerial posts. Schools make physical emasculation unnecessary by doing the job more effectively at the libidinal level. This is, of course, a simplistic metaphor. While there is evidence that girls do better in school than boys and that boys do less well the more masculine they are judged to be, this undoubtedly results more from social than from physical factors. The metaphor understates rather than overstates the facts. School domesticates—socially emasculates—both girls and boys by a process much more thorough than mere selection by sex. School requires conformity for survival and thus shapes its students to conform to the norms for survival.[17] If learning the official curriculum of the school were the principal criterion, this might still not be so bad, although it would substitute the learning of what Whitehead and other philosophers of education have called dead knowledge for true learning. The actual survival criteria are much worse. In addition to the wealth or influence of parents, they include the ability to beat the game, which according to John Holt and other perceptive teachers, is mainly what successful students learn in school.[18]

To say that schools teach conformity and also teach students to beat the game is not contradictory. Beating

the game is one form of conformity. Individual teachers may be concerned with what children learn, but school systems record only the marks they get. Most students learn to follow the rules that schools can enforce and to break those they cannot. But also, different students learn in varying degrees to conform, to ignore the rules, and to take advantage of them. Those who ignore them in the extreme become dropouts, and learn mainly that they do not belong in school or in the society it represents. Those who conform to the rules become the dependable producers and consumers of the technological society. Those who learn to beat the school game become the exploiters of this society. Those on whom the discipline of the school falls lightly, who easily perform its assignments and have little need to violate its rules, are least touched by school. They are, or become, the social aristocrats and the rebels. This, at any rate, is what happened before schools began to break down. Now all kinds of students join in the rush for the door, while schools engage in a similar scramble to recapture their dropouts by any means.

As late as the turn of the century, schools were still a minor institution and all who were not suited for them and by them had other educational options. Fifty years ago, no country in the world had 10% of its teen-age population in school. Schools have grown so fast partly because they happened to be doing what was important to a technological era when this era began. Their monopoly of education has been achieved as one aspect of the monopoly of technology. The main reason we need alternatives to schools is that they close the door to humanity's escape from this monopoly. They insure that those who inherit influence in a world dominated by technology will be those who profit by this domination

and, even worse, those who have been rendered incapable of questioning it. Not only the leaders but their followers are shaped by the school game to play the game of competitive consumption—first to meet and then to surpass the standards of others. Whether the rules are fair or the game worth playing is beside the point.

School has become the universal church of a technological society, incorporating and transmitting its ideology, shaping men's minds to accept this ideology, and conferring social status in proportion to its acceptance. There is no question of man's rejecting technology. The question is one of adaptation, direction, and control. There may not be much time, and the only hope would seem to lie in education—the true education of free men capable of mastering technology rather than being enslaved by it, or by others in its name.

There are many roads to enslavement, only a few to mastery and freedom. Technology can kill by poisoning the environment, by modern warfare, by overpopulation. It can enslave by chaining men to endless cycles of competitive consumption, by means of police states, by creating dependence on modes of production that are not viable in the long run. There are no certain roads of escape from these dangers. There can be *no* road of escape, however, if men remain enthralled in a monolithic secular orthodoxy. The first amendment to the Constitution of the United States was a landmark in history. "There shall be no establishment of religion." Only the terms and the scope of the problem have changed. Our major threat today is world-wide monopoly in the domination of men's minds. We need effective prohibition of scholastic monopoly, not only of educational resources but of the life chances of individuals.

2. WHAT SCHOOLS DO

I learned something in school today.
I signed up for folk guitar, computer programming,
stained glass art, shoemaking and a natural foods workshop.
I got Spelling, History, Arithmetic and two study periods.

So what did you learn?

I learned that what you sign up for
and what you get
are two different things.

Dialogue from Peanuts
Charles Schulz

Schools are supposed to educate. This is their ideology, their public purpose. They have gone unchallenged, until recently, partly because education is itself a term that means such different things to different people. Different schools do different things of course, but increasingly schools in all nations, of all kinds, at all levels, combine four distinct social functions: custodial care, social-role selection, indoctrination, and education as usually defined in terms of the development of skills and knowledge. It is the combination of these functions that makes schooling so expensive. It is conflict among these functions that makes schools educationally inefficient. It is also the combination of these functions that tends to make school a total institution, has made it an international institution, and makes it such an effective instrument of social control.

Custodial care is now so universally provided by schools that it is hard to remember earlier arrangements. Children must, of course, be cared for—if they are really children, that is, and not just young members of the

community taking part in its normal productive and social affairs. Most youngsters still get along without special care, all over the world, in the tribal, peasant, and urban dwellings of the poor. It is only mothers who have been freed from the drudgery of food production and preparation who find it necessary to turn the care of their children over to others. This is because of other differences between modern and traditional societies. Older children are taken out of the home by the school, fathers go to work, and grandparents and other members of the extended family are left behind in rural or older urban settlements. Were it not for the school, child care in the modern family would fall exclusively upon the mother. Schools thus help to liberate the modern woman, but only by imprisoning her child and by tying her and her man more tightly to their jobs so that they can support the schools. Women clearly need not only the liberation schools provide but much more. Men and children, however, need liberation too. The same point holds for all who suffer special discrimination. Each group must formulate its own demands and fight its own battles, but unless they also join forces with others they will win only battles, never the war.

Child care costs money, and although schools provide it relatively cheaply, this is where most of the school budget goes.[1] Time studies conducted in Puerto Rico by Anthony Lauria show that less than 20% of a teacher's time is available for instructional activities. The rest is spent on behavior control and administrative routine. Lauria's data support a statement John Gardner once made, long before he was Secretary of Health, Education and Welfare in the federal government of the United States. He said that everything a high school graduate is taught in twelve years of schooling could easily be

learned in two years, and with a little effort in one. Since child care is the most tangible service schools provide, and since parents are naturally concerned about the quality of such care, this function has a priority claim on school resources. Other functions must compete for what is left after prevailing local standards of safety, comfort, and convenience have been met.

As children get older, child care paradoxically becomes both more extensive and more expensive. Actual hours spent in school increase, buildings are more luxurious, the ratio of paid adults to students increases, and the salaries of these adults also increase. Where there are no schools, children contribute more to the community and require less support as they grow older.[2] High schools, however, take more of the students' time than primary schools, and cost more, too, while most colleges and universities occupy the full time of the student, at an ever-increasing hourly cost as students progress up the academic ladder. The costs of higher education admittedly cover more than mere custodial care, but at upper as well as lower levels the time students spend in school is an important cost factor. Space is also costly; the commodious college campus, insulated from the nonacademic environment, is much more expensive than the neighborhood kindergarten.

Money, however, is the least of the costs of providing custodial care in schools. The really important consequence of packaging custody with the other functions of the school is the extension of childhood from age twelve to twenty-five, and from the sons and daughters of the rich to the youth of the whole society. This, in turn, is only one aspect of the division of modern life into school, work, and retirement.

Children and old people are problems in a society that

has no use for them. They are both in danger and in the way, in modern cities. Such cities are no longer needed, however, for civilized living. The physical products people need could be produced economically in widely scattered, highly automated fields and factories. Only the exchange of professionalized services requires cities; while service institutions, such as schools, restaurants, hotels, hospitals, and office buildings, are needed only in cities. Such institutions do not derive a net benefit from the economies of scale, which permit the use of high technology. Even in the case of hospitals the advantages of high technology are offset by the disadvantages of crowding large numbers of patients together.

So long as modern cities survive, institutional provisions will, of course, have to be made for the care of the old and the young. One general solution might be to keep them largely outside the urban sector. Another would be to rehumanize the city, for example by reserving some streets for pedestrians and relaxing the competitive character of urban occupations. Transitional institutions can also be imagined: co-operative child-care centers, specialized apartment buildings for the old and infirm, new kinds of apprentice programs. The concrete alternatives should be an outcome of how people, given a wide range of choices, decide to live. The important point is that technological considerations impose no serious restrictions on these choices. People can have what they want if they can free themselves of habits and preferences, some of which have been frozen into laws and institutions. Schools play a vital role in the transmission of habits and preferences from one generation to the next.

So long as children remain full-time students, they remain children—economically, politically, even legally. While no formal legal sanctions are available against stu-

dents as such, they can always be deprived of their rights to schooling, and thus to preferred employment and social status. The school schedule remains, also, one of the major supports for age restrictions on the right to vote, to work, to contract, and to enjoy other constitutional privileges and protections. The school itself, as custodian of ever-larger numbers of people, for increasing proportions of their life span, for an ever-growing number of hours and interests, is well on the way to joining armies, prisons, and insane asylums as one of society's total institutions. Strictly speaking, total institutions are those which totally control the lives of their inmates, and even armies, prisons, and asylums do this completely only for certain inmates. Only vacationless boarding schools could strictly be called total institutions, but perhaps the strict definition gives too much attention to the body and too little to the mind and spirit. Schools pervade the lives and personalities of their students in powerful and insidious ways, and have become the dominant institution in the lives of modern men during their formative years.

Studies of prisons and asylums indicate how overwhelmingly such institutions produce the very behavior they are designed to correct. In one experiment, almost all the members of a group of persons diagnosed as hopelessly insane, asylum inmates for over twenty years, were discharged as cured within a few months of being placed in a "normal" environment. In another experiment, a group of persons diagnosed as dangerously insane were allowed to institute self-government among themselves and managed without incident.[3] A similar cure for student unrest would be to stop making children out of people old enough to have children, support them, and fight for them. This would, of course, require other social changes, in addition to the divorce of custodial care from

education at the higher levels of schooling, but they are equally necessary changes if society is to survive.

A second function of schools, more directly in conflict with their educational aims than custodial care, is the sorting of the young into the social slots they will occupy in adult life. Some of this sorting occurs at the high school and college level, when students begin to opt for this or that profession or trade and enter special curriculums of one to a dozen years in length for vocational preparation. Even this aspect of job selection in school is wasteful and often personally disastrous. Part of the waste is in the high proportion of dropouts, not only from professional and trade schools but from the professions and trades themselves, frequently after long and expensive investments have been made. Many people find that medicine or teaching is not for them—something they could have found out much sooner and much more cheaply if they had begun as orderlies, nurses, or teacher-aides. Even those who stay in the field of their choice do not escape extensive waste of time and money. According to the folklore of many occupations, the first several years of work are spent forgetting what was learned about the vocation in school. Counseling and other sincere and systematic efforts are made to minimize this kind of waste, but it is doubtful that, even at great additional cost, they can do more than slow its acceleration. The ever-greater separation of school from the rest of life widens a gap that no amount of effort can bridge.

The major part of job selection is not a matter of personal choice at all, but a matter of survival in the school system. Except for members of minority groups, age at dropout determines whether boys and girls will be paid for their bodies, hands, or brains, and also how much they

will be paid. This in turn will largely determine where they can live, with whom they can associate, and the rest of their style of life. Within this century, any profession could still be entered at the bottom. Today this is difficult even in countries that provide schools for only a tiny minority. In the United States, it is now hard to become a carpenter without having graduated from high school. In New York City even a garbage collector needs a diploma.

While economic status is largely a function of the level at which a student drops out, power in the society depends more upon the sorting that occurs when high school graduates enter college. Admission to Harvard College practically guarantees access to the groups that will control the major hierarchies of the United States. State and local as well as national hierarchies are the products of the college lottery. Even international agencies are ruled by the graduates of a dozen world-famous universities.

Power and wealth are not everything, of course, but almost everything else depends upon them in many parts of the world. Especially where the school system is dominant, respect, reputation, health, even affection of many kinds, can either be commanded or purchased—if they are not tendered as gifts to those who could order or buy them.

The school system has thus amazingly become, in less than a century, the major mechanism for distributing values of all kinds among all the peoples of the world, largely replacing the family, the church, and the institution of private property. In capitalist countries it might be more accurate to say that schools confirm rather than replace the value-distribution functions of these older institutions. Family, religion, and property have such an

important influence on access to and success in school that schooling alters only slowly and marginally the value distributions of an earlier day. Jefferson put it well when he said, in arguing for public schools, that by this means we shall each year rake a score of geniuses from the ashes of the masses. The result of such a process, as the English aristocracy learned long before Jefferson, is to keep the elite alive while depriving the masses of their potential leaders.

Communist countries have, of course, abolished private property, have attempted to abolish organized religion, and have tried to weaken the role of the family. There are few data, unfortunately, to show how much redistribution of values has taken place in these countries, but the general impression is that it is much less than had been expected. One of the strongest supports for this impression comes from the great similarity of school systems in capitalist and communist countries. They perform the same functions and share the same defining characteristics. There is not the slightest doubt that communist schools sort their students into jobs, vocational levels, pay differentials, and power and privilege strata in just the same way as capitalist schools. The only question is whether the prizes go to the sons and daughters of the previously privileged in quite the same degree.

Leaders in communist China are greatly preoccupied with this question. In 1966, schools throughout China were closed in an attempt to make education more egalitarian and down to earth. Mao's own policy statements make clear his desire to rid education of elite control and to make it universally available to the masses. The difficulties encountered in this effort were obviously formidable, however, even for Mao, and it appears that most schools have now reopened with significant but not really

fundamental changes in the structure of the system. How much of this compromise was due to ideological and how much to practical considerations is hard to say. The pressures of building a nation in competition with such superpowers as Russia and the United States are tremendous, and schools appear to be an almost indispensable tool for nation building. On the other hand, the educational controversy in China has never abandoned the rhetoric of schools. Despite all the emphasis on universal access, practicality, and revolutionary objectives, the debate always refers to the reform of the school system rather than to its replacement.[4]

It should now be clear why schools have grown so fast. To the masses, and their leaders, they have held out unprecedented hope of social justice. To the elite they have been an unparalleled instrument, appearing to give what they do not, while convincing all that they get what they deserve. Only the great religions provide an analogy, with their promise of universal brotherhood always betrayed.

Betrayal of the hopes of schooling is implicit in the selection function that schools perform. Selection implies losers as well as winners, and increasingly selection is for life. Furthermore, school is a handicap race in which the slower must bear the growing burden of repeated failure, while the quicker are continually spurred by success. Nevertheless, the finish line is the same for all, and the first to get there win the prizes. All attempts to disguise the reality of this situation fail. Parents know the truth, while teachers and administrators are often compelled to admit it. Euphemisms about the transcendent importance of learning and about doing your best are thus self-defeating. It is no wonder, under these circumstances,

that some children drop out while others work to win rather than to learn.

Consistently punishing half of the children who are trying to learn what society is trying to teach them is not the worst aspect of combining social-role selection with education. Such punishment is an unavoidable result of the relative failure that half the school population must experience while climbing the school ladder in competition with their more-successful peers. Such punishment can scarcely help but condition this half of the school population to resist all future efforts to induce them to learn whatever is taught in school.

But this is only the lesser evil. The greater is that school necessarily sorts its students into a caste-like hierarchy of privilege. There may be nothing wrong with hierarchy or with privilege, or even with hierarchies of privilege, so long as these are plural and relatively independent of each other. There is everything wrong with a dominant hierarchy of privilege to which all others must conform. Birth into a caste, inheritance of wealth, and the propagation of a governing party are all means by which such a dominant hierarchy can be maintained. In the modern technological world, however, all these means either depend upon or are replaced by the school. No single system of education can have any other result, nor can a dominant hierarchy of privilege be maintained in a technological world by any means except a unified system of education.

If schools continue for a few more generations to be the major means of social-role selection, the result will be a meritocracy, in which merit is defined by the selection process that occurs in schools. Michael Young describes this outcome in his *Rise of the Meritocracy*.[5] His picture

of English society fifty years from now is a projection of Galbraith's New Industrial State, with the technocrats in the saddle.[6] His school is a super streaming system, constantly shuffling its students into the channels where their past performance suggests that they belong. The slow students are not kidded in this system; they quickly learn where they stand and where they are going, but they are taught to like it. The quick also know where they are going, and like it so well they end up trying to re-establish a hereditary aristocracy based on merit. This reverse-english twist leads to a happy ending that takes humanity off the hook, but not until the author has made his—and repeated Dante's—point. Any system in which men get just what they deserve is hell.

Schools define merit in accordance with the structure of the society served by schools. This structure is characterized by the competitive consumption of technological products defined by institutions. Institutions define products in a way that is consistent with the maintenance of a dominant hierarchy of privilege and, in so far as possible, with the opportunity for members of the currently privileged class to retain their status in the new "meritocracy."

What schools define as merit is principally the advantage of having literate parents, books in the home, the opportunity to travel, etc. Merit is a smoke screen for the perpetuation of privilege. The ability of IQ tests to predict school performance does not rebut this statement. As Arthur Jensen, the most recent defender of IQ, points out, the intelligence measured by tests is operationally defined as the ability to succeed in school.[7] The significance of Michael Young's book is to show that we would

be even worse off if "true merit" were to replace more primitive means of perpetuating privilege.

The third function of schooling is indoctrination. Indoctrination is a bad word. Bad schools, we say, indoctrinate. Good ones teach basic values. All schools, however, teach the value of childhood, the value of competing for the life prizes offered in school, and the value of being taught—not learning for one's self—what is good and what is true.[8] In fact, all schools indoctrinate in ways more effective than those which are generally recognized.

By the time they go to school, children have learned how to use their bodies, how to use language, and how to control their emotions. They have learned to depend upon themselves and have been rewarded for initiative in learning. In school these values are reversed. The what, when, where, and how of learning are decided by others, and children learn that it is good to depend upon others for their learning. They learn that what is worth while is what is taught and, conversely, that if something is important someone must teach it to them.

Children learn in school not only the values of the school but to accept these values and thus to get along in the system. They learn the value of conformity, and while this learning is not confined to school, it is concentrated there. School is the first highly institutionalized environment most children encounter. For orphans and children who are sick or handicapped this is not the case, and the retarding effects of institutionalizing infants is impressively documented.[9] Orphans learn so well not to interfere with institutional requirements that they seldom become capable of making a useful contribution to society. The argument for schools, of course, is that they strike the balance between conformity and initiative that

the institutional roles of adult life will require. Some of them do. If all of them did, our chances of escaping the contradictions of modern life would be even less than they actually are.

Other values are implicit in those aspects of curriculum which are alike in schools all over the world. These include the priorities given to dominant languages, both natural and technical. Examples of the first are the priority given to Spanish over Indian tongues in Latin America and to Russian over provincial languages in the Soviet Union. Examples of the second are the priorities given mathematics over music, and physics over poetry. There are obviously good reasons for these priorities, but they are reasons derived from the world as it is, ignoring the claims of both the world of the past and the desirable world of the future. More than this, these decisions reflect not even all of the major aspects of today's world, but preponderantly the balance of political and economic power. Fewer people speak English than Chinese and far fewer speak physics than poetry. English and physics are simply more powerful—at the moment.

Another value implicit in school is that of hierarchy. Schools both reflect dominant values and maintain a stratified world. They make it seem natural and inevitable that hierarchies are inherently correlated and cannot be independent of each other. Schools do not have to teach this doctrine. It is learned by studying an integrated curriculum arranged in graded layers.

Finally, after performing child-care, social-screening, and value-teaching functions, schools also teach cognitive skills and both transmit and—at graduate levels—create knowledge. The first three functions are performed necessarily, because of the way schools are organized.

Cognitive learning, although it is declared the principal purpose of schools, occurs only in so far as resources remain after the built-in functions are performed. In urban ghetto schools of the United States, and in rural Brazilian schools, attempting to operate on a budget of fifty dollars per year per child, very little cognitive learning occurs.[10,11] Exceptional teachers can, of course, teach, and exceptional students can learn, within the confines of the school. As school systems expand, claiming an increasing proportion of all educational resources, absorbing more students and teachers and more of the time of each, some true educational experiences are bound to occur in schools. They occur, however, despite and not because of school.[12]

Schools rest much of their case on their claim to teach skills, especially language and mathematical skills. The most commonly heard defense of schools is, "Where would children learn to read?" Literacy has, in fact, always run well ahead of schooling. According to census data, there are always more literate members of a society than persons who have gone to school. Furthermore, where schooling is universal, there are always children attending school who do not learn to read. In general, the children of literate parents learn to read even if they do not attend school, while the children of illiterate parents frequently fail to learn even in school.[13]

In universally schooled societies, of course, most children learn to read in school. Considering when they learn to read and when they begin to go to school, it could hardly be otherwise. Even in a fully schooled society, however, few children learn to read easily and well, although almost all learn to speak easily and well, a skill learned outside of school.[14] Children who do learn to

read well, read a lot for their own pleasure, which suggests that good reading—like other skills—is the result of practice. Data on mathematics give even less support to school. Illiterates who participate in a money economy all learn to count, add, subtract, multiply, and divide, while only a small percentage of people in a fully schooled society ever learn much more. Of those who take algebra in high school, only a small percentage do better than chance on an objective test.[15]

There is a body of data collected by Jerome Bruner and his students showing that children who go to school learn concepts that are not learned by those who do not go to school.[16] The concepts studied were those made famous by Jean Piaget, who found that most French and Swiss children learn at about ages six to eight that water poured from a short fat cylinder into a tall thin one is still the same amount of water. Bruner's students found that African bush children who go to schools patterned after the French, learn such concepts much better than similar children who do not go to school. These experiments did not, however, test the effect of relevant learning environments other than school. Until a unique effect of schooling is demonstrated, with everything else controlled, Bruner's data show only that environments affect concept learning and suggest that the more relevant the environment is to the concept the more effect it has.

Another claim is that schools teach the grammar of language and the theories of mathematics, science, and the arts. Undoubtedly they do, but the real question is whether these things are learned in school more than they would be otherwise. Achievement tests give little support to schools. As in the case of mathematics, only a small minority of students do better than chance on the

formal aspects of any subject matter. Students who are interested in these matters learn them and those who are not do not. Whether interest in them is stimulated by schools remains very doubtful. Einstein, commenting upon a short period he had to spend in school preparing for a degree examination, said that as a consequence he was, for several years afterward, unable to do any creative work.

The pernicious effect of schools on cognitive learning, of which Einstein complains, is best seen by contrasting the impact of schooling on privileged and underprivileged children. The underprivileged, whose home environments are lacking in the specialized resources schools provide, are relatively unsuccessful in school and soon leave it with an experience of failure, a conviction of inadequacy, and a dislike for the specialized-learning resources of which they are subsequently deprived. The privileged, whose home environments are rich in the specialized resources of the school, who would learn on their own most of what the school has to teach, enjoy relative success in school and become hooked on a system that rewards them for learning without the exercise of effort or initiative. Thus the poor are deprived both of motivation and of the resources that the school reserves for the privileged. The privileged, on the other hand, are taught to prefer the school's resources to their own and to give up self-motivated learning for the pleasures of being taught. The minority of Einsteins and Eldridge Cleavers lose only a little time. The majority lose their main chance for an education.

3. WHAT SCHOOLS ARE

First-hand knowledge is the ultimate basis of intellectual life. To a large extent book-learning conveys second-hand information, and as such can never rise to the importance of immediate practice. . . . What the learned world tends to offer is one second-hand scrap of information illustrating ideas derived from another second-hand scrap of information. The second-handedness of the learned world is the secret of its mediocrity. It is tame because it has never been scared by facts.

Alfred North Whitehead
The Aims of Education and Other Essays

It may seem academic to distinguish what schools do from what schools are, but the purpose of the distinction is very practical. The social functions performed by schools are in fact necessary functions. Our argument throughout is that schools perform them badly and that we must discover alternatives to schools. Let us define schools as *institutions that require the attendance of specific age groups in teacher-supervised classrooms for the study of graded curriculums.*

By specifying the age of attendance, schools institutionalize childhood. In schooled societies, childhood is now assumed to be a timeless and universal phenomenon. But children, in the modern sense, did not exist three hundred years ago and still do not exist among the rural and urban poor who make up most of the population of the world. In his *Centuries of Childhood,* Philippe Ariès shows that, before the seventeenth century, children dressed as adults, worked with adults, were imprisoned, tortured, and hanged like adults, were exposed to sex, disease, and death, and in general did not have a special status. The subculture of childhood did not exist.[1] The

medieval Church assumed that children, baptized in infancy, reached the age of reason at about age seven; this meant that they were from then on fully responsible for their acts, not only to men but to God. They were capable, that is, either by positive acts or by neglect, of consigning themselves to everlasting torment. In its time this doctrine was not uniquely harsh. Children were treated no more tenderly in the Arab and Oriental worlds and, for that matter, in Africa and America.

All cultures, of course, distinguish infants and sexually immature youth from adults. All cultures have initiation rites that signal entrance into full adult status. All cultures make some distinction between what adults and nonadults may do and have done to them. This is not to say, however, that all cultures have a subculture of childhood that sharply distinguishes the roles of children from those of adults. Children are not expected to work, except at their studies. Children are not responsible for any nuisance, damage, or crime they commit upon society. Children do not count, legally or politically. Children are supposed to play, enjoy themselves, and prepare themselves for adult life. They are supposed to go to school, and the school is supposed to be responsible for them, guide them, and temporarily at least, take the place of their parents. Childhood explains the priority that schools give to custodial care.

Childhood must also be viewed in contrast with modern, preretirement adult life. Childhood and the adult world of work have been drawing apart. While children have been increasingly indulged, preretirement adults—women as well as men—have been increasingly molded to the world of machines and institutions. Childhood has become more child-centered, more indulgent, while adults have been increasingly constrained. The argument

for schools is that they provide a necessary bridge from childhood to adult life, that they gradually transform the indulged child into the responsible adult. Schools take the child from his garden, by carefully graded steps, to a prototype of the world of work. They enroll the "complete child" and graduate the "complete man."

As in the case of the school, childhood has probably served a useful purpose. The prechildhood treatment of children was, and is, undesirably brutal. Many of the protections childhood has brought to children are important and necessary—so much so that it is vital to extend them not only to other children, but also to adults. Sexual abuse, under conditions that make consent a farce, is one example. The exploitation of labor under similar conditions is another: one party has the choice of working or starving, while the other has to choose merely between one laborer and another. The enforcement or neglect of conditions that stunt the growth or unnecessarily limit the opportunities of children, or adults, need to be prohibited and prevented wherever they occur. But this is impossible if the indulgence of already indulged children, or adults, is endlessly multiplied. Furthermore, while some protections and indulgences are necessary and good, too many are bad, and we have reached and passed many thresholds in the institution of childhood at which benefits become liabilities. Many of these are obvious and need no argument. One that has already been noted is the extension of the age of childhood to include fully mature adults, so long as these adults remain in school. Much of the protest on the part of youth is related to this fact, as is the resentment by adults of this protest. The case for youth is obvious. Old enough to have children of their own and to fight wars, they are encouraged to do only the latter and are denied the right to participate

fully in the economic product of the society. The adult case is also easy to understand. These children, they say, want to remain children and yet to enjoy the privileges of adults. In part, the adults are right. What they forget is that youth did not create the institution of childhood, but were created by it.

Schools, as creators of social reality, do not stop with children. They also create schoolteachers. Before there were schools, there were Greek slaves who safeguarded their young charges in excursions about the city, disciplinarians who kept them at their practice of arms, masters prepared to dispute with them in matters of politics, ethics, and philosophy. Of these, only the disciplinarians survived without major distortion in the early schools. Drill with the pen rather than the sword involved only a change of instrument, and the method was equally effective. Schools stopped being effective in teaching skills when this method was abandoned. The other two roles were totally distorted in their incorporation into school. The caretaker role depended for its educational validity upon not overstepping its bounds. The caretaker/slave had little to say about place, time, or activity. His principal task was to keep his charges within the bounds of safety. The educational value of the activities depended upon student selection and conduct. The master was also transformed into his opposite when placed within the school. His true role was to be questioned and to answer in such a way as to provoke ever-deeper questions. In the school, this role is reversed: the master becomes the questioner and is forced to propound orthodoxy rather than provoke exploration.

Children and teachers do not yet make a school. Without required attendance in specialized space, teachers and children could be a home, a nursery, or a crusade.

Required attendance and classroom walls add the time and space dimensions that imply that knowledge can be processed and that children have an assigned time and place. During infancy, they belong in the home. At kindergarten age they begin to belong, for a few hours a day, in school. The amount of schooltime increases with age, until college becomes Alma Mater, sacred or soul mother, the social womb in which the child develops and from which he is finally delivered into the adult world. Classrooms may be varied to include laboratory, workshop, gymnasium, and year abroad, but this is all scholastic space—sanitized, sealed off from the unclean world, made fit for children and for the transmission of knowledge. In this specialized environment, knowledge must be transmitted—it cannot merely be encountered—since in most instances it has been taken out of its natural habitat. It must also be processed, not only to clean it up but also to facilitate transmission.

The transmission of knowledge through teaching, and its processing to fit both school and school children, seems perfectly natural in a technological age that engineers a product to fit every human need. Once knowledge becomes a product, the graded curriculum follows—an ordered array of packets of knowledge, each with its time-and-space assignment, in proper sequence and juxtaposition with related packages. The graded curriculum is the fourth dimension of the school. As in the case of the other defining characteristics, its quantitative aspects are critically important. Childhood becomes a problem when extended over too many years and too many aspects of life. Teaching becomes a problem when students begin to depend upon it for most learning. Classroom attendance becomes a problem when it builds sterile walls around too much of normal life. Similarly, curriculum becomes a

problem as it approaches international universality. How much required attendance, classroom teaching, and curriculum is tolerable is not a matter for academic discussion. Free people, choosing freely as individuals and in voluntary groups among an ample array of alternatives, can best make these decisions.

Recent international achievement studies demonstrate quite clearly that the universal international curriculum is now a fact.[2] International norms for mathematics and science have been established. These are admittedly the areas of greatest uniformity, but others are not far behind. Nor is the proliferation of vocational schools, black studies, and life-adjustment classes a significant countertrend, for unless these auxiliary curriculums are tied to the core curriculum, they lead to degrees that are meaningless in the marketplace.

The graded curriculum may well be thought of as the very keystone of a system based on institutionalized childhood, teaching, and classroom attendance. Curriculum unites these other elements and determines their impact on students, teachers, and society.

Learning must, of course, occur in some sequence, and there must also be some correlation between different sequences of learning. These sequences and correlations could, of course, be different for each individual. To some extent they must be, and every educator pays lip service to this idea. Nor, on the other hand, are there many who would insist upon avoiding all attempts to correlate the learning programs of different individuals. For a teacher to impose a preferred order on his subject matter is natural and desirable. It is also desirable that teachers learn from each other and adjust their own order of teaching accordingly. But imposing upon teachers an order not of their choosing is undesirable, and requiring students to

follow a particular order, except in deference to a particular teacher, is self-defeating. Only people committed to the idea of a knowledge factory that must run on a prearranged schedule will disagree. The argument that students and teachers must be able to transfer from place to place without losing time is valid only if the synchronized knowledge factory is assumed.

Synchronized learning requires, however, not merely a standard order for each subject but also the coordination of the various subjects. This integrated curriculum creates the school system, which in turn determines the major characteristics of individual schools. Thus the core curriculum of the lower schools is dictated by standard requirements for college entrance. Since the economic value of other curriculums depends upon their relationship to the core curriculum, this curriculum directly or indirectly determines hours of attendance, classroom standards, teacher qualifications, and entrance requirements for the entire school system. Schools that deviate significantly from any of these norms lose their ability to qualify students for college entrance. Even primary school reforms can survive only if they do not threaten the progress of their graduates through the higher levels of the system.

It is by way of the standardized graded curriculum, therefore, that schools become a system that then acquires an international monopoly of access to jobs and to political and other social roles. It can be argued that this monopoly is not by any means complete. Some corporations will still employ the unschooled genius, while Roosevelt and Churchill did not have to pay more than lip service to the schools they attended. But these are exceptions, and if the trend continues, they will not exist for long.[3] Organization by grade, the grading of students,

and the maintenance of grade standards; standardized intelligence and achievement testing; promotion within the system, and certification for employment are all justified by a curriculum that determines the internal structure and operations of a school, relationships between schools, and relationships between school and other institutions.

People who want to define any kind of learning group as a school are, of course, free to do so. There are Summerhills and Pacific High Schools, free schools and schools without walls, an increasing variety of reactions to schools as defined and described above. The minor variations last only as long as special people and special funds are being invested in them. The major departures depend even more upon the unique personalities of their founders. Some of these departures will undoubtedly help to blaze the trails that lead from schools to real alternatives. For the present they serve largely to help define the schools that are the only choice of almost a billion children.

Schools treat people and knowledge the way a technological world treats everything: as if they could be processed. Anything can, of course, be processed, but only at a price, part of which involves ignoring certain aspects of the thing and certain by-products of the process. The price of processing people is intrinsically high. They tend to resist. What has to be left unprocessed may be the most important part of the person. Some of the by-products of educational processing are already evident. The greatest danger, however, lies in the prospect of success. A successfully processed humanity would lose the little control of its destiny that has always distinguished man from the rest of the world.[4]

4. HOW SCHOOLS WORK

REMARKS CONCERNING THE SAVAGES OF NORTH AMERICA

Pamphlet by Benjamin Franklin, ca. 1784

Franklin wrote: At the treaty of Lancaster, in Pennsylvania, anno 1744, between the Government of Virginia and the Six Nations, the commissioners from Virginia acquainted the Indians by a speech, that there was at Williamsburg a college with a fund for educating Indian youth; and that if the chiefs of the Six Nations would send down half a dozen of their sons to that college, the government would take care that they be well provided for, and instructed in all the learning of the white people.

The Indians' spokesman replied:

We know that you highly esteem the kind of learning taught in those colleges, and that the maintenance of our young men, while with you, would be very expensive to you. We are convinced, therefore, that you mean to do us good by your proposal and we thank you heartily.

But you, who are wise, must know that different nations have different conceptions of things; and you will not therefore take it amiss, if our ideas of this kind of education happen

not to be the same with yours. We have had some experience of it; several of our young people were formerly brought up at the colleges of the northern provinces; they were instructed in all your sciences; but, when they came back to us, they were bad runners, ignorant of every means of living in the woods, unable to bear either cold or hunger, knew neither how to build a cabin, take a deer, nor kill an enemy, spoke our language imperfectly, were therefore neither fit for hunters, warriors, nor counsellors; they were totally good for nothing.

We are however not the less obligated by your kind offer, though we decline accepting it, and to show our grateful sense of it, if the gentlemen of Virginia will send us a dozen of their sons, we will take care of their education, instruct them in all we know, and make men of them.

Schools have a hidden curriculum much more important than the one they purport to teach. The purpose of this hidden curriculum is to propagate the social myths, those beliefs which distinguish one society from another and help to hold a society together. All societies have myths, and it is one of the major functions of any educational system to transmit them to the young. Social myths are not necessarily false; in fact, during the golden age of each society they correspond rather well to reality. Social myths are gradually outgrown, however, and in the later stages of a social era they serve largely to sustain beliefs that are increasingly far from what actually goes on in the society.

Let us look at four myths or ideologies that play a prominent role in our society, examine the corresponding realities, and then identify the scholastic rituals that help to bridge the gap between myth and reality. The myths and ideologies selected are those which deal with equal opportunity, freedom, progress, and efficiency.

There is equal opportunity, according to the myths

of modern societies, for every man to achieve whatever his ambitions dictate and his abilities permit. This myth asserts that all levels and branches of schooling are open to all and that students are limited only by their dedication and brains. It proclaims that all occupations and social levels are open to anyone with enough drive and the ability to deliver the goods. Increasingly the school is recognized as the major avenue to occupations and social roles, and the openness of scholastic channels is therefore stressed as guaranteeing access not only to academic but to social advancement. This is the myth of equal opportunity, pretending to make everyone's advancement depend solely upon his own personal qualities.

The reality is that all advancement is at the expense of others. Schools, occupational ladders, and social-class structures are all hierarchies in the shape of pyramids. In school, each higher grade is also smaller. Seldom can grades or levels be skipped. Each successive competition must be survived, therefore, in order to reach the top. In industry the picture is the same. For every president of Standard Oil, ten thousand office boys are left behind.

At what age are the opportunities equal? At birth? It seems unlikely that at birth the son of a president, even though he should begin as office boy, would have no better chance than the son of an office boy. But if not equal at birth, the chances certainly become less equal with every year of life. By the time school begins, no one has irrevocably lost; but as soon as kindergarten is over, grades and IQ scores are recorded, and from then on the door is almost closed for those whose grades and scores are low. This is not because these grades and scores are

valid. Even those who believe in them admit that at this age they are highly unreliable.[1] But judgments have to be made. Judgment about which school, which track, which teacher, all judgments that vitally influence the chances for the future. Once the elementary school is passed, it is nonsense to speak any longer of equal opportunity for those who have not done well enough to go on to a good academic secondary school. One trade-school boy in thousands may wind up as head of a construction company, but this is the great exception. In fact, every step up the ladder for one is a step down for another; one can rise to the top only over the heads of thousands. Corresponding to the myth of equal opportunity there is the reality of enforced inequality, with the odds of staying near the bottom many times higher than the odds of getting to the top.[2]

"But of course!" will be the reply. This is the nature of hierarchy. Everyone understands what equal opportunity means. If this is so, then why not tell it like it is. Call it the social lottery. In truth, it would have to be called the loaded social lottery, with each child getting as many chances as his father has dollars. But this would not suit the purposes served by calling it equal opportunity. Everyone is supposed to think he has an equal chance, whether he does or not. It is better for his morale. For the moment, the question is not whether this should or should not be. This is how it is; and the question is, how is it kept that way? How are people induced to believe, or at least act as though they believed, in equal opportunity, when in fact there is no such thing?

They are induced to believe it by ritual progression up the ladder, the school ladder, the promotion ladder,

the income ladder, the social-status ladder. As long as people are climbing, it is easy to maintain the illusion that all roads lead to the top. One step at a time, that's how one gets there. The fact that there isn't enough time for the man who gets to the top to touch all the steps on the way is easily overlooked. It makes sense that if you climb, step by step, you get to the top.

There are enough steps so that everyone can climb a few. Grades in school are easy enough at first, in rich countries, and almost everyone passes these early grades. By the time the going gets rough the lesson has been learned: there is equal opportunity, but men just aren't all equal. The job ladder works the same way. Everybody except those who really did badly in school goes up a few steps. Then the intervals get longer. People get a little older. It doesn't matter so much any more.

Everyone's income rises a little, even if he doesn't get promoted—annual increments, each year a little more, and by the time the plateau is reached the illusion is also established that everyone has had a chance. Some are just luckier than others. Obviously this is not the whole truth. But people are induced to believe it by ritual progress up the ladder.

The ideology of freedom is that all men have certain inalienable rights: the right of assembly, the right of petition for redress of grievances, the right to be free from unreasonable searches and seizures, the right to counsel, the right not to bear witness against themselves—i.e., to be free from torture in the first, second, or third degree. The facts are that all over the world the flickering lights of freedom are going out. In the communist world, deviationists and enemies of the people have no civil rights. In the capitalist world, over half of the nations that

were democracies twenty years ago now have military regimes, many of which use torture as an everyday instrument of government. The remaining "democratic" governments include South Africa, where "full" civil rights extend only to non-Africans and non-Asians, and then only if they are careful to leave the issue of *apartheid* alone. In the United States, there is also the South, where blacks have the rights that whites deign to give them. In the rest of the country, peoples' rights are increasingly determined by police and national guardsmen. Black Panthers, dissident Democrats, and college students are ever more in danger of having rites instead of rights.

How is belief in freedom maintained in the face of these facts? Largely by the rituals of democratic process. Among other things, the last presidential election in the United States helped people forget the police power used at the Chicago convention by one wing of the Democratic party against the other. Equally, the last national election in France helped people forget the military and police suppression of students and workers that had occurred just a few months before. These dramatic examples, however, are not as important as the daily rituals of democracy in reassuring people about their freedom while domination and suppression are increasing. The professor exhibiting academic freedom by denouncing the establishment, students flaunting hair styles and kicking up their bare feet, sit-ins, paint-ins, sleep-ins, and pot parties—useful as these things are, they serve to reassure people that they are still free when in fact they may not be.

We also have the angry editorial, the enterprising reporter's exposé, the new magazine going the old ones one better, the legislative investigation. Some serve good

purposes. Others merely help to maintain the illusion of freedom. With few exceptions, only those who know how to play the game, those already in positions of privilege even though dissident, are able to use the liberty that democratic process provides. Those who are truly deprived have little real access to democratic process. This is one reason Jefferson despaired of orderly reform carried out within the rules. But the rules themselves, ritually followed, disguise the basis for Jefferson's reliance on periodic revolution. Democratic process, in school and society, helps people accept the discrepancy between the assumption of freedom and the facts of domination and suppression. We do not want to lose or underestimate democratic process, but neither do we want to delude ourselves about how much freedom we have and how secure it is. We can protect and extend the limits of our own and other people's freedom only if we see things clearly.

The myth of progress is that our situation is improving and will continue to improve, without any demonstrable limits upon the degree or scope of future improvements. The facts are that we arc ncar thc limits at which the atmosphere can absorb more heat or the seas more pollution, near the limits of the earth to support more population, near the limits of the patience of the poor to subsist on the bounty of the rich, near the limits of the rich themselves to either tighten further the screws they have fastened upon themselves or to live much longer with the indulgences they have invented. People who do not want to face these facts say that the problems will be solved by new discoveries and inventions. But the discoveries and inventions of the past have merely brought us to our present predicament. Future discoveries and

inventions, similarly applied, can only sharpen this predicament. For regardless of how near or far away the limits are, there can be little doubt that they exist, while the ideology of progress knows no limits. The earth, human population, and human nature are all finite, while progress is infinite. This theoretical problem might not have to bother people if various kinds of progress were in reasonable balance, but they are not. Our ability to kill each other is growing much faster than our productive capacity. The gap between the rich and the poor is widening. Psychological tensions are increasing faster than our ability to deal with them.

The myth of progress is, then, faced with a set of very hard facts, which contradict its assumptions. How are these contradictions reconciled? They are kept from consciousness primarily by the ritual of research—the continuing quest for new knowledge, new insights, new techniques. Research is a very important non-ritual fact, but it is also an important ritual—inducing the belief that new discoveries change the whole picture, that every day is a new day with a new set of rules and possibilities. This is clearly false. Even the most important new discoveries and inventions leave almost everything else unchanged. The invention of breeder reactors stretched the world's supply of fissionable material greatly. Nuclear fusion extends the limits of possible energy sources even more. But these far-reaching developments do not affect the absorption capacity of the atmosphere at all. They have no effect on human population except to threaten its total annihilation. They influence man's ability to think and to govern himself in only the slightest degree. Yet the myth of renewal by research, the belief that major new discoveries can renew all terms of all problems—

this myth and belief permit men to avoid seeing the very hard barriers to further progress that in fact exist.

Research is so identified with school that it affects students even more than it does the general population. The greatest impact of research on students comes by way of its effect on curriculum. One of the hallmarks of modern schooling, which separates it most sharply from its own tradition, is that its offerings are labeled as ever new. Yesterday's knowledge is out of date. In Norway, serious thought is being given to declaring degrees more than five years old invalid. The merit of this proposal is that it belatedly recognizes what was always true, that degrees have little validity. Its rationale, however, is that five-year-old knowledge is no longer valid. Every worker will be obliged to come back periodically to the school to refurbish the knowledge he received the last time. Real education is, of course, a lifetime process. But real education and real research are also continuous, work-related processes. Genuine research and education integrate the new into the much greater mass of the old, and this can be done only in the course of work, in the actual discovery and application of the new. The illusion that knowledge must be contemporary to be valid stands between the generations. This conceit of the young is largely the result of ritualized curriculum renewal as practiced by the school.[3]

The myth of efficiency is that modern man has solved his production problems by means of efficient organization, that other men can do likewise, and that most of man's remaining problems can be solved by a similar approach. The fact is, as Kenneth Boulding, the economist, has recently suggested that gross national product, the current measure of a nation's output, is actually a

measure of economic inefficiency. Employment in the wealthier countries increasingly follows Parkinson's Law: that employment increases as production decreases. More and more people in the wealthier countries are employed in the service sector, doing things of dubious value. Consider government and corporate bureaucrats, salesmen, advertisers, bankers, accountants, lawyers, teachers, policemen, soldiers, polltakers, social workers, for example. There is no doubt that all these people do something that someone values, but there is also little doubt that as many people despise what they do. Lawyers provide the clearest example; for every winner at law there is a loser. The same thing holds, a little less obviously, for all the kinds of workers listed above and for many other services as well. Many physical goods are also of dubious value—military weapons, pornography, billboards, superjets, automobiles, gravestones, schools, meat products, tobacco, alcohol, marijuana, and fluoridated water—all have varying degrees of opposition. The point is not that work is bad or even, in itself, of doubtful value. It is rather that the value of work depends upon its outcome.

How are the discrepancies between the myth and the facts of efficiency kept from public consciousness? The answer is—through ritualized activity.

Schools learned long ago that the way to keep children from thinking is to keep them busy. Classes, clubs, athletics, cultural activities, homework; the devil finds work for idle hands. This is also how attacks on the efficiency of the school are met—more courses, more degrees, more activities, more enrollment. The graduates of school are well prepared to participate in the activity rites of the outside world: more committees, more projects, more campaigns, more products, more industries, more em-

ployment, more gross national product. Not all activity is ritual. But in a nation capable of producing all its agricultural and industrial products with 5% of its labor force, as the United States is, Parkinsonian employment must account for much of the remaining 95%. Ritualized activity must also account for much of the time of adults who are not in the labor force and of students who are in school.

The hidden curriculum of school is dangerous, because it bolsters belief in a sick society—a society dedicated to competitive consumption, which assumes that man wants principally to consume and that in order to consume endlessly he must bind himself to the wheel of endless production. The whole theory of schooling is based on the assumption that production methods applied to learning will result in learning. They do result in learning how to produce and consume—so long as nothing fundamental changes. As means of learning to adapt to changing circumstances, production methods are ridiculous. The need to distinguish these two kinds of learning is kept from our attention mainly by our participation in the scholastic ritual.

5. WHERE SCHOOLS CAME FROM

A single shelf of a good European library was worth the whole native literature of India and Arabia. . . . It is, I believe, no exaggeration to say that all the historical information which has been collected from all the books written in the Sanskrit language is less valuable than what may be found in the most paltry abridgements used at preparatory schools in England . . . I think it clear that . . . neither as the languages of the law nor as the languages of religion, have the Sanskrit and Arabic any peculiar claim to our engagement, that it is possible to make natives of this country thoroughly good English scholars and that to this end our efforts ought to be directed . . . We must at present do our best to form a class who may be interpreters between us and the millions whom we govern, a class of persons Indian in blood and colour, but English in taste, in opinions, in morals and in intellect.

Lord Macaulay
Parliamentary minute on Indian education.

School is a stage in a succession of specialized institutions. Prehistoric rites, myths, and shamans; temples and priestly castes; Sumerian, Grecian, Alexandrian, and Roman schools; monastic orders; early universities, common and grammar schools—all have played a part in the history of the national and international school systems of today. One of the most instructive historical trends is the progressive specialization of content, method, personnel, and location in socially organized human learning. Originally this included much more than what we now call education. Schooling, as everyone knows, includes much less.

Since 1820, archaeology and anthropology have extended the history of man many tens of thousands of years.[1] As far back as the record goes, man has engaged in specialized activities that have much in common with what goes on in schools. Rites and rituals—symbolic practices seemingly unnecessary to the satisfaction of elementary physical needs—have always been part of man's repertoire. As far back as the record goes, we also find

evidence of people and places specialized in and for the use of myth and ritual. Some of the earliest records are in just such places: the caves of southern France and Spain, famous for their paintings of prehistoric animals, were apparently used largely for ritual practices. The only human figures included in the paintings are those of shamans, who combined the teacher's role with those of priest, magician, actor, artist, poet, and ideologue. These, at any rate, are roles combined in shamans of existing tribes whose technology and art resemble those of prehistoric man.

Reasoning both from archaeological and modern anthropological evidence, it appears that prehistoric rites shared certain elements of current curriculums. They had an age-specific character, acting out the myths related to birth, adolescence, and death. They explained and celebrated both the everyday and the unusual aspects of the world. They provided activity for idle periods that followed hunt or harvest. They allowed young people to try on adult roles for size.

The line between prehistoric and historic time is marked by the invention of writing, which corresponds roughly in time to the establishment of cities and the great religions. Education emerged out of the practice of worship and government. Its early home was the temple-court, and its early practitioners were specialized priests. Writing itself was probably invented by such specialists. Shamans and priests are thus in the central line not only of the development of teachers and schools, but of the evolution of man. Brain, hand, and tongue; horde, village, and city; magic, religion, art, and science—these are the milestones of man's physical, social, and spiritual development. The priesthoods of city-based religions in-

herited from their country-cousin shamans a mixture of magic, religion, art, and science, which they began to disentangle and specialize. It is relatively well established that not only writing, but accounting and mathematics, astronomy and chemistry, music, painting, and poetry had their early development in the temple-courts of Egyptian, Sumerian, and other ruling castes, which combined the functions of priest and king.[2] The first formalized teaching of these arts, which still make up most of the modern core curriculum, was a master/apprentice type of teaching. Even earlier, a kind of teaching among equals must have occurred, as one individual shared his discoveries or developments with others. Here is one of the two main roots of the modern school at the very origin of systematic knowledge.

The other, much humbler root makes its first appearance in a Sumerian classroom built to accommodate about thirty children, the discovery of which has led to the speculation that modern modal class size may have been based on the limitations of Sumerian brick and architecture.[3]

Plato and Aristophanes were the first to leave surviving written records of classroom and school.[4,5] These first schools of classical Athens were humble indeed—mere appendages to an educational program that stressed military training, athletics, music, and poetry, and that taught reading, writing, and arithmetic almost as an afterthought. Originally, all education in Athens was tutorial—one aspect of personal relationships that were often erotic as well. As Athens became more democratic, and pupils began to outnumber masters, group instruction gradually replaced the tutorial relationships.

Soon after the first reference in Greek writing to group

instruction in literary arts and skills, schools of medicine and philosophy are also mentioned and, soon afterward, a class of schools conducted by Sophist philosophers.[6] These first models of intermediate schools were based on contracts between a master and a group of parents for the instruction of their sons during a three- or four-year period of their adolescence. The Sophists were the first paid teachers of record, and their aim, appropriately, was practical: to make of their students successful men of affairs.

From these meager beginnings in the golden age of Greece there flourished in the Hellenistic colonies scattered by the conquests of Alexander all over the ancient world, school systems prophetic of our own in organization, curriculum, and the age span of students. Children first learned reading, writing, and numbers, and later were taught gymnastics, music, the classics of literature, geometry, and science. The museums of Alexandria and other cities specialized in the teaching of medicine, rhetoric, and philosophy. Most of these centers, patronized largely by Greek families, were privately financed, although a few small cities had public systems, while others were supported by foundations established by wealthy men. One of the main purposes of these schools was to keep alive the Hellenic tradition in a barbarian world. Only a small minority of the Greek population of the Alexandrian world was ever able to take full advantage of them.

The Romans adopted the Hellenistic school and, with minor modifications, used it for the education of their own elite. From the fall of Athens to the fall of Byzantium, therefore, a tiny minority of the world's population was schooled in somewhat the fashion of today. The

school was not, however, an important institution in Greco-Roman or in Byzantine times. Its importance to us lies in its role in preserving the memory and some of the culture of ancient Greece until the time of the Renaissance, in Western Europe.

Except in Byzantium, the fall of Rome resulted in a reunion of education and religion that lasted for a thousand years. The educational institutions of the Middle Ages were the cathedral schools and the monasteries. More-specialized in their purpose than the ancient temples, they also had a more-limited educational role; they did, nevertheless, introduce a number of important ideas into the history of Western education. In the earliest Benedictine monasteries, space and time became the parameters of learning as well as of living.[7] Every hour of Benedictine life had its appointed place and task. Adherence to this regimen constituted the good life; no external product or other sign presumed to attest the efficacy of the life thus lived.

The subsequent Dominican and Franciscan orders were based on different principles. Dependence upon the charity of others and identification with the poor replaced the bondage of time and space.[8,9] As in the case of the Benedictine rituals, begging and the care of the sick and destitute were not designed as training for subsequent living but as a way of life.

The preparatory principle of education was revived by the Jesuits, who in the sixteenth century extended and rationalized schooling well beyond the limits of Greco-Roman times.[10] The ancient schools had never been more than a small part of an educational program that was a product of tradition rather than of rational forethought. The Jesuits developed a curriculum and

an educational method deliberately designed to prepare men not merely for an ordinary life but for a life of unprecedented scope and challenge. At least part of the subsequent growth of schooling is undoubtedly due to their initial brilliant successes. Originally intended for members of an elite religious order, Jesuit schooling was soon extended to the lay elites of the European medieval world. The rate of this extension and the circumstances under which it occurred are strongly reminiscent of the sudden growth of Greek schooling following the conquests of Alexander. It was the insecurity rather than the dominance of the Greek colonies of Alexandrian times that caused them to build and depend upon schools; it was the insecurity of the Roman Church in the time of Ignatius that accounts for the formation and rapid growth of the Jesuit system of schools. In both cases, the school was seen as a way of preserving a set of values that were losing their dominance.

This chronology of the Christian orders has run ahead of at least one major event in the history of schooling—the foundation of the first medieval universities.[11] Originally devoted primarily to the study of Christian theology, they quickly branched into other fields of knowledge, and long before the Reformation, had become independent institutions in so far as this was possible in medieval Europe. Along with their counterparts in the Moslem world, the universities of Bologna, Salerno, and Paris became the first institutions of any size devoted primarily to the development and propagation of knowledge. They were also, of course, the direct predecessors of modern universities, and thus of the upper layer of the present school system.

Luther and his followers, coinciding so neatly in time

with Gutenberg's invention of movable type, gave a vast stimulus to the growth of the lower schools in northern Europe. The large-scale printing of bibles, and the doctrine that salvation was directly derivable from them, made the teaching of reading a moral imperative for Protestants who could afford it. The industrial revolution, coming so closely on the heels of the Reformation, supplied the last condition necessary for the rapid proliferation of schools, providing not only the means, but also a secular rationale, for widespread literacy.[12]

Mere growth in the number of schools did not result in school systems. This dimension of schooling came with the development of the national state. Thus, while public schools first burgeoned in the federated United States, the first integrated systems of schooling developed in France and Prussia. The Prussian development, although later, was the more clear-cut and became an important international model. In Prussia and later in Germany, the development of the school system was coterminous with the development of the national state and was deliberately designed to be one of its principal pedestals.[13]

One aspect of the German school system was the teaching of High German, the language of the school and the unifying language of the state. A common, graded, integrated curriculum was another—designed to serve the military, political, and manpower needs of the nation. A hierarchically organized teaching profession was still another. Most important of all was a carefully thought-out philosophy of education, reflected in school organization, logistics, curriculum, teacher recruitment, teaching methods, and scholastic ritual, and aimed at producing a citizenry tailored to the specifications of the architects of the German national state. No other national system

has been so systematically designed. But all nations, in copying to a greater or lesser degree the major features of the German system, have in effect adopted its objectives and its methods. England has perhaps copied them least, but even England's former colonies have followed Germany more than England.

In France, the idea of a national school system first arose partly in opposition to the Jesuits, who in the sixteenth century were among the principal educators of the elites.[14] Despite the suppression of the order in 1763 and the attempts of the legislators of the French Revolution, public schools made little headway. After the restoration of the monarchy, the Jesuits and, at the primary level, the Christian Brothers again played an important role in French education. The educational reform law of 1834 called for friendly relations between Church and state, but the resulting collaboration did not survive the crisis created by the French defeat in 1870.[15] The power of Prussian arms was attributed by many to the efficiency of their national school system, and no effort was spared to initiate a similar system in France.

Public schools in the United States have also had a long and complicated history. Despite the early establishment of public schools in New England, Pennsylvania, and Virginia, these schools remained for a long time under local control and, except in New England, the privilege of a relatively small minority.[16,17] The original New England schools were quasi universal without being compulsory, because their promoters shared a common conception of man, God, and the world. Even in New England, public schooling became much less than universal with the influx of non-Puritan immigrants beginning early in the nineteenth century. It was, in fact, this

lapse from a brief tradition of universal schooling that led Horace Mann to formulate the modern American concept of the public school.[18] Mann's public schools required attendance because persons of different origins, values, and faiths had to be brought to share the common conception that the pilgrims had taken for granted. These two approaches to universal public schooling illustrate the contradictions that have brought a glorious promise to a dismal end. Thomas Jefferson,[19] Orestes Brownson,[20] and John Dewey[21] saw universal education as the means of equipping men to discover their beliefs and to create their institutions. St. Ignatius of Loyola, Johann Gottlieb Fichte, and Horace Mann saw a similar process as the means of shaping men to the requirements of social goals and institutions assumed to have prior validity.

These ideological strains combined to make public schools popular with both the privileged and the deprived. For the latter, they held the promise of equal opportunity; for the former, the promise of orderly progression under control of the elite. To a degree, both promises were realized, but the contradictions inherent in them have become steadily more obvious as the balance of power has shifted from citizens to the state. In their time, Locke and Jefferson prevailed. John Dewey's more recent effort to put man back in the saddle was merely given lip service.

The organizational, legal, and procedural steps that have welded tens of thousands of nominally independent local school districts and thousands of colleges and universities into a national school system are the logical outcome of a philosophy that views schools as serving national ends. The popularity of such a philosophy, in a century that has seen the number of nations in the world

more than tripled, is not surprising. The proliferation of nation-states is clearly one of the major factors in the growth of the international school system. Regardless of reasons, however, the actual development of such a system is one of the amazing facts of human history. Schools are, of course, only one of the technological institutions that have spread from Europe and North America over the rest of the world; but all the others are more easily explained, while none has spread like schooling. Universal schooling has become part of the official program of almost every nation. Every state must have its university, every city its high school, every hamlet its primary school. All nations look to the leading nations for models of curriculum, scholastic organization, and scholastic standards. Capitalist and communist nations compete in schooling their populations, with as little argument about the standards of competition as in the Olympics.

How is all this to be explained? Technology, the profit motive, and the world struggle for power explain most of the growth of international institutions. None of them directly explains the case of schooling. Similarity of constitutions and codes of law can in some cases be explained as the residue of empire and in others as ideological emulation. The spread of hospitals and medical technology can be attributed to the demonstrated efficacy of at least some aspects of modern medicine. There is nothing comparable in modern schooling; schools are as free of the obligation to demonstrate their efficiency as were the Benedictine monasteries.

European world domination during the eighteenth and nineteenth centuries helps to explain the existence of school systems in former colonies. Japanese schools can

also be explained in part as a colonial phenomenon, developed as part of a general Western pattern and adopted to avoid colonization. Schools have clearly lagged the most in those parts of the world least influenced by European and American industrialization. Schools have served a major purpose in the consolidation of the new national states that grew out of the wreckage of empire. Schools also serve the elites of these new nations, providing access to international politics, economics, and culture. This does not, however, explain the international popularity of mass education. The real explanation can be traced back to the two previous historic explosions of schooling—the Alexandrian and the Jesuit. As noted, both of these occurred at times when traditional value systems were in jeopardy. This is again the case, but this time the values involved are more basic and more universal than those of Hellas or medieval Europe. In question now are the assumptions of a society based on hierarchy of privilege. The technology that invalidates these assumptions has created the antidote for its own effects: a school system that promises universal access to the goods of technology but denies it in fact.

Modern technology relieves man, for the first time in history, of the need to earn his bread by the sweat of his brow. All preindustrial societies required close to 80% of the labor force to be engaged in agriculture. Now, using existing techniques, 5% of the labor force of a modern society could produce all of the agricultural and industrial goods currently consumed.

Even today, 10% of the labor force of the United States produces 90% of its agricultural and industrial output. And this is almost entirely prior to the application of existing methods of automation and in the face

of widespread job-protective pressures from organized labor. Nevertheless, the United States is producing record agricultural surpluses while paying farmers billions of dollars to restrict production. Additional billions of dollars' worth of industrial goods are being produced for commercial export, over and above the value of goods imported. A huge bill of military goods is being produced, while massive space and research programs are underway. If labor and management could agree upon the objective, 5% of the United States labor force could within a very few years produce the goods currently being consumed by the domestic civilian population. This bill of goods, although badly distributed, leaving many people deprived, is nevertheless enormously wasteful in its average composition. It provides an excessive and otherwise unhealthful diet, clothing that is discarded because of style changes rather than wear, so-called durable goods that are made to wear out in a few years, a tremendous packaging component that merely multiplies the pollution problem, and an unbelievable quantity of junk that serves only to relieve the boredom of people whose lives, devoted to the consumption and production of goods and services, have been emptied of real meaning. We would live much better on half as much. Such a society does not require a hierarchy of privilege for any of the reasons that have justified such a hierarchy in the past.

Modern institutions have assumed the burden of maintaining and justifying a continuing hierarchy of privilege. Among these institutions, the school plays a central role. It initiates each generation into the myths of technological production and consumption, the ideas that what is to be consumed must first be produced and that what is

produced must be consumed. Not only goods, but services and knowledge itself become commodities. It celebrates the rituals that reconcile the myths and realities of a society that merely pretends to be for all. It prepares men for specialized roles in specialized institutions, selecting and shaping them in terms of both skills and values. By its own hierarchical structure, it accustoms men to accept a single integrated hierarchy of power and privilege.

School qualifies men for participation in other institutions and convicts those who do not meet the requirements of school of not deserving desirable roles in other institutions.

6. INSTITUTIONAL PROPS FOR PRIVILEGE

In less than a hundred years industrial society has molded patent solutions to basic human needs and converted us to the belief that man's needs were shaped by the Creator as demands for the products we have invented. This is as true for Russia and Japan as for the North Atlantic community. The consumer is trained for obsolescence, which means continuing loyalty toward the same producers who will give him the same basic packages in different quality or new wrappings.

Industrialized societies can provide such packages for personal consumption for most of their citizens, but this is no proof that these societies are sane, or economical, or that they promote life. The contrary is true. The more the citizen is trained in the consumption of packaged goods and services, the less effective he seems to be in shaping his environment. His energies and finances are consumed in procuring ever new models of his staples, and the environment becomes a by-product of his own consumption habits.

Ivan Illich, Celebration of Awareness.

Schools are not the only institutions that promise the world and then become the instruments of its denial. This is what churches, to give one plural label to all religious institutions, have always done: packaged the free gift of God, or nature, so that a price could be exacted for it, and then withheld it from people unable or unwilling to pay the price. Churches were remarkable among other institutions, until recently, only for their hypocrisy. Other traditional institutions never pretended to offer a universal gift. Even the prehistoric practitioners of religious magic did not do so. It is the unique mark of the great religions that their founders opened the doors of the spirit to all and that their priests then succeeded in holding these doors open with one hand while charging admission with the other.

Except for churches, traditional institutions were always openly run for the benefit of those who ran them. Courts, kingdoms, armies, empires, and enterprises belonged to their possessors and shared their benefits only with a few and only for a fee. Two non-religious institu-

tions have recently begun to make the claim of offering universal access: first, nation-states and their subsystems such as schools, and second, modern production enterprises.

Something for nothing is not the issue. No religious leader has ever promised something for nothing, but only that the door would open to all those who would follow the path. This is the promise that churches have reneged on in failing to keep their own doors open and that many modern enterprises and public bureaucracies falsely proclaim.

As provision for human needs is institutionalized, the institutions in question define a product and control access to it. They progressively (1) define the product or service that satisfies the need (e.g. schools define education as schooling); (2) induce general acceptance of this definition among the needy (e.g. people are persuaded to identify education as schooling); (3) exclude part of the needy population from full access to the product or service (e.g. schools, at some level, are available to only some people); (4) pre-empt the resources available for satisfying the need (e.g. schools use up the resources available for education). The above generalizations hold for health, transportation, and many other kinds of human needs, as well as for education.

Health is progressively defined and conceived as access to the services of physicians and hospitals and to the products of the drug industry. This access is notoriously unequal. The cost of hospitals, doctors, and drugs is increasing faster than the resources available to pay for them. It can also be argued that the health of mature populations, those whose birth and death rates are converging, is getting worse as expenditures for hospitals,

doctors, and drugs increase. We are merely achieving a longer sick-life by means of these expenditures. People may indulge themselves more as more remedies become available, but if more resources were devoted to preventive measures, sickness as well as death rates would decline.

In the case of transportation, the facts are even clearer. The private automobile has almost displaced its competitors in many countries. In the United States, saturation is reaching the point of declining utility, even for car owners. Yet half the adult population remains without dependable access to a private car and has a harder time getting transportation than if cars had never been invented. Even in Los Angeles, which reputedly has more cars than people and is drowning in its own exhaust, there are as many old and young people who cannot or are not allowed to drive as there are qualified drivers.[1] These people, even those who belong to families that include qualified drivers, must wait upon the convenience of their chauffeurs, or vice-versa.

Provision for a category of human need is institutionalized to the extent that there is a prevailing standard product or service, a standard production and distribution process, and a standard price (with the concept of price including all significant conditions of access). It is worth noting that the people priced out of the market are convinced not only of their unworthiness to participate in it, e.g. their inability to pursue college studies or to wear stylish clothes, but also of their unworthiness to participate in the privileges that college education and stylish clothes imply.

Until democracy was popularized and technology institutionalized, claims of universal political and economic

participation could not be made. Now such claims sound plausible and are widely believed. The makers of these claims come with specific products designed to meet specific needs. They elaborate a package that becomes ever more complex, more exclusive of access, and more expensive. More basic, however, than product elaboration is the identification of need with product. The words education and school, health and hospital, automobile and transportation become inseparable. People forget that there were educated men before there were schools, healthy men before there were hospitals, and that men walked and rode before they drove or flew.

As institutions grow, more and more people accept the identification of need and product. In medieval Europe, only the Jews and the Moors failed to identify salvation with the Catholic Church. Women, who throughout history have borne their babies in the fields, are now recruited into maternity wards. Peasants who have never seen schools vote for the candidates who promise them.

Women and peasants are not irrational. They see that those who go to hospitals and schools are better off. While they also see that those who are better off have greater access to schools and hospitals, they frequently confuse cause and effect. This is not surprising, since the most astute researchers are often unable to disentangle them. Only in rare cases can the efficacy of a medical or educational treatment be conclusively demonstrated.

Product elaboration effectively prevents universal access, even to the simplest products. Pins and needles are packaged in ever-fancier collections. Salt becomes a monopoly and a form of tax. One of Gandhi's first struggles in India was against the salt monopoly maintained by the British government.[2] The Italian government still

maintains a monopoly on salt except in Sicily, where salt is produced. What happens to schools, hospitals, and automobiles is common knowledge; people are priced out of the market not only directly but by increasingly complicated rules—drivers' licenses, entrance examinations, insurance requirements. There are good reasons for all the rules, but their proliferation tends to shrink the proportion of qualified consumers.

There are, of course, opposing processes. Because of consumer credit, rising incomes, growth of public systems of schools and hospitals, etc., net access to modern institutions may even gradually increase. Beyond question, however, the excluded portion of the population, even if declining in number, gets steadily worse off as the monopoly of an institutional product is established. No resources remain for alternative products. As school budgets grow, support for educational alternatives must decline. Not only do school dropouts find progressively fewer educational resources, they also have fewer job opportunities. And finally, they have fewer excuses. As automobiles increase in number, there are fewer trains and buses; those which survive are more expensive, less satisfactory, and less profitable.[3]

During the past decade, the number of new owners of automobiles throughout the world increased by no more than twenty-five million. Perhaps a roughly equivalent number enjoyed for the first time the benefits of modern medical services. The number of school children may have increased by a hundred million. But the population of the world increased by over half a billion during the decade, so that the numbers without any of these services increased much more than the numbers with them. Even more were priced out of the market during this period.

The price of automobiles increased substantially, while the cost of medical services and schools multiplied several times. Meanwhile, per-capita income, on a worldwide basis, rose very little. Even if there had been no population growth, and other things had remained equal, more people would have been priced out of the markets for modern goods and services during the 1960s than were added to them.

Nor can the above figures be written off by labeling the sixties as a bad decade, in which major institutions did not function as they are supposed to. In a world dominated by competition for privilege, there is no other way in which institutions can function. The already privileged continue to demand better schools, better hospitals, better cars. As the number who enjoy these commodities increases, there are ever more people to be supplied with ever more-expensive packages, making it increasingly difficult to extend similar privileges to an ever-widening ring of a growing population. Even without population growth, the above factors—plus ecological limits—might make it impossible ever to universalize even the current standards of living of Europe and America.

The excluded are not the only, perhaps not even the principal, sufferers. Those who participate, but to a limited degree, feel sharper pain. Imagine the anguish of pious folk whose relatives languished in purgatory while those of more fortunate neighbors were professionally prayed into heaven. Imagine the torment, today, of persons whose relatives die because donors of kidneys and hearts are co-opted by those who can pay. The fortunate feel no pain but they may be hurt worst of all, for they get hooked on a game that has no end and that no one can win. The struggle of the rich against old age and death is

a grotesque example. Much worse, if less macabre, is the status scramble, which as it spreads to more products and more people, poisons the air, the water, and the earth and sucks the very meaning out of life. A squirrel in a rotating cage is no more hopeless or ludicrous than the Smiths and the Joneses trying to keep up with each other.

When Veblen wrote his account of conspicuous consumption over seventy years ago, it was part of a theory of the leisure class.[4] Confined to this class, competitive consumption may have been morally offensive, but it remained socially tolerable. Extended to the masses, competitive consumption destroys man, his society, and his environment. A limited leisure class could consume at the expense of the masses. Open-ended consumption can occur only at the cost of the consumer. But man can no more live in a squirrel cage than can a squirrel. Society cannot survive class conflict stoked to increasing heat by international warfare, universal advertising, and competitive schooling. The world cannot absorb the waste it now receives, let alone the amount implied by present trends.

One critically important aspect of the competitive consumption of institutionalized products is competition among nations. The early products of modern institutions—people as well as things and services—were exported from Europe to the New World and to European colonies, thus providing opportunities for all members of the populations of these European nations. Those who could not attend the new schools or buy the new goods could migrate to the New World, be drafted as soldiers to police the colonies, or take over the land of those who left. They were therefore priced out of the new markets only temporarily. The sons of these conquerors of new land became, in fact, the pioneers of new levels and types

of human consumption. The presently developing nations are not, with some exceptions, able to displace or conquer weaker peoples. Far from being able to involve their total populations in export trade, migration, or conquest, they are instead required to compete inside their domestic markets with imports of foreign products, including manpower. Far more of the population of underdeveloped nations, compared with those which developed earlier, is priced out of schools, hospitals, and modern transportation. This part of the population is progressively alienated from the elite of its own nation, from those who do have access to the products of modern institutions, foreign or indigenous. The alienated masses become, in turn, a demographic drag, an economic liability, and, ultimately, a political opposition.[5–10]

Most institutions continue to serve the interests of their inventors and at the same time the interests of those who were originally peripheral to them, only at the cost of an even more-peripheral group.

In the days when political empires were the salient institutions, the above statement would have excited no interest. The privileges of Roman citizenship were extended only as additional territories were conquered. Marx applied the principle to capitalist institutions. We merely generalize the principle to other institutions and possibly free it of dependence on the notion of deliberate exploitation. Most of those attempting to universalize schooling and hospital care sincerely believe that they act in the interest of the as yet unschooled and uncured. Earlier missionaries, conquerors, and even traders frequently acted with the same conviction.

The difficulty is that we are the prisoners of our institutions rather than their masters. Seldom do we con-

sciously design them, and when we do, we can scarcely finish the process before bowing down in reverence. So in their thrall are we that we tremble lest we lose them inadvertently and fall helplessly back into barbarism. Actually this fear is largely confined to the privileged, and what we really fear is that the specific bases of our own privilege might get lost in the institutional shuffle.

There is, then, a political as well as a psychological aspect of the difficulty. There are those who benefit from present institutions and who consciously desire to preserve them. Among these are owners, managers, political leaders, and other holders of power, including the common citizens of privileged nations. But many with power have no conscious desire to monopolize it, and many over whom power is wielded give in to the illusion rather than the reality of power. Man cannot free himself from existing institutions without struggle, but neither will struggle avail unless preceded by imagination and invention. One of the major problems is that the developed nations now have an effective, if not necessarily deliberate, monopoly of the means of modern invention.

Theories of political revolution are not sufficient. Such theories assume that if a new class gains control, the society will change in accordance with the values of this class as expressed in its ideology. In practice, we see that a spate of revolutions throughout this century have left most of the specialized institutions that constitute societies intact. The schools and hospitals of communist states are no different from those of capitalist states. Even the recent revolution in Cuba is attempting to extend health and education services to the masses largely by means of traditional school and hospital systems. The agricultural and industrial institutions of communist and capitalist

states tend to converge, despite great efforts on both sides to make them different. According to prevailing theory, technology provides the force that defeats these efforts, but technology scarcely explains the case of the school, of the church, of the family, or of many other institutions that have, temporarily at least, defeated the efforts of revolutionary governments to change them.

Yet there is ample evidence that institutions are by no means eternal. During this century, monarchies have disappeared, political empires have broken up, churches have lost their power if not their membership, labor unions have risen and declined, entrepreneurs have been replaced by managers and technicians, major industries have disappeared and been born. Many of these changes are almost totally unexplained; others, especially the political changes, have resulted from specific plans, sometimes based on a general theory of political revolution. Man has shown himself capable of creating and destroying institutions, on a planned or an unplanned basis, with or without theory. At the same time, he remains the prisoner of his institutions to an almost unimaginable degree. He can break his thralldom only by first understanding it thoroughly and then by deliberately planning the renovation and replacement of his present institutional structures. This is a necessary—not a sufficient—condition. Struggle cannot be avoided, but struggle without adequate prior understanding and planning has again and again proved futile.

Understanding and effective action will require a general theory of institutional change. We must develop conceptual tools for the analysis of institutions in order to understand the historical process by which they were introduced, the sociological process by which they be-

came acceptable, and the limitations that they now place on the search for alternatives (not only limitations of power and resources, but also limitations upon the creative imagination). We must develop a language in which we can speak with precision about the needs of modern man—a language freed from the one that is shaped by those institutions men have come to accept as the definers of their needs.

7. ARE DEMOCRATIC INSTITUTIONS POSSIBLE?

If we continue to believe that the goals of the industrial system—the expansion of output, the companion increase in consumption, technological advance, the public images that sustain it—are coordinate with life, then all of our lives will be in the service of these goals. What is consistent with these ends we shall have or be allowed; all else will be off limits. Our wants will be managed in accordance with the needs of the industrial system; the policies of the state will be subject to similar influence; education will be adapted to industrial need; the disciplines required by the industrial system will be the conventional morality of the community. All other goals will be made to seem precious, unimportant, or anti-social. We will be bound to the ends of the industrial system. The state will add its moral, and perhaps some of its legal, power to their enforcement. What will eventuate, on the whole, will be the benign servitude of the household retainer who is taught to love her mistress and see her interests as her own, and not the compelled servitude of the field hand. But it will not be freedom.

If, on the other hand, the industrial system is only a part, and relatively a diminishing part, of life, there is much less

occasion for concern. Aesthetic goals will have pride of place; those who serve them will not be subject to the goals of the industrial system; the industrial system itself will be subordinate to the claims of these dimensions of life. Intellectual preparation will be for its own sake and not for the better service to the industrial system. Men will not be entrapped by the belief that apart from the goals of the industrial system—apart from the production of goods and income by progressively more advanced technical methods—there is nothing important in life.

John Kenneth Galbraith,
The New Industrial State

In the admitted absence of an adequate language of institutions, the hypothesis that institutions can be democratic may appear premature. The hypothesis of this chapter, however, is that institutions can be identified in which the tendency toward domination can be restrained[1] and that encouragement of this kind of institution can foster the growth of a just and democratic society.

Institutions are so identified with hierarchy, control, privilege, and exclusion that the very notion of democratic institutions seems strange. Jeffersonian democracy was based on the relative absence of large institutions, and came to grief with the growth of corporations and public bureaucracies. According to Galbraith and others, today's technology requires large institutions. As indicated by the preceding quotation, Galbraith's theme in *The New Industrial State*[2] parallels in many ways the argument of this chapter. His argument is much more detailed and much more carefully qualified; without the support of his documentation, the positions taken here

would be much less tenable. Galbraith does not, however, suggest an institutional dichotomy of the type outlined in this chapter. In *The Affluent Society*,[3] which is in a sense a companion volume to *The New Industrial State*, Galbraith suggests the need for a massive shift of resources from private to public enterprise. Again, the major difference from the argument of this chapter lies in Galbraith's much greater caution, coupled with an immensely greater documentation of his assertions. For Galbraith, all hope seems to lie in a shift in basic values. In the absence of such a shift, little else is possible. He may be right. But this chapter suggests that if such a shift should begin to occur, an appropriate program of institutional development might lead to something better than mere battle between institutional and humanistic social goals.

Historically there have been at least quasi-democratic institutions: the Greek city-state, the New England town, the Jeffersonian republic; some of the early temples, churches, and religious fraternities; the Chinese market networks.[4] There are also some modern institutions that seem to serve democratic purposes: postal systems, telephone exchanges, and road networks, for example. If Chinese markets and road networks do not appear to qualify for institutional status, this is at least partly because of the way we have been trained to think about institutions.

The history of institutions is a history of domination. Armies, temples, courts, and empires established the institutional mold, and despite exceptions, their pattern has continued to determine man's thinking almost to the point of defining deviations from this pattern as non-institutional. Even people who admit that an organization

that is not hierarchical or exclusive might be called an institution, will argue that hierarchy and selective membership increase institutional efficiency. They probably do—for purposes of domination. Institutions that are better at dominating their members may also be better at dominating their rivals. Despite Pericles' eloquent claim for the superiority of Athenian democracy, Sparta won the war. The relatively democratic Greek city-states were later conquered by much less-democratic Rome. The record begins to get fuzzy with England's triumph over Spain and with the results of the two world wars. But even English history credits the better discipline of her navy, obtained partly by means of the lash, and the record is not yet closed on the battle between dictatorship and democracy. Currently the loudest clamor for control comes from the leadership of the democracies.

Admission that large, hierarchically controlled institutions may be better at dominating others will not satisfy the adherents of hierarchy. They claim greater productive efficiency as well. This is a little like claiming that big sharks have more efficient digestive systems than little sharks because they succeed in eating them. Is General Motors more productive because it is bigger, or bigger because it is more productive? The answer is neither. It is bigger because it is the product of a merger; its size gives it the resources to dominate other companies that remain independent. It is not, in general, a more efficient producer, or it would not buy so many large and small components from smaller companies. Its size does help it to dominate the market, which in turn permits some economies of scale in production. General Motors is currently the most efficient player of the game in which it is engaged, just as the United States and Russia are cur-

rently the leaders in the world struggle for domination. No one would claim that both of these nations are models of efficiency in all other respects.

Consider American Telephone and Telegraph, in contrast with General Motors. It is just as technical, just as profit-oriented, just as large as General Motors, but there is a great difference in what the two companies do for and to their clients. The telephone company installs a phone and there it stays, whatever its age, shape, or color, unless the customer, for special reasons of his own, decides he wants a different model. The telephone subscriber pays a few dollars a month and, unless he has teen-agers, forgets about his phone until someone calls him or he wants to call someone else. The telephone doesn't have to be washed, waxed, or serviced, except rarely, requires no insurance, and is not liable to theft. It is not, on the other hand, a source of pride or envy, of concern or comfort, of thrill or trepidation. It is just there, in case it is needed to call next door or halfway around the world, imposing no constraints on what is said and not intruding itself in any way into the use that is made of it. Anyone who has a dime or a friend or an honest face or an emergency can use it, even if he can't afford or doesn't want a phone of his own. And the essential service the user gets, the value it has for him, has nothing to do with what he pays or who he is. Clearly, people who are better off are more conveniently served, but the telephone network is essentially democratic—so long as it serves individuals rather than computers, corporations, or military systems.

How different the Cadillac or Chevrolet, not so much owned as owning its possessor. Long before we purchase, the model, color, style, horsepower, power steering, power windows, to say nothing of other options, domi-

nate the family council. Subsequent payments dominate the family budget as much as the new car dominates family life. Triumphs and tragedies succeed each other in rapid succession as it passes or fails one test after another. Utility is our last concern. We join car clubs to avoid exposing the new member of the family to the dangers of the parking lot. Gasoline mileage is merely a point of debate with the neighbors. Emission of lead and other air-borne poisons we do not even think about.

Human nature? Perhaps. But elsewhere people compete on horses, or on foot, or with sticks or stones, without surrendering their lives (including employment, taxes, education, and the condition of the air, water, and land on which they live) to the producers of these horses, sticks, or stones. And yet, human nature is involved. The automobile, like the modern house or household utility, is too big a toy to be resisted. Offered, even in exchange for submission to its supplier, it is as hard to resist as were the early cults with their idols, incense, and temple prostitutes. Life is dull, and what else is there to relieve the tedium?

This is one of three traditonal ways of dominating men. The others are force and the withholding of necessities. Force is relied upon mainly between nations. Necessities are withheld to insure the services of the lower classes. The grown-up plaything game is used to keep the palace guard in line. International competition, interclass competition, and interpersonal competition are all related. The first requires the military institution, the second the police and penal institutions, and the third requires General Motors. What these institutions have in common is the advantage they try to establish for one group or individual over another. What all forms of advantage have

in common is that they exact a price for the advantage as well as for the product that provides it. When the advantage is permanent, this price must be paid continuously. When the advantage is on all counts, the price is total. The point is made elegantly in the Faust legend, and the theme appears throughout human mythology. It provides the touchstone for distinguishing democratic from dominating institutions.

Democratic institutions offer a service, satisfy a need, without conferring advantage over others or conveying the sense of dependence that institutions such as welfare agencies do. They take the form of networks rather than production systems—networks that provide an opportunity to do something rather than make and sell a finished product. Public communication and transportation systems are examples, as are water works and sewers, electricity and gas distribution systems, and general markets that facilitate the flow of various kinds of goods. Public utilities are democratic institutions if they are truly public and provide something really useful.

Everyone has access to a true public utility, either free of charge or at a fee everyone can afford. Access is at the option and initiative of the user, who may also leave the service when he wishes. The most useful products, such as electricity or water, can be used for a variety of purposes. So can roads or the mails. Public utility networks show true economy of scale. The bigger they get and the more of the population they serve, the more useful they are for everyone. Water and sewer systems, which might seem to be exceptions, are seen not to be when public health is considered. Superhighways, as opposed to road networks, are false public utilities. They are actually the private preserves of car owners, built partly at public

expense. Utilities serve basic, universal needs. Everyone needs water, power, communication, transport, food, raw materials, a place to exchange fabricated products, and many other things. Nevertheless, basic needs are limited. They cannot be indefinitely multiplied. They can, therefore, be satisfied without exhausting all available time, labor, raw materials, and human energy. After they are satisfied, there are things left for people to do, if and when they like, and there are remaining resources for doing them. The managers of democratic institutions can and must be largely responsive to the expressed desires of their clients.

Institutions that confer or maintain advantage over others fit a description almost diametrically opposed to that above. They tend to be production systems rather than networks. If networks are involved, they have the secondary purpose of distributing a particular product. Access is limited, and access costs are frequently high. Once on, it isn't easy to get off; participation is often either obligatory or addictive.[5] The product tends to be specific, elaborate, and all-purpose. There are important diseconomies of scale. At some point, extension of the service to new clients becomes a disservice to former clients. The needs served are not basic but at least partly induced. Once induced, however, these needs are open-ended and can never be fully satisfied. Surfeit leads to excess rather than to satiation. Dominating institutions tend, therefore, to become total, to exhaust the life space of human beings and the life-sustaining capacity of the biosphere. The managers of dominating institutions must take and maintain the initiative. Clients must be seduced, manipulated, or coerced. True initiative or choice on the

part of clients tends to disrupt the maintenance requirements of dominating institutions.

Most actual institutions fit these opposing prototypes only partially. Some fit fairly well, including certain public utilities on the one hand and military establishments, prisons, and asylums on the other. Most products, services, and institutions fall somewhere in between. Automobiles, modern houses, and home appliances are not merely pawns in a status game, but are also useful. Making long-distance calls on credit cards, on the other hand, may be pure oneupmanship. The management of the telephone company and its institutional advertising differ little from those of General Motors, which also produces buses as well as private cars. The buses are, however, almost incidental. The policies of General Motors and its role in the society are determined by the private automobile, considered not primarily as transportation—as Henry Ford viewed the Model T—but as status symbol. With the development of the video-phone, the telephone company could easily embark on the same route. A videophone is not for everyone, and might seem to require private viewing space. This in turn could lead to elaboration not unlike that which has afflicted the automobile. If the choice were left to management, there is little doubt that AT&T would follow the route of General Motors. The management of a true public utility must be at the service and command of its clientele. The management of a dominating institution must manage its clientele as well as its personnel. The choice is a fateful one. It is, hopefully, not too late for the public to choose.

The choice is not between high and low technology. It is not necessarily between private and public management, of either "public" utilities or "private" factories for

necessary products. It is a choice of shopping lists, of the kinds and varieties of products that will be available. An unlimited market basket for the rich is not compatible with freedom for either the rich or the poor. But this metaphor is inexact. The "unlimited" market basket can be filled only with those products of high technology that enough people can be induced to buy. It can, of course, be filled with custom-made products for those who can afford them, but even these will be the products of an inherited artisanship living on the past. A vigorous artisanship cannot survive in unrestricted competition with high technology. The choice ultimately is between two completely different styles of life. One is egalitarian, pluralistic, and relatively sparse in the kinds of products and services it provides. People have to do things for themselves, but have time and freedom to do what they want. The other kind of life is based on a unified hierarchy of privilege maintained by international, interclass, and interpersonal competition. The kinds of competition are limited and highly structured, but the prizes are relatively glamorous, at least on the surface.

It may seem idealistic in the extreme to believe that people who have the second option already in their hands will voluntarily exchange it for the first. Yet there are signs that this could happen and the choice may not be entirely voluntary. Pollution of the environment, pressure from the underprivileged, and the horrors of war may help to decide the issue. But blind forces cannot achieve intelligent solutions of issues. Only intelligence can do that. This is why education is so important, and why it cannot be left to schools.

Schools are themselves dominating institutions rather than opportunity networks. They develop a product that

is then sold to their clients as education. Concentrating on children gives them a less-critical clientele, to which they offer the prizes that other dominating institutions produce. Parents want these prizes for their children, even more than for themselves, and can be sold a rosy future even more easily than a current illusion. Seen at a distance, the fallacies of competition are harder to perceive clearly. Foreigners can have what we have if they will follow the course we have followed. Workers can achieve our standard of living if they will educate themselves to earn it. Our children can have what we couldn't have if they will prepare themselves to produce it. These propositions sound so plausible and yet are so patently false when viewed in perspective. An open-ended consumption race must always result in a hound who gets the rabbit, a bunched pack in the middle who get some of the shreds, and a train of stragglers. This must be the outcome in terms of nations, of classes, and of individuals. Schools not only cloud this perspective, they actively foster the illusions that contradict it. They prepare children precisely for interpersonal, interclass, and international competition. They produce adults who believe they have been educated and who, in any case, have no remaining resources with which to pursue their education.

Schools will have to be replaced by opportunity networks that provide universal access to essential educational resources—including things and people.

8. NETWORKS OF THINGS

An Expedient was therefore offered, that since Words are only Names for Things, *it would be more convenient for all Men to carry about them, such* Things *as were necessary to express the particular Business they are to discourse on. And this Invention would certainly have taken Place, to the great Ease as well as Health of the Subject, if the Women in Conjunction with the Vulgar and Illiterate had not threatened to raise a Rebellion, unless they might be allowed the Liberty to speak with their Tongues, after the Manner of their Forefathers: Such constant irreconcileable Enemies to Science are the common People. However, many of the most Learned and Wise adhere to the new Scheme of expressing themselves by* Things; *which hath only this Inconvenience attending it; that if a Man's Business be very great, and of various Kinds, he must be obliged in Proportion to carry a greater Bundle of* Things *upon his Back, unless he can afford one or two strong Servants to attend him. I have often beheld two of those Sages almost sinking under the Weight of their Packs, like Pedlars among us; who when they met in the Streets would lay down their Loads, open their Sacks, and hold Conversation for an Hour together; then put up their Implements, help each other to resume their Burthens, and take their Leave.*

Jonathan Swift, Gulliver's Travels

There are things with general and things with special educational significance. Those of special educational value are again of two kinds: those which embody symbols and those which produce, translate, transmit, or receive information encoded in symbols. All objects serve as means of communication, but as Swift points out, some serve it better than others. Among those which serve it best are records, books, tapes, anything used for the storage of symbols. Records are relatively so easy and cheap to store and to keep that they can be organized for quick access enormously more efficiently than the things they represent. This is the virtue of human brains, but also of computers, libraries, microfilm stores, and the like. Large collections of records, such as central libraries or national archives, are like collective memories serving societies as brains serve individuals. Further organization of such record collections, by means of computers, is certain to increase their utility greatly and to warrant the comparison with human brains. Effective access to records is sure to become even more necessary to the educated man than

it is today. Even today, records are very significant extensions of educated brains. Much that could be kept in human memory is deliberately passed on to these supplementary memory systems.

One of the things that makes almost unlimited universal education potentially so cheap is the great economy with which record systems of many types can now be organized for very rapid access by almost unlimited numbers of people. Anyone who learns to use these systems, for which only elementary skills are needed—at least for certain levels of use—is then capable of carrying on his own education to almost any degree. This has always been true for people who knew how to read and to find books. The new development will simply make it easier. It may be worth noting that this has also always been true for anyone who knew how to observe and to find information. Reading merely made things easier, just as computers now do. They make things so much easier, however, that education can now become universal.

The quality of this education will depend only upon the quality and completeness of the records that are available to the public. Information upon which corporate and national advantage presumably depends will not be available. Neither will other information deemed vital by some groups for the maintenance of their advantage over others. These are problems that organization alone cannot solve.

Libraries are partial models for the organization of records and similar objects. Only an extension of the library system is necessary to enable these kinds of educational objects to be located and placed at the disposal of learners. But the scope of the extension required is very great. Libraries do not yet take full advantage of the

ease and economy with which most records can now be reproduced. They are, of course, seriously handicapped by property rights and consequent restrictions on reproduction. These restrictions and the novelty of cheap reproduction methods account for the carry-over of the custodial tradition, which opens libraries to the charge of being more concerned with their records than with their clients. This tradition will have to be overcome, as will the tradition of serving an elite rather than the general public. The reading public is an elite, and because libraries were founded on books, an elite as well as a custodial tradition has limited their educational scope. It might not even be a good idea to use the name library in the network of educational objects that must become one of the major institutional alternatives to schools.

In addition to vastly expanded directories and repositories of all kinds of records, we need effective access to objects that have special value in the transmission of information. Among these are the instruments that play records, produce them, or transmit their message. Books are among the few records that do not require special decoders. In the production of books and papers, however, instruments are indispensable: pencils, typewriters, mimeograph machines, or presses. Universal access to these instruments is just as important as the ability to read what has been written. This is why freedom of the press was included in the American Bill of Rights. Its original purpose was to protect the rights of common people such as Thomas Paine to make their ideas public; only later did it become primarily a protection of the commercial press.

Most records other than books require instruments for their production and also for their use. Musical instru-

ments and microphones may be needed to produce and record sound, and record players to hear it. Typewriters and computers are needed for the production and reading of punch cards, tapes, disc-packs, and other types of computer records. Cameras and projectors are another pair of basic instruments, which can be combined with telescopes, microscopes, and many other devices, and can use television or telephone lines as transmitting devices. Then there are simpler kinds of materials for producing records, such as paint and brushes, knives and chisels, knitting needles and string—a great variety of common tools and materials.

Message coding and decoding devices shade off into general types of instruments or machines that transform one kind of energy into another. Musical instruments and printing presses, for example, are not so strictly communications devices as tape recorders or typewriters. All general types of energy transformers have special educational value, not only because of their general usefulness in facilitating communication, but also because they reveal some important features of the world: clocks, for example, reveal the relationship between motion and time, motors between motion and electricity, telescopes between distance and size. Names for relationships of this kind—but not confined to the world of physical science—make up much of the basic vocabulary of educated men.

Tools, instruments, and machines are less available now to most of the people of technological societies than they used to be. Specialized large-scale production removes them from the common scene. Artisans and mechanics can still be found in South America, Asia, and Africa, but in Europe and North America they are disappearing

rapidly from public view. Not only children, but also neighbors, friends, clients, and passers-by are deprived of access to firsthand demonstrations and opportunities to experiment with tools and to see the insides of the gadgets that now come out of factories encased in shiny shells. Worse than this, many modern devices can no longer be taken apart without destroying them. They are made not to be repaired but to be replaced. As a result, modern man is becoming richer in devices and poorer in his understanding of them.[1] The multiplication of product shells and factory walls, behind which tools, instruments, and machines are hidden, has the same effect educationally as the hiding of records behind the veils of national security and corporate privilege. The result is to deny people the information they need to act intelligently in their own interests. The reasons behind all this secrecy are also the same, even though the conscious motives may be different. Manufacturers guard their equipment and their products from the eyes of their customers, perhaps not consciously to keep them ignorant, but certainly in order to maintain an advantage in which ignorance is a critical factor.

Secrecy is by no means confined to capitalist countries. Professionals, managers, and specialized workers guard their privileges as jealously as owners. The techniques of modern production play into their hands equally well and are indeed partly responsible quite apart from any conscious motivation. Large-scale production has, in and of itself, profoundly anti-educational implications, as Jane Jacobs points out in her *Economy of Cities*.[2]

So long as large-scale production continues to monopolize tools, instruments, machines, and other products that have special educational value, it will be necessary to

include such products in educational directories and to arrange for general access to them. Vocational schools are one attempt to supply this access, but they are far more expensive and much less educational than junk yards. Vocational schools can never serve the needs of the entire population, while junk yards could, although today junk yards are in some respects more difficult of access.

Toys and games are a special class of objects with great potential for offsetting the educational disadvantages of a technological society. They can simulate many real objects and situations, sometimes to advantage and sometimes not. Traffic rules in the classroom, for example, may be a dangerously safe simulation of a truly dangerous situation. But simple toys and games, made easily and widely accessible, could provide skill, practice, and intellectual insights with an effectiveness and economy not easy to match. Games have three great educational assets: First, they are a pleasant way of learning many skills, the practice of which might otherwise be onerous. Second, they provide a means of organizing activities among peers that make minimum demands upon leadership or authority. Finally, they are paradigms of intellectual systems, being based on elements, operations, and rules, just as mathematical systems and other intellectual models are. People familiar with games can easily be introduced to a basic understanding of the most important models of science and mathematics. Games are, of course, open to the objection of stressing scientific and technological outlooks over those of nature and the humanities. Games are also open to the objection of pitting persons against each other and of producing losers and winners. It is doubtful, however, whether competition can or should be organized out of life. Games can be so

organized as to equalize advantages and thus the pleasures of winning. While everyone still knows who is best, it is usually rather difficult for one person to be best at everything.

Organizing access to toys and games falls largely into the ambit of libraries. Physical sports constitute an important exception, with problems similar to those involved where access to nature and natural things are involved.

Nature is not only becoming more distant, it is also being increasingly denatured, by exploitation and pollution on the one hand and by the sterilization of adventure on the other. The exploitation and pollution of the natural environment have been well publicized, and in terms of man's continued enjoyment of nature are of great importance. Educationally, however, cleaning up the environment may be worse than getting it dirty. Protecting children from dirt, animals, birth, sickness, death, and other natural things distorts their sense of what is real and natural. For the typical city child, nature is man-made, like everything else. Even as an adult, he has decreasing opportunities to discover the truth. Jet planes and highways keep nature at a distance, and even after he gets there, modern man's dude ranch and stage-managed safari will do little to penetrate his urban aplomb. Only a few rivers, forests, and mountain ranges remain unspoiled, and these are being invaded. Nature can no longer be left to herself, but has to be protected by man against man. Educational access complicates the problem of conservation, but education should be the main function of nature in the life of man. If proper boundaries are established between man and nature, and if his weapons are removed before he enters her, nature can continue to be man's mentor. For many people, a new

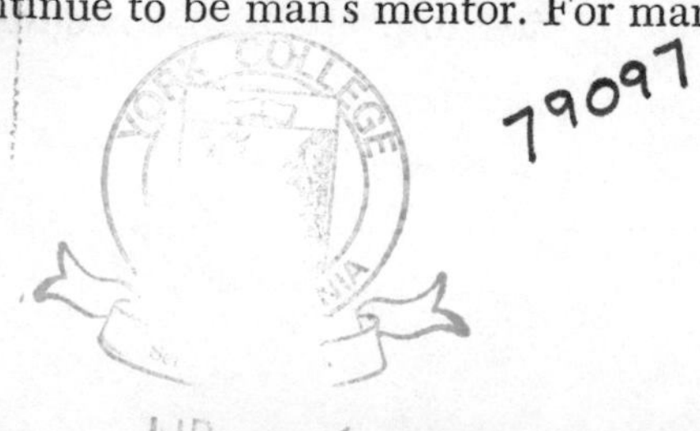

guide will have to be written and new kinds of encounters devised. It is surprising and hopeful, however, to see what small enclaves of nature, truly protected, turn out to be viable.

Access to records, tools, machines, games, natural preserves, and other extraordinarily useful educational objects is relatively easy to organize. Logical classifications already exist. Directories can easily be developed; storage in libraries and arrangements for other kinds of access can be made without major difficulty. But this leaves the whole rest of the world, not as concentratedly educational perhaps, but outweighing in its total educational value all the special kinds of objects put together. The barriers to this world of ordinary objects are of several kinds. One is characterized by the automobile. Cities and many rural areas have become so unsafe for pedestrians, especially for children, that streets and roads—the physical paths to the world—are off limits to many of the world's inhabitants. If streets could again be opened to pedestrians, the city itself could again become a network of educational objects, the natural school that it has been throughout history. A second barrier, however, would still lie between the customers' area of the various shops, and the workrooms where most of the really educational objects and processes are shut away. In older cities these barriers do not exist. The tradesman works where he sells, open to public view. In the modern city, however, there is yet a third line of defense: Many machines and processes are not there at all but hidden outside the city or in places where only the persons who already know can find them. Directories that will locate this world for people who want to learn about it are indispensable, but even directories may not be easy to prepare, and access will be

still more difficult to arrange. For these most interesting objects are also the most carefully guarded—the scientific, military, economic, and political objects hidden in laboratories, banks, and governmental archives.

Secrets seem natural and inevitable in the world to which we are accustomed, but the cost of keeping them is very great. Science, for example, used to be a network of people working all over the world and exchanging information freely. One of the original premises of science, which has never been repealed, was that progress depends precisely upon the open sharing of the results of scientific work. Now the members as well as the artifacts of the scientific community have been locked into national and corporate prisons, impoverishing even the citizens of these nations and the stockholders of these corporations. The special privileges they gain are more than offset by the barriers to the growth of knowledge. In a world controlled and owned by nations and corporations, only limited access to educational objects will ever be possible. Increased access to those objects that can be shared, however, may increase men's insight enough to enable them to break through these ultimate educational barriers.

9. NETWORKS OF PEOPLE

Learning is but an adjunct to ourself,
And where we are our learning likewise is.

William Shakespeare

Although people could learn much more than they do now in a world where things were freely accessible to them, it would still be helpful to have the assistance of other people. Each person might eventually learn to type, given a typewriter, but each might learn to type in a different way. Having a typist who could demonstrate the skill would help to avoid this, especially if more than one learner took advantage of the same model. If that happened, those two could compare notes and thus learn something from each other. If, finally, there were, in addition to the skill model and the two learners, someone who had taught typing before, compared the progress of various learners, and drawn some valid conclusions, this person might also be useful in reducing the time required to learn to type.

The indispensable resource for learning to type is, of course, some model of the typewriter itself. The skill model, while not indispensable, might nevertheless reduce the learning time by quite a bit, and improve the final product as well. The fellow learner, the peer, is also

important, especially in providing motivation to learn and the opportunity for practice. Less important than the others is the typing teacher.

Schools reverse this kind of logic. They do not, it is true, try to teach typing without a typewriter, but they frequently try to teach foreign languages without the help of anyone who can speak them, without anyone to speak to in them, and without anything to say in them that could not just as well be said in the native language of the learner. Geography is similarly taught, without benefit of people or things from the places in question. Music is taught without instruments or musicians, science and mathematics by people who do not know them. Schools assume that the indispensable resource for learning is the teacher. Ideally this teacher should have the essential equipment for the practice of the skill and should also be able to demonstrate the skill, but these are secondary considerations. The need for learning peers is given lip service, but little use is made of peers in the learning process.

Schools are not just willfully perverse. Learning a skill, learning to practice it with someone else who is learning it, and learning how others have learned it are three different things, sometimes related but also frequently not. Schools try to find teachers who combine all three kinds of learning, but understandably they often fail. The combination is much scarcer than its elements. When they do succeed in finding the scarce combination, schools use it as if it were not scarce at all. The experienced teacher is required to act as skill model and as practice partner for individual students, to say nothing of the many duties that are unrelated to learning or teaching. The scarcest skill of the teacher is usually the ability to diagnose learn-

ing difficulties, a skill acquired by observation of learning under various circumstances. In school, the use of this scarce skill must share time with all the other functions built into the teacher's role. Most unions and school administrators oppose even specialized roles for veteran teachers who have acquired diagnostic skills. This is how schools succeed in taking plentiful learning resources and making them scarce. They package them all together, then stand the package on its head.

What schools do, nevertheless, provides an excellent model for the organization of educational resources. The model has merely to be used in reverse. Educational resources must be administered independently of each other and given priority in reverse order to that of the school: First attention must be given to the availability of information in the form of records, the instruments that produce and interpret these records, and other objects in which information is stored. Second priority must be given to the availability of skill models, people who can demonstrate the skill to be acquired. Third priority must go to the availability of real peers, fellow learners with whom learning can actually be shared. Fourth and last priority must go to the provision of educators who by virtue of experience can facilitate the use of the more essential learning resources. It might appear that educators are of first importance, if only to see that the other resources are properly valued and used. It is evident, however, that this is what educators, when incorporated into schools, do worst, not because they are educators, but because schools give them powers that corrupt their judgment.

Skill models are different from educational objects in two important respects: First, they must personally con-

sent to their use as educational resources. Second, they frequently have enough additional flexibility and other secondary advantages to make it worth the trouble to gain this consent. In this technical age they are not strictly necessary, since their skills can all be demonstrated on records of one kind or another, but they are convenient. The superior flexibility of human models was recently demonstrated in Patrick Suppe's experiment in computerized instruction at Stanford University.[1] The computers were programmed to teach reading and numbers to beginning first-graders. The computers worked well—so long as one teacher stood behind each child to deal with his unexpected responses. Typical of these was the insertion of a pencil under the keys that operated the computer. The computer could, of course, be reprogrammed to deal with each one of these unanticipated reactions, but at the end of the third year of the experiment the programmers were lagging further behind the children than at the beginning. Computers may be able to teach other computers, but it appears that human learners may, for a time at least, continue to be better served by human models.

Skill models are in plentiful supply. There are almost always more people in any vicinity who possess a particular skill than there are people who want to learn it. The major exceptions occur when a new skill is invented or imported into a new territory. When this happens, skill models proliferate rapidly and are soon in balance with the demand for their services. Only schools and similar monopolistic institutions make skill models scarce. Schools try to forbid the use of models who have not joined the teachers' union. Some of the most famous musicians in the world, who fled from Germany at the time

of the Nazi terror, were not allowed to teach music in the schools of the United States. Unions and professional associations also restrict the unauthorized use of skills, frequently creating serious shortages of vital services. Nurses, for example, are scarce in the United States primarily because the training curriculum has been extended again and again by schools of nursing, placing the cost of training beyond the means of the girls for whom the profession offers opportunities for social mobility. Restrictions on the practice of a skill are usually justified in terms of professional standards and protection of the public. Sometimes these claims are true, but more often they are patently false. The best skill models are frequently those who have just learned a skill. Children learn to read from older siblings, sometimes with ridiculous ease. English schools were really economical for a time, when Joseph Lancaster introduced the systematic use of older students to teach younger ones. This system worked better than schools usually do and was very much cheaper. It shares with other forms of schooling the fatal flaw of not allowing the learner to choose his model, his subject matter, and his place and time of instruction.[2]

Access to skill models should be organized so as to give each learner the widest choice of models and each model the greatest latitude in accepting or rejecting learners. This requires, first, an absence of restrictions and, second, a directory of skill models of all kinds. There should be no special restrictions. Model/pupil relationships are subject to risk and abuse, as is any kind of human relationship, but the general laws and customs that cover all such relationships provide the best available protection. Learning in and of itself creates no additional hazards. The advantage of permitting the learner to seek and find

a model from whom he will learn is, in general, worth all the additional risk that such latitude entails. Not learning what needs to be learned is likely to involve the greatest risks of all.

Developing directories of skill models is not intrinsically difficult. Truly convenient and comprehensive directories might be so valuable, however, as to warrant considerable investment. Responsibility for developing and administering such directories should probably be vested in a public utility. Skill models willing to offer evidence of their skills might be offered free registration. Those who chose not to do this could, nevertheless, retain the freedom to make such arrangements as were possible using their own means of publicity.

Having learned a skill, people need someone with whom to practice. But peers are important even before practice. Who would bother to learn a skill unless there were others with whom to share it, fellow explorers of the new ground opened by the skill? Many skills are learned primarily with peers, taking advantage of the skill models in the general environment. Often, peers and skill models are hard to distinguish. In ordinary interpersonal relations there is neither need nor advantage in distinguishing skill models from peers. On the contrary, learning occurs best when such distinctions are not made. There is, however, an important distinction that can be ignored only if the individuals involved are willing to ignore it. Peers are by definition equals, deriving mutual benefits from their relationship. They can play tennis together, go exploring together, study mathematics together, or build a camp together. If they are peers, they contribute more or less equally to each other's objectives. Helping a smaller brother or sister learn what he wants

to learn is different. It may be equally enjoyable for a while, but the enjoyment palls more quickly. Peer relationships are freely chosen, freely kept. Skill-modeling frequently requires some sort of compensation for the model if the relationship is maintained as long as the learner would like. A method for compensating skill models is therefore needed, although it is not needed in relationships of peers.

Finding peers is merely a matter of knowing where they are and being able to get there, write, or call on the telephone. Neighborhoods free of major hazards are all that most children need for the purpose. As skills develop, however, the better ballplayers go farther afield to find worthy competitors, the botany bug outgrows his neighborhood pals, the serious ballet addicts find their ranks thinning out.

Schools supplement neighborhoods, as things are now organized, but schools create as many barriers to peer groups as opportunities for them. In schools, peer groups form around the goals of teachers or around the interests of dope pushers. Student-initiated groups concerned with education have a hard time competing with either. But, for teen-agers, the neighborhood no longer serves as an adequate base for contacts. If it did, the telephone and the automobile would be more readily dispensable.

For adults, with their frequently highly specialized interests, even the largest cities cannot always provide true peers. The best illustration of this is the scientific community, which must be world-wide for the most fruitful peer encounters to occur. The scientific community also illustrates how peer matches can be fostered or frustrated.

The logical structure of science provides a framework

for identifying persons of similar interests. Its journals provide means of communication. Its rules of logic and criteria of evidence provide the parameters for fruitful encounters. Its achievements unfailingly generate new problems, which beckon explorers with common interests. All these advantages of science as a network of related interests that provide an ideal basis for peer-group formation, have now been offset by institutional barriers. National and corporate interests now dictate who may speak or write to whom, in what terms, when, how, and where. Only the model of a scientific community is left, available for other interest groups that have been less successful in forming fruitful peer groups than scientists used to be.

The advantages of science in fostering communication among peers are no more natural than the forces that have now disrupted them. The modern "logical" structure of science did not exist a century ago. Neither did its current journals, nor its present rules of logic or standards of evidence. The beginnings were already there, but, two centuries ago, even those were only dim foreshadowings.

Fortunately, other communities of interest do not have to retrace the steps of science. The example and the products of science make it possible to short-cut these steps. Today any area of interest can be so described that a computer can match the persons who share it. Learners in search of peers need only identify themselves and their interests in order to find matches in the neighborhood, city, nation, or world. The computer is not indispensable. In the neighborhood, a bulletin board will do; in the city, a newspaper; in the nation, a national magazine; in the world, an international journal. All these media and others are and should be used to find peer matches, but

computers can make the matching easier and more flexible.

The operation of a peer-matching network would be simple. The user would identify himself by name and address and describe the activity he wanted to share. A computer would send him back the names and addresses of all who had inserted similar descriptions. People using the system would become known only to their potential peers.

Abuses of our matching systems are easy to visualize. They range from the danger of master data files compiled by government agencies for the control of citizens to the danger of sex perverts' misusing information posted on bulletin boards. As in the case of model/pupil relationships, these dangers increase as contacts increase, but they are not increased by the educational purposes of these contacts. Monitoring systems provide one type of safeguard, but also raise the question of who monitors the monitors. Providing potential users of a communications medium with ample information about the dangers of its use, and with suggestions for countering these dangers, is the best short-term safeguard. In the longer term, only progress toward a just society, which would alter people's motives toward one another, can give us a world both safe and free.

As in the case of skill models, a public utility might provide free service for the finding of peers. This would be justified not only in educational terms but also as buttressing the right of free assembly. The same right should also be extended to include prohibition of involuntary assembly, in the form of compulsory attendance at school. If freedom of the press and free assembly were taken seriously, and public means provided to make them

available to everyone, compulsory school attendance, military service, and other common current compulsions would become unnecessary.

As schools are replaced by networks of educational objects, skill models, and peers, the demand for educators, rather than declining, will probably increase. These educators will perform different functions than are now performed in school, and not all of them will be the same people. The need for those with real ability in administration, teaching, and scholarship will increase, and their rewards in terms of educational achievement, professional freedom, and income will also increase. Schoolmen whose skills are primarily in the hiring, supervision, and firing of teachers; public relations with parents; curriculum making; textbook purchasing; maintenance of grounds and facilities; and the supervision of interscholastic athletic competition may not find a market for their skills. Neither will all the baby-sitting, lesson-planning, and record-keeping teachers, unless they have skills that can be turned to other uses, or unless they leave education for more honestly designated employment. This is no put-down of school teachers and school administrators as people. Schools put them in impossible positions, just as they do students.

At least three kinds of professional educators will be in strong demand: first, architects and administrators of the educational resource networks that have been briefly described; second, pedagogues who can help design effective individual educational programs, diagnose educational difficulties, and prescribe effective remedies; and third, leaders in every branch of learning.

Educational-resource networks are simple in principle and will be effective only if they are kept simple in oper-

ation. The kind of simplicity required, however, is frequently the mark of genius. People who can multiply the services available to others and still stay out of their way are relatively rare people.

The designers of the new networks will have to understand knowledge, people, and the societies they live in. They will have to be dedicated to the idea of student-directed, individualized education. They will have to understand the barriers to the flow of relevant information and how to reduce them without generating offsetting counteractions. They will, above all, have to be able to resist the eternal temptation of subtly directing the studies of their clients instead of opening ever new and possibly dangerous doors for their investigation.

Teachers were greatly honored before there were schools, and will be again when they are freed to practice their profession without the constraints of forced attendance, mandatory curriculums, and classroom walls. The core of an independent educational profession will be the pedagogue, a bad word now but one that will come into its own when students, parents, and teachers are free to make responsible educational decisions. They will find then that they need advice and assistance in selecting learning programs, choosing skill models, discovering peers, finding leadership in difficult endeavors. Unlike the network administrator, the independently practicing pedagogue will not have to suppress his opinions and values in favor of those of his client. He will be free to make value judgments, because his clients will also be free. He will have no way of shaping their decisions except through the persuasiveness of his advice. And he had better be right as well as persuasive, for his clients will hold him responsible. This profession is

not for the fainthearted, but the competent pedagogue will find in it the rewards of the old family doctor, the man who made the reputation that modern medical specialists are still living on. There will, of course, be room for many pedagogic specialties, such as testing and educational psychiatry, which will be in less demand as the damage done by schools declines. Eventually the new pedagogic profession may succumb to the overspecialization that now afflicts medicine, but by that time it will have made its contribution.

The role of the educational leader is more elusive than that of the network administrator or the pedagogue. This is because leadership itself is hard to define. Walter Bagehot's description of a leader as a man out in front when people decide to go in a certain direction, has not been improved upon.[3] It takes nothing away from the leader who positions himself for relevant reasons.

Leadership, like education, is not confined to intellectual pursuits. It occurs wherever people do things together, and especially when the going gets rough. This is when true leadership distinguishes itself, usually depending more on relevant prior learning than on the personal qualities so dear to the world of fiction. There is no valid test of leadership, even past experience. As Thomas Kuhn points out in *The Structure of Scientific Revolutions*, even in fields as rigorous as physical science, the most distinguished leaders are periodically proved basically wrong.[4] There is, on the other hand, no substitute for leadership, and leaders remain one of the vital educational resources that learners must be helped to find. Leaders will, of course, recommend themselves, and this must be depended upon even in systematic attempts to match learners with leaders.

In practice, there will always be a fuzzy line between skill models and leaders. Both are specific to the content of what is being learned or done; both are subject-matter specialists. Mountaineers cannot substitute for physicists, and vice-versa. The directories and administrative means that serve to locate skill models can also be used to locate leaders, who will identify themselves by the claims they make, the terms they insist upon, and the behavior they exhibit in actual encounter. Networks can be helpful in finding potential leadership, but the true commodity will always be recognized only after the fact.

There are other kinds of human beings who can be called educational resources only by stretching the concept. These people are nevertheless more important educationally than all the resources described above. They are mothers, fathers, children, lovers, and all the other kinds of people who distinguish human beings from featherless bipeds. These people cannot be treated as educational resources, because they are primarily something else. Familial, erotic, economic, and political relationships cannot be organized as if their main purpose were educational. All, however, have enormously important educational implications, which cannot be neglected even though they cannot be manipulated for specific educational purposes. Unless people enjoy, in the main, good human relationships, they can neither be educated nor educate themselves. The most fundamental educational resource, then, is a world in which most people have good relationships with others. Perhaps paradoxically, universal education may itself be the principal means of realizing such a world.

It should be emphasized again that distinguishing the various kinds of human educational resources makes

sense only in economic and administrative terms. It would be an error for individuals to treat each other or themselves as restricted to one or another of these categories. For economic reasons, however, these or similar distinctions are vital. The packaging of educational resources determines whether these resources are scarce or plentiful, expensive or cheap. And this in turn determines whether education, and all other privilege, is to remain the prerogative of the few or whether education and justice are to be made available for all.

10. FINANCING UNIVERSAL EDUCATION

The way to establish an institution is to finance it.

Justice William O. Douglas

In a just world, or in a world trying to achieve justice, public expenditures on education should be inversely proportional to the wealth of the student. Private expenditures on education are made almost entirely on behalf of the better off, so that equal total expenditures on education would require that public funds for education go in a higher proportion to the poor. Even this would not equalize educational opportunity, since the parents and the homes of the better off represent an investment in their education that needs to be offset. Finally, the poor suffer the handicap of the culture of silence, the inheritance of magic and myth designed to insure their continued docility. It is this, rather than deficient genes, that handicaps the learning of their children; this plus the punishment of failure and disapproval, which is their customary lot in schools. These disadvantages, not inherent in them and not of their own making, require additional expenditure on the education of the poor. If all the public funds alloted to education in every nation were spent exclusively upon the poor, it would still take

many generations to offset the handicaps that generations of exploitation have imposed upon them.

It should be clear that even the first step in equalizing educational opportunity among social classes requires an allocation of educational resources outside the school system. The only ways of making sure that poor children get even an equal share of *public* funds for education are either to segregate them completely in schools of their own, or to give the money directly to them. The first of these alternatives has been tried and has conspicuously failed.

The United States Supreme Court's anti-segregation decision of 1954 was based squarely upon the finding that the prior, "separate but equal" doctrine had not worked. No country in the world fails to provide both more and better schooling to its more-privileged children.

Putting financial command of educational resources in the hands of learners does not solve all the problems of allocating these resources, but it is an indispensable step toward a solution. Not only the problem of equalizing opportunity across class lines but many other problems discussed above become manageable with the aid of this principle. Schools would stand, adjust, or fail according to the satisfaction of their clients. Other educational institutions would develop in accordance with their ability to satisfy client needs. Learners would choose whether to learn on the job or full-time, which skills they wanted to learn, at what age they wanted to use their educational resources, and how.

This presupposes a system of lifetime educational accounts administered in early childhood by parents, in which resource credit could be accumulated and over

which the learner, from a very early age at least, would have a veto power.

In the world as seen by Adam Smith, this would solve all the problems. In the real world, there is still an imperfect distribution of the supply of the real resources required for education, and there is, furthermore, imperfect knowledge of what resources are needed and where they are to be found. This imperfect knowledge is not confined to learners. The would-be suppliers of educational resources also lack knowledge of where their potential clients are and of what they need. There is finally the age-old problem of imperfect character: people who want something for nothing and those who will sell anything to make a profit. If perfect competition and complete knowledge existed, they would offset the problem of man's venality. Since they do not, it remains to compound the evil.

A system of personal educational accounts and a system of public educational utilities, such as those suggested in the two preceding chapters, would complement each other. They could be combined in a number of ways. One way would be to make the public utilities self-supporting, as the postal system is supposed to be, charging each user for the approximate cost of the service rendered him. Another way would be to make the services of the resource networks completely free. This would require dividing public funds for education between the support of the proposed utilities and provision for the proposed personal accounts.

Besides these alternatives, various mixtures are possible: providing some services free while charging for others or charging some people and not others, according to age, income, or other criteria. The possible com-

binations are too numerous to permit exhaustive discussion, but a few are worth mentioning. The networks might, for example, provide a directory service free, locating skill models, objects, peers, etc., but do nothing further to economically facilitate access. This would leave it to the learner to buy or borrow the indicated book, or pay the skill model, out of his personal account. Alternatively, libraries and stores of educational objects in common demand might be maintained for the free use of the public; reading and mathematics teachers might be publicly paid to teach elementary skills.

These alternatives contemplate only the use of public funds derived from tax revenues and divided between educational-resource networks and personal educational accounts. Additional financial arrangements are conceivable. An educational bank might be established, in which educational services could be deposited and from which educational credit could be received. Skill models, for example, might elect not to be paid in cash but to accumulate credit for themselves and their children. Learners might borrow from the bank either credit with a skill model who is accumulating credit, or cash to pay one who wants cash, and the learner might later repay the bank either in cash or in service as a skill model for someone else.

An educational bank could not compete in the market with banks less restricted in their activities and in a better position to enforce the repayment of loans. Government support for such a bank, or for any free service by an educational-resource network, or even for the establishment of such a network, would constitute an educational subsidy. The use of taxes for education is, of course, already a subsidy, but if educational tax funds

were diverted entirely into educational accounts, there would be no subsidy for one kind of education over another. Today there is. Graduate schools are highly favored over elementary levels. Science is favored over other subjects. Nor are subsidies confined to the public sector. Monopolistic industries are able to pass on the costs of educating both their employees and the public, because they can set their prices to absorb such costs. Government bureaus have even greater latitude. The military have almost unlimited funds for training and almost unlimited capacity to educate the public, not only by spending money but by manipulating information. The mass media are currently subsidized by the advertisers of products and services, while producing corporations in turn are able to charge the public for the education they impose upon them. Some educational subsidies are paid directly out of the public purse. Others are collected by private corporations under permissive public laws. All are expressions of public policy more or less openly admitted.

Educational policy would be most open to public view if all public funds were channeled into personal educational accounts, and all educational institutions, including the proposed resource networks, had to be self-supporting. At present levels of expenditure, this would provide every man, woman, and child in the United States with two hundred and fifty dollars per year to spend on education. It would also force all elementary and high schools, universities and graduate schools to charge tuition high enough to pay all costs. At first sight, many a scholastic career would appear to be nipped in the bud. But each newborn child would have a lifetime fund of seventeen thousand dollars to finance his personal

education. Each twenty-year-old could count on twelve thousand dollars, each forty-year-old on seven thousand dollars, each sixty-year-old on two thousand dollars. This is the average amount of schooling the American public is buying now, through taxes, for each of its citizens.[1] It is roughly equivalent to a college education. The fact that so few people get it merely underscores the inequality of the present distribution. Actually, few of those who now receive more would be seriously hurt if public funds were divided equally. All but a few would be able to finance their additional education privately. Poor children, on the other hand, would have five times as much educational support as they now receive. On the average, these poor children would get the same amount they now get up to age fifteen. They would then, however, still have four times as much left. Many poor children become able to profit from formal training only at about this age, although this may be only because the present system of schooling is so poorly adapted to their needs.

What about those who, today, spend at a much faster rate? Would the average middle-class child who now uses up his quota of public funds by about age twenty-one be retarded by having to keep within his annual quota? Under at least three circumstances he would not: First, his family might supplement his allowance. Current private investment in education in the United States is only one fourth of public expenditure, one fifth of the total. Second, he might not attend schools but get his education elsewhere at lower cost. Third, he might borrow against his lifetime allowance. Under favorable circumstances this would appear to be relatively safe. If the student's family were fairly well off but reluctant to invest their own money, they could probably, in one way

or another, insure against the risk of failure. If, on the other hand, the family were poor but the student able and promising for his chosen career, insurance might be bought at public expense to cover his risk.

What about people who didn't use their allowance? The taxpayers might be allowed to benefit. Allowances might be increased in subsequent years. Families might be permitted to pool their allowances. Adults would probably learn fairly quickly to use what they had coming, and this could work to the great benefit of education, the adults themselves, and their society. Adults acting on their own behalf would be shrewd buyers of education. Their demand would bring educational resources into the market that younger people would also use, once the demonstration had been made. Many now-passive middle-aged and older people would come alive and begin to take a more-informed interest in their own and in public affairs.

How would educational allowances actually be spent? What would happen to schools? How would profiteering be controlled? Answers depend very much on development of the resource networks previously described. Capital investment in these networks would have to have a prior claim on public funds for education, even if this investment were to be repaid by the fees charged for service. If these networks were well designed and operated, they would influence the investments of many learners, especially adults at first. Many of these adults would be parents, however, whose children would also soon begin to use the networks.

Schools would, for a time, continue to be used by parents dependent on the custodial care they offered and by students far enough along to be dependent upon them.

Schools could not, however, continue to function at the level of today, since the public funds available to the age group they serve would be less than one third of the public funds that schools receive now. A few schools might survive—old, established private schools and a few public schools in rich suburbs whose patrons could afford to keep them up and could also afford not to worry too much about the economic future of their children. Most people would soon discover more-efficient ways of learning and more-pleasant ways of spending time than in school.

Charlatans and profiteers might have a field day for a time. But, if the networks functioned properly, they would soon be checked, not by suppression primarily, but by the competition of honest suppliers and skill models, aided by competent pedagogues advising parents and students. Controls of the type offered by better-business bureaus would be sufficient, too inefficient to do much harm, but available for use against a real mountebank.

The money that is now so insufficient for schools would be more than enough to support an enormous network of educational objects and to partially support a number of skill models, pedagogues, and educational leaders far in excess of the number of teachers employed today. Many would work only part time as skill models and educational leaders, practicing their skills and pursuing their explorations for other purposes as well. Educational counselors working full time could serve a clientele of a thousand persons, giving each on the average a couple of hours per year.

Financial magic? Not at all. The cost of custodial care would in large part be transferred back from the public

to the private purse. Most of it is now provided for people too old to need it—old enough to work and, in many cases, better off working.

While no financial magic is involved, two major social problems would obviously increase if schools were disestablished. Younger children would have to be cared for, while older ones would have to find employment. Some older children could be employed in the care of the younger. Some, not suitable as caretakers, would nevertheless be excellent models of athletic, musical, and many other skills that younger children really want to learn. Still others could build playgrounds, not once for all, but day by day, in streets and vacant lots and fields and forests; places that can be made at least temporarily safe for younger children through the efforts of older ones.

Not all older children, of course, should be employed in looking after youngsters. Some should help their elders or even substitute for them part time, freeing some of them—the ones with appropriate interests and talents—to spend time with the younger children or to direct the activities of the teen-agers. While teen-agers should work, they should not be confined to routine work. An enormous number of ecological and social research projects could be carried out by young people. An equal variety of artistic projects, from painting the town to the production of plays and festivals, could not only engage the young but benefit the old.

The core of all these projects, the principle underlying the work of older children and the care of younger ones, should be the creation—or re-creation—of the good life. There is not really so much difference of opinion about what that is, especially where children are involved. The

problems, rather, are those of overcoming barriers, finding staff, financing. But the disestablishment of schools would release a lot of money and a lot of talent.

Starting from where we are, how could this money and talent be redirected? Under the principles proposed above, public funds for education would be redirected from schools to students, teachers, taxpayers, or businessmen.

Educational accounts would channel funds that now go directly to schools through the hands of students. Students might still spend them on schools, either because the law gave them no option or because the schools succeeded in hoodwinking them or because the schools, under the impact of necessity, succeeded in providing what people wanted. In all probability, schools would get a steadily declining share of the educational dollar if it went directly to students.

Students would probably elect to spend some of their dollars directly on teachers, by-passing the schools, but there are also other ways in which teachers could profit at the expense of schools. Any significant weakening in the regulatory power of schools would tend to have this effect; their power to compel attendance, for example, or to certify compliance with curriculum requirements. If students were to receive credit by examination without attending classes, teachers would be in increased demand as tutors. For them to increase their earnings would, of course, require a transfer of the savings resulting from reduced school attendance to a tutorial account. Most school laws would not have to be changed to make this possible.

One way of transferring funds from schools to taxpayers is merely to reduce the resources earmarked for edu-

cation. Another way, however, is to shift educational emphasis from children to adults. Since there are more taxpayers than parents, education distributed over the adult population would tend to match educational benefits with tax liability. The taxpayer, of course, would get back a dollar earmarked for education in place of one that had no strings attached, but this might have good educational by-products. The taxpayer would insist upon maximum control of his dollar and would spend it on education valued by him rather than dictated by another.

There are several ways to shift the educational dollar from schools to businessmen. Educational accounts are one. Performance contracts are another. Such contracts have recently been written by a number of schools with enterprisers who guarantee to teach a testable skill and who are not paid unless they do. Still another way to benefit business is to shift the burden of teaching from people to reproducible objects, be these books or computers.

There is an understandable reluctance on the part of educational liberals to make common cause with taxpayers and businessmen. Some academicians claim, for example, that mass media, especially television, already have more educational influence than schools, and that weakening the schools would merely strengthen the hold of business interests on the minds of men, women, and children. Galbraith even argues that the academic community is one of our main hopes of escaping the worst implications of the new industrial state. The evidence does not support him. There is no major issue—war, pollution, exploitation, racisim—on which the academic community, as such, has a discernible stand. There are intelligent, courageous men in schools and universities, as

there are elsewhere, but they receive no effective support from their institutions. In the exceptional case, in which an institution has shielded an unpopular dissident, it has also muffled his voice. The worst causes, on the other hand, have had no difficulty in recruiting academics to their support while institutions of learning have entered into contracts with all kinds of other institutions for all kinds of purposes.

But this does not meet the argument that jumping out of the school fat might land us in the television fire. If one believes in people and in freedom, this would still be a step forward. No one is compelled to watch television and everyone knows who is talking and why. People learn, if they are given a chance, although not always what we want them to learn. God had to gamble on people and has frequently lost. Without this gamble, however, there would be no humanity.

If educational liberals are unwilling to co-operate with taxpayers and businessmen, they must submit to an ever-waxing educational bureaucracy whose efficiency is steadily declining. If, on the other hand, real education were to result from this proposed unholy alliance, this would in itself reduce the danger of economic domination. Responsibility is best divided between private and public interests if policy is made by those who do not stand to gain by its implementation and carried out by those who do. Taxpayers, businessmen, and educational liberals can be satisfactory allies if none are permitted to write the rules under which all will operate.

It would be a mistake, however, to conclude that a competitive market in educational resources would necessarily result in good education. If everyone were already educated it might, but this is to assume the end

we are seeking. Starting from where we are, certain educational institutions would have to be subsidized.

One of the most important tasks would be to induce parents and employers to reassume their proper educational responsibilities. Every thinking person knows that real education occurs primarily at home and at work, but a number of facts have conspired to rob this truth of its former general acceptance. The modern organization of society, by offering free schooling, rewards both parents and employers, in the short run, for reducing their normal educational roles. In addition, schools benefit politically potent parents, while business gains from any reduction in production costs. Similarly, the competitive consumption in which modern households engage induces them to save on costs for which there is nothing to display. Except perhaps in certain academic households, bright children are harder to show off than shiny automobiles.

This kind of dominantly economic competition among producers and households is itself the product of a particular kind of legal structure. Until this is changed, some kind of subsidy will be needed to put educational processes back where they occur most rationally and economically—in the home and on the job.

Another place where a great deal of effective education used to occur was in the practice of the arts. Before modern technology took over, all production involved the practice of art. What we now call the fine arts were integrated with the practice of other crafts, and people learned not only by working with more-experienced masters but also from associates practicing related arts. In the early stages of industrialization, now rapidly passing, this kind of learning was disrupted. It could now

be re-established, since the demand for industrial labor is rapidly declining, but only if people who learn, teach, and practice the various arts are given a dependable claim on the goods and services produced by modern technology. Unrestricted competition between men and machines is not a natural phenomenon, but one that has been deliberately engineered in modern societies. Most countries of the world are frustrated in their efforts to bring this competition about. Modern countries may find it no less difficult to undo, but they must undo it if the arts are to reclaim an educational role that can in no other way be performed. There is no comparable way of teaching everyone the essential skills of hand and foot, ear and eye, mind and tongue.

In addition to the revival of traditional educational institutions, the modern world requires the new ones, which have been described as networks, or directories of educational objects, skill models, learning peers, or professional educators. Public utilities charged with administering educational networks could be self-supporting, once established, and might even be established with minimum public investment, but some experimental operation and testing would probably have to be publicly subsidized.

Schools cannot be disestablished and education made available to all while the rest of the world remains unchanged. Competition among nations, classes, and individuals will have to be replaced by co-operation. This means placing limits upon what any individual or group can consume, produce, or do to others—limits that are being widely transgressed today by many individuals and groups. Acceptance of such limits implies an increased self-insight into what the real interests and pos-

sibilities of groups and individuals are. More than that, it implies a sacrifice of short-term interests for those which are more enduring. This is not the kind of behavior for which the human race is noted. It remains quite probable, therefore, that it will not be learned except under the impact of catastrophe. There is no need, however, to plan for catastrophe, while there is every need to plan for its avoidance.

11. THE REVOLUTIONARY ROLE OF EDUCATION

Men had better be without education than be educated by their rulers; for this education is but the mere breaking in of the steer to the yoke; the mere discipline of the hunting dog, which by dint of severity is made to forego the strongest impulse of his nature, and instead of devouring his prey, to hasten with it to the feet of his master.

Thomas Hodgkins, 1823.

Effective alternatives to schools cannot occur without other widespread changes in society. But there is no point in waiting for other changes to bring about a change in education. Unless educational alternatives are planned and pursued, there is no assurance they will occur, no matter what else happens. If they do not, the other changes are likely to be superficial and short-lived. Educational change, on the other hand, will bring other fundamental social changes in its wake.

True education is a basic social force. Present social structures could not survive an educated population even if only a substantial minority were educated. Something more than schooling is obviously in question here. People are schooled to accept a society. They are educated to create or re-create one.

Education has the meaning here that deep students of education and of human nature have always given it. None has defined it better than Paulo Freire, the Brazilian educator, who describes it as becoming critically aware of one's reality in a manner that leads to effective

action upon it.[1] An educated man understands his world well enough to deal with it effectively. Such men, if they existed in sufficient numbers, would not leave the absurdities of the present world unchanged.

Some such men do exist—men who understand reality well enough to deal with it effectively. Today they exist in small numbers, most of them engaged in running the world for their own convenience. If, in any society, the proportion of persons so educated were twenty percent instead of two, or thirty instead of three, such a society could no longer be run by a few for their own purposes, but would have to be run for the general welfare. The laurels of leadership lose their appeal if spread over more than a few. Whenever, as in Pilgrim New England, ancient Athens, or early Rome, a reasonable proportion of the population have been educated, in the sense of understanding their reality well enough to act effectively upon it, their societies have been truly democratic.

Nation-states as they exist today could not for long survive an educated population. Nations made up of educated citizens would tend to merge with other nations. This could, of course, begin to happen within the nominal framework of the nation-state. Geographical boundaries would not have to change. When immigration and tariff restrictions change sufficiently, political frontiers become meaningless.

Class distinctions would also tend to disappear in educated societies, as indeed they have tended to do in certain periods of history. This does not mean that individual differences of value-position or privilege would disappear. In a changing society, new differences would occur as rapidly as old ones were equalized. It would be difficult, however, to identify differences resulting from con-

stant mobility with either class, race, or any other socially identifying label. An educated society would become and remain highly pluralistic, with many loosely related, fluid hierarchies based on a large number of independent value criteria. Some people might be rich, some powerful, others popular, still others loved or respected or strong, but not very many could be all of these for very long.

An educated population would make not only their nations but also their specialized institutions responsive to the needs and desires of clients and workers, in addition to those of managers. Any sizable educated minority would never put up with inadequate health and education services, environmental pollution, political policy control by military-industrial cliques, or advertiser control of mass media, to say nothing of traffic jams, slums, and the host of other absurdities that afflict modern societies.

No educational magic is implied. Not even educated people could solve these problems in their present context. What they could and would do is recognize an impossible context and change it. They would realize, for example, that competitive consumption is an impossible way of life for more than short periods or small minorities. Once this were grasped, much of our present production and employment would be seen as not only unnecessary but actually harmful. War materials are an obvious case, but schooling, pretentious short-lived consumer durables, advertising, corporate and governmental junketing, and a host of other products and activities are scarcely less so.

One difficulty in doing anything about these matters is that the present way of life of so many privileged people depends upon keeping things as they are. Education

alone cannot solve this problem. It can help people see what shifting sand their present security rests upon. It can help them visualize feasible alternatives, although something more may be required to realize them. This is merely to say that education alone cannot bring about revolutionary social change. It can go much further, however, than people who confuse education with schooling are accustomed to think.

The world of schools conceives the problem of education as one of inducing students to learn what they are supposed to know. From this point of view, it seems nonsensical to think of people as being blocked from knowing and learning. Yet clearly they are. Most of the people of the world sweat their lives out on land that belongs to others, constantly in debt to their landlords, with no control over the prices of what they buy or sell, helpless in their misery and kept helpless not only by denial of information and opportunity to learn but by deliberate distortion of the facts of their lives. Witch doctors, priests, politicians, and purveyors of profitable nostrums vie with each other to keep these people sunk in their ignorance and unaware of their true condition. They are aided in these attempts by the physical misery in which their victims are forced to live, misery so great and so hopeless that it must somehow be justified, somehow disguised, in order to make it bearable.

Education for these people does not consist primarily in learning to read, but in learning to understand and do something about their miserable situation. This may involve learning to read, but it must obviously include other things, without which the ability to read would not be of any real value. Suppose that a few children in such an environment do learn to read and thus escape. This

does nothing to help those who stay behind to breed more children.

Much of what people in this situation need to know, in order to basically improve their lot, is actively withheld or hidden from them. Paulo Freire found in working with Brazilian peasants that they immediately learned to read words with real meaning in their actual situation.[1] But Freire's clients had no sooner learned to read than they organized peasant leagues through which they tried to bargain with their employers. Although they were scrupulously careful to observe the law and the customs of the region, their employers, government authorities, and the Church united against them. Their leaders were fired and jailed, while the Church denied its sacraments to members of the league until Protestant missionaries began to make converts among them.

Freire calls the rural culture of Latin America a culture of silence. By this he means that the rural masses, having been deprived of any real voice in the matters that concern them most, have forgotten how to speak or even to think about these matters except in terms of the rationalizing mythologies supplied by their superiors. In Freire's terms, they have lost the "word." The term is used here as it is in the first verse of the Gospel according to St. John: "In the beginning was the word and the word was with God and the word was God." What the members of the culture of silence have lost is their God-given birthright of naming—and thus understanding and controlling—their world. To understand how the word might be lost to a whole class of men, it is necessary only to remember the origins of this class in the institution of slavery. Slaves were allowed to sing, to chant, to chatter, and to gossip, but they were not allowed to say anything

serious about their own condition or about the society that kept them in this condition. For generations, the children of slaves were raised without reference to such matters, and even with conscious repression, by parents, of references that innocent children might make. It is easy to see how the word was lost to slaves and their successors.

The current practice of religion as it affects the peasants and urban workers of Latin America illustrates very aptly how the word remains lost to these populations. In the rural areas, this religion is Catholicism, but in many regions it is Catholicism in name only. Actually it is often merely an overlay of popular saint culture upon a base of indigenous witchcraft, the content of the Catholic and witchcraft elements of the amalgam varying from one region to another.[2] The social functions performed by these amalgams are the same, however, with no discernible differences in efficacy. They all effect cures, control anti-social impulses or re-establish order when the controls fail, and provide a structure of meaning for celebration of birth, death, marriage, and other critical events in the lives of individuals. More important from a social point of view, they legitimize ownership of the land by the rich, condone and justify the privileges enjoyed by the elites at the expense of the poor, and exalt the charitable acts of the elite and their symbolic roles in religious, political, economic, and familial affairs. They provide the peasants with a set of afterlife rewards to console them for their misery in the present life and represent their current sufferings as the will of God and acquiescence in these sufferings as the height of virtue.

There are, of course, many Catholic priests in Latin America whose behavior contradicts every line of the

above description, who castigate the rich and assist, arouse, and lead the peasants in their search for justice. These priests are sometimes killed, more often locked up as mad, and still more often assigned to innocuous duties or dismissed. Occasionally their work is welcomed and supported by bishops who agree with them.

When Latin American peasants move to the cities and become urban workers, they are converted in large numbers to a variety of fundamentalist Protestant sects. Even Catholic employers frequently prefer these converts as workers and hire them selectively. They are likely to be more sober, more faithful to their wives and families, and more earnest about their work, about keeping their children in school, about acquiring possessions, and about getting ahead in the world. Their behavior supports perfectly Weber's hypothesis on the relationship between Protestantism and industrialization. The personally permissive nominal Catholicism—so perfectly adjusted to rural Latin America and so sharply in contrast with its counterparts in rural Ireland and northern Spain—is poorly suited to São Paulo, Buenos Aires, Mexico City, and the lesser industrial centers of Latin America. So is the more-sophisticated urban Catholicism of Latin American cities, with its emphasis on the rights of labor, the obligations of the employer, and, in general, on social justice in the modern industrial world. The teachings of some of the older Protestant sects are no more in the interests of urban employers than modern Catholicism, and these sects make fewer converts among the workers.

It may seem odd that workers join the sects whose teachings are in their employers' interest rather than their own. This is only partly because employers select as workers the members of these sects. It is also because

relatively powerless workers psychologically need a religion that will reconcile the contradictions between their employers' interests and their own.

We take as great pains to hide the facts of life from our children as the Brazilian landlords and urban employers do to hide them from their peasants and workers. Like them, we not only hide and distort facts but invoke the assistance of great institutions and elaborate mythologies. Facts of life are not confined to sex; about this we are becoming less inhibited even with children. But relative incomes of families on the block, the neighborhood power structure, why father didn't get his promotion or mother her chairmanship, why Jimmy is smoking pot or Susie is having an out-of-town vacation: these things, which children perversely want to know, are obviously not for them. Neither is ballet at the expense of reading, karate in place of math, or the anatomy of flies as a substitute for botany out of a book. Schools are obviously as much designed to keep children from learning what really intrigues them as to teach them what they ought to know. As a result, most children learn to read and do not read, learn their numbers and hate mathematics, shut themselves off in classrooms and do their learning in cloakrooms, hangouts, and on the road.

We ourselves are no better off than our children. Attempts to get the contents of cans and boxes clearly labeled are treated as attacks on private enterprise. Any real probing of foreign policy is labeled subversive, while the basic facts are hidden behind the screen of national security. The enemies of every military power in the world know more about its military capacities and intentions than is available to the makers of its own laws. Spies, bellhops, charwomen, valets, and ladies' maids are the

privileged exceptions to the conspiracy of secrecy in which we live.

There are, of course, the best of reasons for all the secrecy and mystification. Children might be permanently scarred by premature exposure to death, suffering, sex, or the sordid facts of economic and political life. Mechanics might be embarrassed if car owners were given detailed descriptions of their own motorcars. A little knowledge is dangerous, not only for laymen, but for their doctors, lawyers, and accountants. If customers were allowed to know what they are buying, competitors could also find it out. If national security barriers were lowered, the enemy would learn even more at lower cost. These reasons range from valid to ludicrous, but even the valid ones are valid only in the context of the society in which we live. In this society, Paulo Freire is a threat and so is the free education of our children and of ourselves. At present, this education is not free. People are systematically prevented from learning those things which are most important for them to know. They are deliberately misled by institutional distortions of facts and by the propagation of religious, political, and economic mythologies that make it extraordinarily difficult to get a clear glimpse of relevant truth. Protestants see clearly through the Catholic smoke screen. Capitalists have no difficulty in seeing how the communists brainwash their victims. Englishmen and Frenchmen see through each other's machinations without the slightest trouble. Only our own camouflage confuses us.

The secular significance of the great religious teachers of the past can be seen in the important role of disclosure in true education. Apart from the transcendental content of their teaching, Moses, Jesus, Mohammed, Gautama,

Lao-tse—to mention only a few of the most famous—disclosed major truths to millions of people. Each of their teachings was, of course, subsequently used to obscure the very enlightenment they brought, to justify what they denounced, and to convict those whom they justified. Nevertheless, the truths they revealed could never again be totally hidden. Today's injustice stands convicted by their teachings, and today's ideals are built upon them. Their teachings were not esoteric. Many of their contemporaries must have seen what they saw, felt what they felt, but lacked the security to trust their judgment, the courage to speak their minds, or the charisma to attract disciples.

In our time, the great teachers have spoken in secular terms. Marx, Freud, Darwin, to again name only the most famous, have revealed to millions truths that many others sensed but could not equally well express. Thanks in part to the great teachers of the past, today's significant truths lie closer to the surface. They are there for many to see. The veneer that covers them is frequently transparent; the hypocrisy with which they are disguised is often so blatant as to be insulting. Today no genius is required to discover, reveal, and proclaim the truths that could set men free. But it still takes doing. This is the role of the true teacher, the one educational resource that will always be in short supply.

Today's educational tasks do not, in the main, require genius, but they may require heroes. Some room for talent, if not genius, remains. To bring the truths of modern science, economics, politics, and psychology to the masses without simplistic distortion will take some doing. Nevertheless, the sincere desire to do this remains a scarcer commodity than the ability. There are good rea-

sons why desire great enough to lead to action, should not be in plentiful supply. Those who seriously undertake to bring truth to others who, because of their large numbers, are most capable of bringing fundamental change—such people run a considerable risk. The Gandhis and Martin Luther Kings do not die in bed. Ché Guevara took weapons into the jungle and followers who could protect themselves and him. He was, beyond doubt, a hero and a martyr. Those who go armed only with the truth will be still more dangerous and also more vulnerable. No one, while he himself remains safe, can in conscience call for heroes. But the heroes have always appeared and—when the time is ripe—will again.

12. STRATEGY FOR A PEACEFUL REVOLUTION

Whereas it appeareth that however certain forms of government are better calculated than others to protect individuals in the free exercise of their natural rights, and are at the same time themselves better guarded against degeneracy, yet experience hath shown, that even under the best forms, those entrusted with power have, in time, and by slow operations, perverted it into tyranny; and it is believed that the most effectual means of preventing this would be, to illuminate, as far as practicable, the minds of the people at large, and more especially to give them knowledge of those facts which history exhibiteth, that, possessed thereby of the experience of other ages and countries, they may be enabled to know ambition under all its shapes, and prompt to exert their natural powers to defeat its purposes.

Thomas Jefferson
"A Bill for the More General Diffusion of Knowledge"

Strategy for the replacement of schools with universal access to educational resources involves the formulation of specific demands, a statement of the broad goals that justify these demands, and a general plan of action for getting these demands accepted and the goals achieved.

Demands for the just application of existing laws are more easily pressed than legislative programs, and should be used as an entering wedge. In some parts of the United States the federal poverty program has given poor people access to the courts, and they have not been slow to take advantage. Welfare rights, tenant rights, and other civil rights have been won for an increasing number of clients by lawyers paid by the state. Some kinds of action toward deschooling already have a long history, especially legal objections to compulsory schooling by dissident religious sects. More recently, such objections have been based upon non-religious grounds, including the claim that children are not receiving the education that schools purport to give. Suits claiming an equal share of public resources earmarked for education have also been filed,

based on the promise of equal protection of the laws contained in the fourteenth amendment. Recently the Supreme Court of the United States has denied the right of employers to impose educational requirements upon candidates for promotion unless they can be shown to be specifically job-related.[1]

We need legislation that would parallel the first amendment to the Constitution of the United States, prohibiting any law with respect to an "establishment of religion." Institutional monopoly of education, especially by the state, has all the evils of a state church, compounded by the fact that a secular school system is sometimes claimed to be neutral with respect to basic values. Since such a claim is obvious nonsense, the defense of a national school system falls back upon the overriding needs and prerogatives of the state. But this involves a contradiction with democratic theory, which holds the state to be the instrument and not the molder of its citizens. The school, in modern times, has become more powerful than the church of the middle ages. The career and, therefore, the life of the individual depend upon his success in school. The law makes him a criminal if he does not attend it. He is subject to its influence far more than medieval man was ever subject to the church. The case for a prohibition of educational monopoly is stronger than the case against a state church, which in times of crisis could oppose the state and claim heavenly authority for its position. The comparable claim to academic freedom is relatively feeble. Churches on the wane did infinitely better against the Nazis and Fascists than universities in the fullness of their power. The school is an instrument of the state and creates subservience to it.

Along with prohibition of an established school, we

need an extension of anti-discrimination laws to include schooling. We must forbid favoritism based on schooling as well as on race or religion, and for the same reasons. Where and how one has been schooled is as irrelevant to one's capacity to do a job as race or religion. All affect aspects of job performance that are of interest to the employer but that the law has decided, in the cases of race and religion, are not his legitimate concern. Neither is the school the job applicant went to, or whether he went to school at all, if he can demonstrate the ability to do the job. We are so used to schools that this statement appears strange, yet the logic is simple. We now reserve the best-paid jobs for those whose training has cost the most. If schooling were privately financed, this might be superficially justified in ethical terms, but its economics would still be ridiculous. The public has indeed been schooled to believe that a more-expensive item must be better, but economists explain this on the assumption of price competition among suppliers. Schools have precisely the opposite kind of competition. Even Harvard would be suspect if it were cheap.

In order to equalize educational opportunity, we would have to distribute educational resources in an inverse ratio to present privilege. The argument against such a policy is that it would spend the most money on those with the least aptitude and would produce the least total education. This argument can be challenged, since aptitude judgments are based on success in a school system that discriminates against the poor, but in the end such arguments will not decide a political issue. Many people believe that public resources are equally shared, and if not that they ought to be. A law requiring equal sharing of public educational resources is thus a third

item in a legislative program. A system of individual educational accounts would be the only feasible way to enforce such a law.

These three laws would effectively disestablish the school system as an educational monopoly. They would not, however, prevent the development of a new one. By creating an educational market, they would open the way to already powerful economic institutions that might easily take advantage of their power to establish a new monopoly of educational resources.

Effective extension of anti-monopoly laws to the field of education, and effective enforcement of anti-monopoly laws in general, would therefore be a necessary fourth demand. Since such laws are now relatively ineffective in other fields, this demand is far from routine.

Political demands that, if accepted, would result in revolutionary social changes, are formulated not with an expectation of immediate acceptance but for the purpose of creating a revolutionary situation. A demand for the effective enforcement of anti-monopoly laws illustrates this better than the demand for the prohibition of the school monopoly. The latter demand might conceivably be accepted, somewhere, without immediate revolutionary consequences, since it is not schools as such, but a monopoly of enlightenment about the relevant facts of privilege and power that permits privilege and power to continue to be monopolized. But this is the actual issue. The political evil of schools is that they make educational opportunity available only in rough proportion to existing privilege, while conveying the belief that this is not the case.

Commitment to revolutionary change cannot be based entirely upon the recognition of existing evils. A belief

that change would be for the better is also necessary. While alternatives to schools have been fairly well spelled out, the broader outlines of a future society in which these alternatives would have to be realized have been only sketchily suggested. Not too much more can be done in the context of a book on education, but the following paragraphs indicate very briefly the premises on which my utopia is predicated.

Defining freedom, in its clearest if not its most complete sense, as freedom *from* rather than freedom *for*, leads to a definition of basic values and factual propositions in largely negative terms. The question becomes, as Paul Goodman says, not what shall we do but what will we tolerate.[2] Philosophies that state in positive terms what is and what should be, seem to lead to the constraint of one human being by another, to the imposition of enlightenment upon the heathen. A philosophy based on the right of maximum freedom from human constraint begins by denying the right of any man to impose either truth or virtue upon another.

The implications of such a philosophy of freedom are very far-reaching. They include, for example, denial of the right to monopolize anything that other men need, since such monopoly is and always has been used to constrain their freedom. Needs, moreover, cannot be restrictively defined as those things immediately needed to sustain life. Denial of information, for example, leads to denial of fresh air, pure water, and nutritious food.

A social and educational philosophy based upon proscription rather than positive values may appear to contradict both the Christian and the liberal traditions. Both, I believe, have been perverted. Jesus said, "I came to fulfill the law," and the Mosaic law, in so far as it applied

to human affairs, was written in terms of "thou shalt not." What Jesus taught was simply that fallible human beings can fulfill the law only by going all the way, with others. Because this is uncomfortable doctrine, being your brother's keeper has been swung all the way around from going all the way with him to constraining him—for his own good—to your way; or to God's way, as you interpret it. Liberalism has been even more blatantly perverted. It began as a doctrine of freedom from constraint by others. It has become the forced feeding of persons who have been fenced away from food. Today's welfare programs are obvious attempts to find cheap substitutes for simple justice. We give back to the poor only a fraction of what we take away from them in monopolistic practices, many of which are actual violations of unenforced laws.[3]

Negatively defined freedom is not opposed, as it may superficially appear to be, to a richly positive realization of the good life. It is opposed only to forcing any one concept of such a life upon those who do not share it. Actually, negatively defined freedom provides the only universal basis for positive co-operation. There is no other way of guaranteeing to each human being the opportunity to join with others in any kind of co-operation that does not deny equal opportunities to others.

A world that is to be made by people and not for them cannot be inherited. This rules out political revolution as a means of achieving such a world, since political revolution implies a seizure of concentrated power. Power has often been seized on the pretext that it would be distributed, but it never has been. In progress toward a free, just world, power cannot be seized; it must be destroyed, or rather dissipated, since destruction implies violence, which in turn invites retaliation. A world

totally without power is of course impossible, but power can be greatly decentralized, with any necessary concentrations carefully controlled.

Theories of political revolution provide some basis for a more-general theory of institutional revolution, but important revisions and additions are needed. Political institutions are unique among others in the priority they give to the use of violence. In political matters, ideology and rationality tend to be subservient to power and violence. In the case of other institutions—even including the religious—ideology and rationality are relatively more important. This may not always be apparent in the declining days of decadent institutions bolstered by naked power. It is nevertheless true that people choose their markets, their schools, their hospitals, and their transport somewhat less blindly, somewhat more in consideration of costs and benefits—including sentimental attachments—than they choose and defend their citizenship. Changes in non-political institutions are, at least on the surface, subject to rational discussion. Major changes in non-political institutions are at times carried through without violence, although this might be less the case if so-called legitimate violence were not a monopoly of political institutions. It is conceivable, at any rate, that revolutionary change in non-political institutions could take place without violence, could be semirational, and could be affected by analysis, research, and debate. Socialization in the Scandinavian countries and Britain and the formation of the European Common Market provide examples of changes that have taken place in relative peace, though certainly not without pressure and the threat of violence.

Scientific and religious revolutions are worth looking

at for ideas. In mature sciences, one major theory controls research and teaching in the field until gradually its deficiencies become more and more widely recognized, it fails to satisfy an increasing set of requirements made upon it, and it is finally discarded in favor of a more successful rival. The necessary conditions for this kind of peaceful change are easy to identify. There is a common language that members of a branch of science use and jointly understand. There is regular communication among scientists. There is an ultimate court of appeal, namely empirical evidence produced under controlled and published conditions. Finally, there are agreed-upon canons of reason and logic. These conditions are hard to match outside the mature sciences, but they provide useful standards, which have actually been approximated in the examples of peaceful institutional change cited above. Thomas Kuhn's recent book and the controversy it has engendered show that even scientific revolutions are vastly idealized in the above account.[4] They do proceed without major violence, however, and with an apparent rationality, at least after the fact.

Religious revolutions have not so commonly been peaceful, but some have been: the spread of Buddhism, for example, of Theosophy, and of more-militant faiths in certain parts of the world. New religious faiths have swept over large areas at a rapid rate, and the conditions under which this has happened have something in common, both with each other and with the conditions under which scientific revolutions have occurred. Sweeping religious changes have always occurred among miserable people, under deteriorating social conditions leading to disillusionment and despair. The other condition for their occurrence has been a powerful and attractive new rev-

elation of truth. Sometimes, but not always, charismatic leaders and disciples have proclaimed the new truth. As in the case of science, common language or translation, communication, and commonly accepted standards of reason and logic are necessary conditions for a religious revolution. The logical standards are not, of course, the same as those of science, and the ultimate test of truth is different. Not evidence for the senses but evidence for the emotions is the touchstone of religious truth. Deeply felt needs must be satisfied. Nevertheless, the parallels between scientific and religious conversion are much more impressive than the differences. Religious revolutions, too, may hold lessons for a theory of institutional revolution.[5]

The annals of violence itself support the idea that violence need not accompany change. Military history is full of instances of battles that were not fought because one side had a demonstrable preponderance of power. Usually this was the side that began with the most power, but not always. A peaceful revolution is not one in which the holders of power give up meekly. This is truly romantic nonsense. A peaceful revolution is one in which the nominal holders of power discover that they have lost their power before they begin to fight.

There is no assurance that institutional revolution can be peaceful. There is only a hope, and not necessarily a very good one. The peaceful character of revolution is not, however, the only consideration. It is important partly because of its critical relation to an even more important criterion. This is that revolution be effective, that it achieve its purposes. The history of political revolution is a history of betrayal, both of the idealists who helped create the conditions for it, and even more of the

common people on whose behalf it was made and who themselves made the major sacrifices. Revolution will result in only those positive changes that are in the course of being made when the revolution occurs. If it consists in nothing but these changes, so much the better.

13. WHAT EACH OF US CAN DO

One makes the revolution
because it is the best way to live.

Danny the Red

Most of us are not cut out to be heroes, but heroes will be of no avail unless we support them. What we can all do, and must do if there is ever to be a just world, is to begin to live as we would have to live in such a world. If this sounds as if it has been said before—it has. Every great religious leader has said it in one form or another. This makes it neither untrue nor irrelevant, but it is, on the other hand, the best evidence of both its relevance and its truth. If it promises no new magic, guarantees no ultimate victory, but claims only to put humanity back on the main path out of the past, this also is evidence of its truth and relevance.

Power and security, whether based on magic, religion, or science, have always been false beacons leading to the repeated shattering of human hopes. They are false because the attainment of either ultimate power or security would be the final end of everything worth while in human life. People have repeatedly pursued these goals—the prophets of Israel called it idolatry—but people have

also, again and again, recognized their idols and turned away from them.

Our modern idols are science and technology, and their temples are the institutions that propagate their worship, and profit from the proceeds. The promise of this modern cult—every man a king, with his private palace and his royal chariot—has captured the fancy of most of mankind. Suppose, even, that it were realized. What would there be to do? Only an endless exchange of royal visits, comparing the quantity and quality of royal plumbing, and an endless drag race of royal chariots, starting from countless crossroads. Eliminate the crossroads, with over- and underpasses, and the whole point of the game would be lost. It would be like checkers with the red and the black playing on separate boards.

But this dream of universal royalty is a pipe dream—only a few can win. Does that make the game worth playing? Not for those who lose. And for those who win? Already they are establishing private arsenals in their suburban redoubts and servicing their Cadillacs with bottled air while they drive through valleys of smog that grow longer and wider and deeper by the day.

So what can people do? They can begin to live as they would have to live in a sane, just world. They can begin again to guard their health, avoiding poisonous air, water, and food and the overeating and underexercise that more than defeat the miracles of modern medicine. There are other millions, of course, who undereat and overexercise because they are forced to work so hard in order to eat at all. What can they do? They can do different things, depending on whether they have the co-operation of the affluent or not. In either case it comes to a matter of sharing—but sharing can be either mutual or unilateral.

People can either increase or decrease their consumption and production, depending on whether they are now doing more or less than their share of the world's work and using more or less than their share of the world's goods. They can share their possessions or their needs. They can conserve, among other things, the natural environment they live in.

Lowering consumption, sharing, and conserving are three actions most of us can take, and yet, jointly, they constitute a powerful revolutionary program. Consider the consequences if this program were consistently practiced in Europe and North America only by those who believe in its principles.

There would be an immediate sharp drop in demand, especially for the more elaborate goods and services. Ever since World War II, production in the North Atlantic community has been directed more and more to the sale of luxury goods, including food, clothing, shelter, and transport for those already fed, clothed, sheltered, and transported much better than most. No small part of the problem of the American economy today is the failure of young people from the upper middle class to establish themselves in the style their parents would gladly support. If only those who share the basic values and beliefs of these young people would follow their example, the market for automobiles, housing, and appliances would collapse. The resulting unemployment would involuntarily curtail the consumption of other people, who would then come to see on what a false foundation their pseudo prosperity had been built. For these people, sharing and conservation would at first be forced consequences of involuntary unemployment, but once—or once more—ex-

perienced, they would begin to recommend themselves on their own merits.

Sharing and conservation, applied especially to goods that are supposedly durable, would vastly multiply the economic effect of a mere curtailment of excess consumption. Conserved and shared, there is enough clothing, shelter, and transport in the North Atlantic community to last for a decade. Much of it would need repair and improvement, but this could be supplied without generating much demand even for new raw materials.

Exchange of services, rather than their purchase, whether voluntary or forced, would further deflate the market for goods, services, raw materials, and land. The gross national product of the United States could be cut in half without any reduction in the supply of goods and services that actually benefit anyone. What would happen to the foreign commitments of the United States under these circumstances is another matter, but most of the people of the world would be better off if these commitments were curtailed. What now looks like a scarcity of real resources in much of the world would turn out to be an ample supply, with only the problem of rational use and distribution remaining to be solved. Once faced directly, stripped of its deliberately obscuring façade, this problem, too, might be rationally attacked.

This last statement makes more sense if we remember the political psychology of the great depression. During the thirties, masses of people became aware of the contradictions involved in some people owning and controlling what they could not use and other people needed. Only the fascist movements saved Europe from the consequences of this insight, and only the war saved America. Would fascism occur again if conspicuous con-

sumption broke down for a second time? The fear and even the covert threat of this prospect keeps many otherwise constructive people immobilized. But only those who do not learn from history are fated to repeat it, and learning does not mean that because one opportunity is missed all others must be forgone.

This is not intended to minimize the dangers that a breakdown of the present system, absurd as it has become, would necessarily entail. These dangers are great, and any way of minimizing them should certainly be grasped. They cannot be avoided, however, by pretending that they result merely from calling attention to the need for basic change or by pretending that the only change needed is to improve the operation of our current institutions. These institutions are basically unsound. They are designed not to meet people's needs but to keep people under control. It would have been safer to change them in the 1930s, before we had the atom bomb. It is safer to change them now than to wait until still more esoteric weapons are invented. The risks of change are great, but the risks of delay are greater.

What, it may be asked, is to prevent the defenders of the status quo from again using totalitarian nationalist parties, international provocation, and war as the means of preserving or re-establishing the present order? Certainly nothing will prevent them from trying. Only enough people deeply committed to a world of sanity and justice, co-operating wisely in their efforts to achieve such a world, would have any chance against those who will assuredly use all means to perpetuate their power and their privilege. But the power of elites declines rapidly when they are forced to rely on violence. They lose the support of even those of their fellows who enjoy their

privilege but are unwilling to purchase it once they become aware of its true price. There is no doubt that those who fight for justice, even passively, will pay a price in heightened suffering if privilege is challenged. But the history of Europe during the latest great war provides many examples of how people can protect each other even in the face of overwhelming power ruthlessly applied.

No one can know in advance how, in his own case, the battle will be joined. In some places, mere withdrawal from excessive consumption and peaceful sharing and conservation in co-operation with like-minded people will produce a majority capable of taking power by legal political means. In other places, civil disobedience as practiced by Gandhi and Nehru in India and by Martin Luther King and his followers in the United States may be necessary. In still other places, the guerrilla tactics that characterized the resistance in Nazi-dominated Europe from 1940–45 may be forced upon people who refuse to continue to support injustice. Strategy and tactics at the three levels of democratic politics, passive resistance, and guerrilla warfare have some important things in common. They all depend upon co-operation rather than coercion. They depend upon local, as opposed to central, leadership. They depend upon a relatively equal sharing of burdens, responsibilities, and rewards. But these are also characteristics of a sane, just world. This is how a worth-while, viable world will have to be run. People will therefore learn how to run it in the course of bringing it about.

There is probably no other way of creating a society that is of, by, and for the people than through personal co-operation in which each person first orders his own

life in the light of shared principles, and then co-operates with others who share these principles. This is how all communities that have enjoyed a reasonable period of sanity and justice have been established—the early United States, Costa Rica, and Uruguay, the ancient Greek and Roman republics, to name only those I know something about.

The Soviet state and the first French republic, established on even nobler principles, but by the replacement of one central power with another, were never able to enjoy the fruits of the sacrifice entailed by their revolutions. Their struggles for power engendered, predominantly, new struggles for power. No sooner, even in the case of communities originally founded on voluntary co-operation, were power and responsibility concentrated than the downfall of these communities began.

What individuals must do, then, is not merely to curtail consumption, share, and conserve. They must also learn how a just world is organized and governed. For while a great deal is known about past attempts, none of these attempts succeeded, and thus, evidently, not enough was known by those who made them. They were all helped to fail by power seekers, who did their successful best to corrupt them, but they were also helped to fail by the neglect, overconfidence, laziness, interest in other matters, and perhaps most of all, by the ignorance of their members. Brutus and Cassius understood the danger that Caesar represented, but they were too few. Jefferson understood and tried to share his understanding by universalizing education, but was betrayed, unwittingly perhaps, by Horace Mann and other inheritors of the public schools he pioneered.

Perhaps the most important single thing that indi-

viduals can do is to take back their responsibility for the education of their children. Children learn very young how power is used by the strong in their relations with the weak, and it is at least possible that this early learning shapes the individual's behavior in all his subsequent relations with those who are stronger or weaker than he.

There is so much that each of us can do to create a just world that the problem is not one of elaborating the ways, but rather one of defining principles of selection. One thing that all ways have in common is some kind of sacrifice. The affluent must enjoy less than they could enjoy. The poor must demand more than they can safely demand. Everyone must learn ways of living and perceiving that are new to him, must risk his own security to help his neighbor in trouble. Affluent parents will have to deny an automobile for each teen-age son and daughter. Poor parents will have to vent their frustrations elsewhere than upon their children. Both will have to allow their children to take risks from which they could protect them.

A strategy of sacrifice must necessarily be selective. People can consistently sacrifice only those things for which the reward exceeds the sacrifice. Especially is this true, since the strategy of sacrifice here described is as necessary after the revolution as during the heat of the battle. A just society cannot first be won and then enjoyed. It must be won anew every day, and must therefore be enjoyed while it is being won.

For sacrifice is not opposed to enjoyment but is its proper alter ego. Health, strength, love, and respect, for example, can be enjoyed only while being earned—or for

the briefest time thereafter. Even wealth and power are easily squandered.

Each individual, then, must choose the kind and degree of sacrifice that he can sustain, that for him is rewarding. Some must even be allowed to sacrifice their earned share in a sane, just world. Most people, when they come to understand what is at stake, will not find it so difficult to choose a burden they can bear with pleasure—a discipline they can enjoy. What follows is not intended to restrict, but to amplify, these choices.

One form of sacrifice that many people find rewarding is to trade quantity for quality. When, as frequently happens, this entails choosing the products of artisanry over manufactured goods, the revolutionary consequences in an industrial society may be very great. There is no doubt that manufactured goods are cheaper, in most instances, so that more can be enjoyed for a given amount of money. But one original painting may give more satisfaction than a dozen prints, and this can be true even though the painter is a member of the family. The principle holds for food, clothing, furniture, home construction, and the assembly of jalopies from junk-yard parts. Among the affluent, hobbies can generate demand for tools and new materials more expensive than the finished products. They do not have to, however, nor need art be left to hobbies. It can be a way of life for entire communities, and could be used to advantage by and for the poor on a scale not yet imagined.

The average American household above the poverty line, contains not less than a thousand dollars' worth of unused durable goods, which with a little work, could be made more useful and attractive than goods the poor can afford to buy new at the prices they have to pay.

This represents a potential capital of four thousand dollars for each poor American household, the transfer of which would benefit the donors (they could use the space), the poor, and the entrepreneurs who effect the transfer. These entrepreneurs would probably have to have a social rather than an economic motivation, or else a very good façade. Too crass an approach might foul the wellsprings of "charity." Nevertheless, the use of the term entrepreneur is not mere allegory. There would not only have to be middlemen to effect the transfer in question, but thousands of them might come from the ranks of neighborhood businessmen who cannot compete, in the sale of new goods, with nationally organized chains.

In addition to its stock of unused goods, the better-off American household has several thousand dollars' worth of unused space, above what is usually needed for its part-time members and occasional guests. If this excess space were fully utilized, the poor could be as well housed as the affluent. Complete utilization may be hard to imagine, but there are many ways in which a substantial part of this space could be salvaged, which would benefit everyone except real-estate speculators and snobs. Much of this idle space is owned by older people whose families are grown and gone and who cannot sell because the families who could buy do not meet the ethnic requirements of their neighbors. This problem could be overcome by enough acceptable people willing to buy houses as agents for those who suffer discrimination. Another large block of housing space is immobilized because people are afraid to rent rooms or apartments to tenants they feel might expose them to unpleasantness or even danger. This problem could also be overcome by a proper matching of homeowners and tenants.

The two tactics suggested in the paragraph above are opposed in the sense that the first is based on deceit, while the second is based upon restoring trust. This does not make them incompatible. If both were used successfully in the same neighborhood, each would result in the more complete use, and therefore in the greater value, of the neighborhood. Nor are the two tactics politically incompatible. Most people understand the distinction that a man's home is his castle, in which he should be able to choose his associates, while his neighbor's home is not. Nor are the two tactics morally incompatible. It is not that the end justifies the means, but rather that the means chosen in each case appear to be the best available. If this is not actually the case, the suggestions are invalid.

This principle for the selection of means has a broad range of application. Even the law against murder recognizes the right to kill in self-defense or in the defense of others. There are few judicial systems any more that would convict a Jean Valjean for stealing bread to avoid starvation. New laws, on the other hand, complicate current choices. Should people send their children to schools that actually harm them even though the law requires that they do so? Should not people help those who are suffering political persecution even though the law has labeled them criminal? Neither the law nor the prevailing moral code provides a fully dependable criterion for action. In Nazi Germany, both law and current morality required people to collaborate in the murder of their Jewish neighbors. When such major issues as power and privilege are at stake, both laws and mores are used as weapons.

Nevertheless, neither private morality nor the slogan of political revolution—that the ends justify the means—

will do. Choosing the best available means is not itself a foolproof formula. But there may often be no other way of choosing courses of action than to apply relevant economic, political, strategic, legal, or moral criteria to the available choices. If the criteria are chosen and applied as others agree they would be applied in the sane, just world that is the goal of action, there may be no better guide.

A third principle is implicit in the above idea of the best available means, namely, the principle of co-operation. It is essential for people to choose and to act as individuals, since only the true consent of individuals can validate the concept of justice. Nevertheless, purely individual action is ineffective and hard to sustain. Individuals must find ways of acting together, but they must personally choose these ways rather than be coerced by superior power. Leadership there can and probably must be, but the leaders rather than the followers should be drafted, and should follow the policies of those they lead.

Co-operation that results in community, physical or functional, has especially great advantages. The future world must be based on community and, throughout most of the modern world, community has been lost. Even the traditional communities that remain may have to be re-created, since it is doubtful that people given a real choice will settle for the drudgery and hierarchy that characterize most traditional communities. But there are also important strategic advantages in community effort. Communities can often legitimately take over much of the lawmaking and police power. They can also serve as examples of sanity and justice to the outside world.

In all the above there is, obviously, nothing new. Even

what may seem original is merely a new dress on an old-fashioned idea. We have become used to thinking of reality in terms of pentagons and atom bombs or, before that, in terms of armies, navies, banks, and corporations. People's movements are thought to belong to the dark ages. Yet the oldest part of the United States is less than two hundred years old; the independent nations of South America have scarcely more than a century of history, while those of Africa and Asia, including Israel, were founded by popular movements only a few decades ago. The Viet Cong, among others, seem to have a pretty good thing going right now.

It is true that, up to now, military action has often been decisive, but the present rulers of China won their battles with weapons captured from the enemy, while in India there was no military showdown at all.

Three things are new that lend substance to what used to be, and still is called, utopian dreaming. First, drudgery is out of date. Second, modern institutions require increasingly universal co-operation. Third, universal education is now possible. It was only yesterday that the labor of four people was required to feed five. England had to fence people off the land in order to fill her factories. Today most people are in the way, both in the factory and in the field. Food and all other physical products can be produced more efficiently without them. People are indispensable, however, as passive clients and supporters of the production complex—taking what they are offered and doing what they are told. Without their co-operation, the current system for control of production and distribution would collapse. Increasingly, people are becoming aware of these facts—realizing that their bodies are no longer required for mass production and that they

are being asked instead to surrender their judgment and their will to its dictates.

But to whose dictates? Production is a mindless thing. It knows no imperatives as to what shall be produced, where, when, and for whom. The invisible hand is somebody's hand behind the curtain. More and more people are beginning to realize that they should be deciding these things, along with others, and that actually everyone has an equal right to decide them. When everyone understands this, universal education will be well on its way. There will still be a lot to learn: how to do one's share, how to claim one's share and no more, how to cooperate with others in things that cannot be done alone. These lessons will never be completely learned, but when everyone has a reasonable opportunity to learn and to apply them, things will begin to move.

All this, if it were mere exhortation, would still be whistling in the dark. But things are happening. Charles Reich, in *The Greening of America*, says that a people's revolution has begun. Young people all over the world are tuning out the system and turning themselves on. Older people, including many who are concerned by the tactics of the young, still share their sense of the absurdity of the world they live in. The deprived, especially those who live in the prosperous countries, are opening their eyes and flexing their muscles. The great masses of the deprived, in Africa, Asia, and South America, are still largely quiescent. When they begin to stir, the thunder may at first roll softly, but it will be heard. We can turn it on.

NOTES AND REFERENCES

Foreword

1. In 1961 Ivan Illich, Feodora Stancioff, and Brother Gerry Morris founded CIDOC, originally called the Center of Intercultural Formation, in Cuernavaca. During its first six years, the center was devoted mainly to educational programs for missionaries to Latin America. This period ended at about the time Illich published an article called "The Seamy Side of Charity" in the Jesuit magazine *America,* which called into serious question the very idea of sending North American missionaries to Third World countries. Since 1967, CIDOC (Centro Intercultural de Documentación) has concentrated on the analysis of various modern institutions, especially the school. During this period, CIDOC has hosted the seminar on alternatives in education that I have directed.
2. The current rate of population increase in Costa Rica is three times the current world rate. United Nations, Demographic Statistics, Annual Reports.
3. George Dennison, *The Lives of Children: The Story of First Street School* (New York: Random House, 1969).
4. Jonathan Kozol, *Death at an Early Age* (New York: Bantam Books, Inc., 1968).
5. Floyd H. Allport, *Institutional Behavior* (Chapel Hill, N.C.: Chapel Hill Press, 1933).

Chapter 1

1. Enrollment figures by grade, compiled by UNESCO, show that only in a minority of even those more advanced countries that have such data do more than a small fraction of the students enrolled in the first grade complete elementary school. UNESCO, Enrollment Data, Annual Reports, Paris.
2. For a further development of the "ladder" image of society, see the concluding chapter in Raymond Williams, *Culture and Society, 1780–1950* (Harmondsworth, Middlesex: Penguin Books, Ltd., 1958).
3. *La instrucción pública en Puerto Rico, ayer, hoy y mañana*, Department of Public Instruction, Commonwealth of Puerto Rico, 1968.
4. *Ibid.*
5. Monographs, International Institute for Educational Planning, Paris.
6. From data compiled by the Organization for Economic and Cultural Development for member countries. OECD, Paris. See, for example, Background Study No. 1, for the Conference on Policies for Educational Growth.
7. This estimate is based on two studies commissioned by the United States Office of Education in 1969. Two groups of educators, working independently, were asked to set forth the currently unmet needs in American elementary and high school education. The costs of meeting these needs were then calculated in terms of current unit costs as published in the USOE annual report. The independent estimates were within a few billion dollars of each other. These studies have not been published. Their results were made available by Kenneth Parsley, Director of the Office of Organization and Methods of the USOE, Department of Health, Education and Welfare, Washington, D.C.
8. National accounts data, United States and other countries. Published annually by the United Nations.
9. In comparing the cost of education in school and on the job, all school costs are attributed to the education that occurs in school, while only training time on the job is charged to the edu-

cation that occurs at work. Our analysis of the functions of schooling might appear to invalidate such an attribution, and for other purposes it would. For this specific purpose, of comparing educational costs in school and at work, it seems justified. The money the public pays for production is paid for the products of work. The money paid for schooling, as far as the public is concerned, goes for education. In neither case does the public get what it pays for, but in comparing costs it must be assumed that it does.

10. These calculations were made by the author, based on school cost data from the annual reports of the U. S. Office of Education, supplemented by information contained in such special reports as the Coleman study on equal opportunity. There are no official data on enrollment by family income nor on expenditure by family income, but there are many bases for estimate and for cross-checking the validity of estimates. I believe that I have been in all instances conservative, and invite others to make independent estimates and to check my calculations.

11. Based on an Evaluative Report on Title I entitled "Education of the Disadvantaged," published by the U. S. Office of Education, fiscal year 1968. This report found, among other things, that less than one dollar of every three allocated to Title I projects, which were supposed to supplement the education of children whose families had incomes below $3000 per year, was actually spent on these children. The rest was spent on other children of higher family income enrolled in the same school system or on general support of the system.

12. These calculations were made by Ivan Illich, based on official enrollment and expenditure data supplied by the Bolivian government. They were reported to a specially constituted policy board of the Bolivian government, by Illich personally, and were accepted as valid. They reflect primarily the fact that only a tiny percentage of the population survives the early elementary grades, and that all the cost of secondary and higher education must be attributed to this tiny minority.

13. Based on compilations prepared by the U. S. Office of Education, which in turn are based on financial data reported by the various states, and published annually by USOE.

14. Frederick Harbison and C. A. Myers, *Manpower and Educa-*

tion: Country Studies in Economic Development (New York: McGraw-Hill, 1965).

15. Analysis of demographic data in many developing countries shows that the number of children born to women during their total childbearing period declines markedly for women with more than four to six years of schooling, especially in urban areas. A detailed study of declining birth rates in Japan shows that while schooling and urban residence are both related statistically to lower birth rates, the most critical factor is a shift in the vocational basis of family support from traditional rural to modern urban occupations. Irene Taeuber, *Population of Japan* (Princeton, N.J.: erson, N.J.: Littlefield, Adams & Co., 1959).

16. From data compiled by the Economic Commission for Latin America, Santiago de Chile.

17. Richard Hoggart brilliantly describes the psychological effects of schooling on scholarship students recruited from England's working class in *The Uses of Literacy* (Oxford: Oxford University Press, 1957).

18. John Holt, *How Children Fail* (New York: Dell Publishing Co., 1964).

Chapter 2

1. Unpublished study of pupil/teacher relations using ethnographic (participant-observer) methods. Anthony Lauria, Planning Department, Puerto Rico Department of Instructions, 1968.

2. In this light see the history of labor opposition to high schools, in Merle E. Curti, *The Social Ideas of American Educators* (Patterson, N.J.: Littlefield, Adams & Co., 1959).

3. R. Gurjoy, unpublished paper read at the Conference on Development Planning, sponsored by the Public Administration Department of the State University of New York, held at Saratoga Springs, November 11–24, 1969. For similar evidence see the various books of R. D. Laing.

4. Paul Bady, "L'enseignement en Chine," *Esprit*, 37e année 399, Janvier 1971, pp. 73–88.

5. Michael Young, *The Rise of the Meritocracy* (New York: Pelican Paperbacks, Penguin Press, 1970).

6. John Kenneth Galbraith, *The New Industrial State* (New York: The New American Library, Inc., 1967).
7. Arthur R. Jensen, "How Much Can We Boost IQ and Scholastic Achievement?" *Harvard Educational Review* (Winter 1969).
8. A. S. Neill's Summerhill and schools patterned after it may be partial exceptions.
9. W. Dennis and P. Najarian, "Infant Development Under Environmental Handicap," *Psychological Monographs* 71:7.
10. The failures of ghetto schools in the United States are detailed in more documents than can be listed. Among them are:

Report on Equality of Opportunity in Education, U. S. Department of Health, Education and Welfare (U. S. Government Printing Office, Washington, D.C., 1966).

Herbert Kohl, *36 Children* (New York: The New American Library, 1968).

Jonathan Kozol, *Death at an Early Age* (New York: Bantam Books, Inc., 1968).

11. The failures of Brazilian rural schools are best illustrated in the dropout figures. More than half drop out before the beginning of the third grade, and according to many studies conducted by UNESCO among other organizations, dropouts at this level have not achieved functional literacy.
12. Paulo Freire and Paul Goodman, two current philosophers of education proceeding from quite different premises, both provide carefully reasoned support for this point of view. Paulo Freire is a Brazilian educator known for his success in teaching peasants to read and write effectively with a minimum investment of time and facilities. A gross oversimplification of his position is that people learn only in the process of becoming conscious of their true-life situation—coming to see this situation clearly under circumstances that permit them to act effectively upon it. Schools could never provide their students with the action potential that this program requires. It is interesting that Dewey called for something like this action potential in his proposed experimental schools, which never actually came into being.

Goodman's position, in equally oversimplified form, is not easily distinguished from Freire's. Goodman holds that people learn what they need to learn in the course of real-life encounters. Professions and trades are learned by practicing them. Scholars develop

in communities of scholars. Schools can teach only alienated knowledge: knowledge divorced from both its origins and its applications, and therefore dead knowledge.

The effect of transmitting dead knowledge, according to Freire, is to domesticate rather than educate. Domestication is training in conformity and the development of either magical or mythical attitudes toward those aspects of life which contradict the pressures toward conformity. According to Goodman the attempt to transmit dead knowledge either has no effect or leads to a sense that the world is absurd. Both men are probably right. The real world of the Brazilian peasant is perhaps too grim to be seen as absurd and must, therefore, be either repressed or enshrouded in magic. The New Yorker, on the other hand, may be protected enough to be able to view the grimness of his world through the semitransparent veil of absurdity.

Paulo Freire, "The Adult Literacy Process as Cultural Action for Freedom," *Harvard Educational Review,* Vol. 40, No. 2, May 2, 1970, pp. 205–25. Also *Pedagogy of the Oppressed* (New York: Herder & Herder, 1970).

Paul Goodman, *Growing Up Absurd* (New York: Alfred A. Knopf, 1960).

Joel Spring, "Education and the Rise of the Corporate State," CIDOC, 1970.

13. The 1910 United States census, which included Puerto Rico for the first time, showed a majority of the adult population to be literate, though fewer than 10% had attended school.

14. The Coleman *Report on Equality of Opportunity in Education, supra,* shows that home background, including the education of parents, explains much more of the difference in student achievement than the quality of schools attended by these students as measured in costs, teacher preparation, etc.

15. Analysis of achievement-test scores for all students who took high school algebra in the Puerto Rico public schools in 1964 shows a random distribution of answers on all items except the four or five easiest, which were essentially simple arithmetic problems. Other student populations may do somewhat better, but both Project Talent, conducted by Flanagan et al. at the University of Pittsburgh, and Torsten Husén's, *Achievement in Mathematics in Twelve Countries* (International Educational Achievement

Association Project of the Institute of Pedagogy, Hamburg, Germany) show that differences between school systems and between countries are relatively small. Item analyses are not available for these other populations.

It will be noted that statements of fact in the text are frequently supported with Puerto Rican data. This is partially because the author worked for fifteen years with Puerto Rican school data, but also because very few school systems have data as comprehensive, in as much detail, and so well analyzed. This, again, is because Puerto Rico has one of the largest integrated school systems of the world. In the United States only New York City's is larger. Another reason is that school systems in general are not given to quantitative evaluation. Puerto Rico has limited resources, but from 1946 to 1968 enjoyed a very progressive government. Finally, its school system had a series of outstanding directors of evaluation culminating in the work of Charles O. Hammil, who is responsible for most of the analyses cited.

16. Jerome S. Bruner, Rose R. Olver, Patricia M. Greenfield, et al., *Studies in Cognitive Growth,* A Collaboration at the Center for Cognitive Studies (New York: John Wiley & Sons, Inc., 1967).

Chapter 3

1. Philippe Ariès, *Centuries of Childhood* (New York: Vintage Books, 1962).
2. Torsten Husén, *International Study of Achievement in Mathematics,* 2 vols. (New York: John Wiley & Sons, Inc., 1967).
3. Ivar Berg, *Education and Jobs: The Great Training Robbery* (New York: Praeger Publications, 1970).
4. Richard Hoggart, *Uses of Literacy: Changing Patterns in English Mass Culture* (Oxford: Oxford University Press, 1957).

Chapter 4

1. Joseph M. Hunt, *Intelligence and Experience* (New York: Ronald, 1961).
2. "Another alternative to working class solidarity offered is the

idea of individual opportunity—of the ladder. It has been one of the forms of service to provide such a ladder, in industry, in education, and elsewhere . . . Yet the ladder is a perfect symbol of the bourgeois idea of society, because while undoubtedly it offers the opportunity to climb, it is a device which can only be used individually: you go up the ladder alone. . . . My own view is that the ladder version of society is objectionable in two related aspects: first, that it weakens the principle of common betterment, which ought to be an absolute value; second, that it sweetens the poison of hierarchy, in particular by offering the hierarchy of merit as a thing different in kind from the hierarchy of money or of birth." Raymond Williams, *Culture and Society, 1780–1950* (Harmondsworth, Middlesex: Penguin Books, Ltd., 1958), pp. 317–18.

3. New knowledge has meaning only in the perspective of the past. Schools were once such champions of this principle that the word scholastic still carries opprobrium in certain circles. Modern schools have done a complete turnabout. They pay lip service to meaning and reserve their obeisance for relevance. Nor can they blame students for this. Having made themselves the gateway to all other secular delights, they cannot wonder that students storm the gates.

Chapter 5

1. Joseph Campbell, *The Masks of God,* 3 vols. (New York: Viking Press, 1969).
2. H. I. Marrou, *A History of Education in Antiquity,* tr. by George Lamb (New York: Mentor Books, 1964).
3. Edward Chiera, *They Wrote on Clay* (Chicago: University of Chicago Press, 1938).
4. Richard L. Nettleship, *The Theory of Education in the Republic of Plato* (New York: Teachers College Press, Columbia University, 1968). See also, Marrou, op. cit., Chapter VI: "The Masters of the Classical Tradition."
5. Aristophanes, *The Clouds,* in *The Plays of Aristophanes,* tr. by Benjamin Bickly Rogers, ed. by William Barton (Chicago: Encyclopaedia Britannica Press, Great Books of the Western World

No. 5, 1952). See also, Marrou, op. cit., Chapter IV: "The Old Athenian Education."

6. Marrou, op. cit.

7. David Knowles, *The Monastic Order in England* (Cambridge: The University Press, 1941).

8. M. H. Vicaire, *Histoire de Saint Dominique*, 2 vols. (Paris: Cerf, 1957). W. A. Hinnebusch, *History of the Dominican Order* (New York: Alba, 1966).

9. Kajetan Esser, *Anfange und Ursprungliche Zielsetzungen des Ordens der Minderbruder* (Leiden: E. J. Brill, 1966).

10. H. Outram Evennett, *The Spirit of the Counter-Reformation* (New York: Cambridge University Press, 1969).

James Broderick, *The Origin of the Jesuits* (Garden City, N.Y.: Doubleday & Co., 1960).

11. Paul Goodman, *The Community of Scholars* (New York: Random House Press, 1962).

12. In addition to the invention of printing, the fifteenth century brought on an expansion of commercial activities, which created a demand for a different kind of instruction. "Reading and writing" schools appeared in England and northern Germany. These were opposed by the clergy, and a compromise was reached under which they were allowed to continue, but forbidden to teach Latin, thus preserving the clerical monopoly on elite education. Luther deplored students going to these schools when, with the breakdown of monastic education and the old Church system, studies no longer led to places in the ecclesiastical bureaucracy. In sixteenth-century England the reading and writing schools were establishments in which "letter writing and practical accounting were taught, for a new class" (Raymond Williams, *The Long Revolution, supra*, p. 151).

13. Johann G. Fichte, Addresses to the German Nation (New York: Harper & Rowe, 1968).

14. Cf. Louis René de Caradeux de la Chalotais, *Essay on National Education* (London: Edward Arnold, 1934).

F. de la Fontainerie, *French Liberalism and Education in the Eighteenth Century. The Writings of La Chalotais, Turgot, Diderot and Condorcet on National Education* (New York: McGraw-Hill, 1932).

15. Cf. Mona Ozouf, *L'École, l'Église et la République, 1871–1914* (Paris: Armand Colin, 1963).
16. Merle E. Curti, *The Social Ideas of American Educators* (Paterson, N.J.; Littlefield, Adams & Co., 1959).
17. Joel H. Spring, "Education as a Form of Social Control," the first of a series of conferences given at CIDOC in February 1970. (Cuernavaca, Mexico: CIDOC Doc. 70/221, 1970).
18. Horace Mann, *The Republic and the School: Horace Mann on the Education of Free Men,* ed. by Lawrence A. Cremin (New York: Teachers College Press, Columbia University, 1957).
19. Thomas Jefferson, *Crusade against Ignorance: Thomas Jefferson on Education,* ed. Gordon C. Lee, New York, Teachers College Press, Columbia University, 1961.
20. Cf. Michael Katz, "From Voluntarism to Bureaucracy in American Education," in *Formative Undercurrents of Compulsory Knowledge,* Cuernavaca, CIDOC, 1970, p. 2/14.
21. John Dewey, *John Dewey on Education: Selected Writings,* ed. by Reginald D. Archanbault (New York: Random House, 1964).

Chapter 6

1. Mark Arnold Foster, "Poison in the Air," *Manchester Guardian Weekly,* August 15, 1970.
2. Mohandas K. Gandhi, *Autobiography* (New York: Beacon Press, 1957). *The Essential Gandhi,* ed. by Louis Fisher (New York: Vintage Paperbacks, Random House Press, 1962).
3. Janet Reiner, Everett Reimer, and Thomas Reiner, "Client Analysis and the Planning of Public Programs," *Journal of the American Institute of Planners,* Nov. 1963. Bernard J. Frieden and Robert Morris, eds. Urban Planning and Social Policy (New York: Basic Books, 1968).
4. Thorstein Veblen, *The Theory of the Leisure Class* (New York: Mentor Books, 1954).
5. This has failed to occur only in areas where development has progressed very rapidly, with correspondingly heavy imports of foreign capital and manpower. Israel, Puerto Rico, and Taiwan—significantly, all very small—are the only unequivocal examples.

In these areas, war, migration, and strategic location, respectively, have made it possible to engage the entire population in the development process, thus avoiding the social split and alienation of the non-participating element. These exceptions, therefore, prove the rule—unless it can be shown that all nations would accept similar relationships with the developed world and that comparable rates of foreign investment could be achieved on a world-wide scale.[7]

Japan and the communist nations are special cases. The latter, by taking over the pricing mechanism, were able to force their total populations into their institutions. By doing so, they succeeded in avoiding the dilemmas of the Third World, but the procrustean character of their institutional frameworks and the attendant difficulties are well known. These difficulties resulted, in considerable part, from the wholesale adoption of precommunist institutions, unadapted to the purposes they were supposed to serve. By fiat, these institutions involved the whole population, but not in ways that resulted in high levels of motivation for socially constructive activity.

Japan's ability to maintain the character of her traditional social structure gave her a less costly means than that of the communist states. Employers were responsible for employment security, and employees were willing to accept the wages offered.[8] But Japan also shared the advantages of the nations that pioneered economic development, in that she enjoyed a substantial political and economic empire, which permitted her to export goods, services, and manpower.

What this means for development strategy is that developing nations must invent their own institutions. Obviously these institutions must be able to use foreign components—machinery, materials, techniques, knowledge, even trained manpower. What must be indigenous are the basic institutions that determine who gets what, when, and at what price. They must not only be indigenous, however, but also new. The church and the hacienda will obviously not do, since they originally opened the door to foreign institutions. The feudal plantations of northeast Brazil, for example, originally provided a role, however humble, for the inhabitants of that area.[9] The importation of modern machinery reduced the demand for labor, while the importation of modern drugs increased

its supply to the point where the masses of this region are now starving. A return to the hacienda would merely accelerate the current rate of starvation.

What must be new and indigenous are the institutional patterns —which determine how major classes of needs will be satisfied; how people will be fed, clothed, sheltered, educated, and protected from danger, disease, misfortune, and exploitation.[10] Much of the technology of the modern world will be required, but it will have to be applied in a way that meets the needs of the needy.

This is impossible within the framework of the institutions of the developed world. Using the same institutions, the Third World could never catch up. The educationally more-advanced nations must forever remain better educated if schools are to be the means of education. And Brazil, spending fifty dollars per student per year, can never have the schools that in North America cost a thousand dollars. Transportation can never catch up unless the less-developed nation installs more-efficient factories than the developed nation. But seldom can the less-developed nation install a factory even nearly as good. If this is done in a particular case, major and expensive components must be bought from the developed nation at a price that forces this case to be an exception. The follower must, therefore, not only remain behind but fall further behind as long as he adopts the means of development of the leader.

The underdeveloped society requires more-efficient institutions than those of the developed: more food, clothing, shelter, learning, and protection per unit of input than modern agriculture, manufacture, construction, schooling, etc., can supply. This is possible only by departing from different premises. India may never be able to produce the U.S. diet, but only the producers of Coca-Cola, scotch whisky, corn-fed beef, and the doctors and dentists who live on the consumers thereof really benefit from this diet. Better clothing, shelter, education, and protection than the standard products of the North Atlantic community are no more difficult to design than is a superior diet. Neither is there great difficulty in designing better means of producing these goods and services than the ones now in vogue.

6. Gunnar Myrdal, *Rich Lands and Poor* (New York: Harper & Row, 1958).

P. A. Ehrlich, *Population Bomb* (New York, Ballantine Press).

Alfred Sauvy, *Fertility and Survival: Population Problems from Malthus to Mao Tse-Tung* (New York: Collier, 1962).
7. UN Annual Statistics on Rates of Development and Investment from Foreign Sources.
8. James C. Abegglen, *Japanese Factory* (New York: Free Press, 1965).
9. Celso Furtado, *Development and Underdevelopment,* tr. by Ricardo de Aquilar and Eric C. Drysdale (Berkeley: University of California Press, 1963).
_______________, *Economic Growth of Brazil,* tr. by Ricardo de Aquilar and Eric C. Drysdale (Berkeley: University of California Press, 1963).
Albert O. Hirschman, *Journeys Toward Progress: Studies of Economic Policy Making in Latin America* (New York: The Twentieth Century Fund, 1963).
10. Ivan Illich, "Outwitting the Developed Countries," *The New York Review of Books,* New York, 13(8), November 6, 1969. Also in Illich, *Celebration of Awareness,* Chapter Eleven (New York: Doubleday, 1970).

Chapter 7

1. Alex Bavelas and others have experimented with small groups in which communication is variously channeled. While there is no direct relationship between Bavelas' work and the hypothesis proposed here, there are certain parallels that suggest a possible common theoretical explanation. Alex Bavelas, "Task Oriented Groups," Journal of the American Acoustical Society, 1950; 22, 727–30.
2. John Kenneth Galbraith, *The New Industrial State* (New York: Signet Books, 1967).
3. John Kenneth Galbraith, *The Affluent Society* (Boston, Mass.: Houghton Mifflin, 1958).
4. G. William Skinner, "Marketing and Social Structure in Rural China," from *Peasant Society, A Reader* (Boston, Mass.: Little, Brown and Company, Inc., 1967).
5. It might be argued that electricity, for example, is as addictive as are the household appliances that use it. Judged in terms of withdrawal symptoms, this might appear to be so, but a sharper cri-

terion of addiction is the need for ever more of a product in order to produce the same degree of satisfaction. Here, electricity in the absence of appliances or other devices, does not qualify, while the appliances clearly do. Water works the same way. People do not drink more or wash more except as more clothes, better detergents, or water-wasting washing machines are introduced.

Chapter 8

1. José Ortega y Gasset, *Revolt of the Masses* (New York: Norton, 1932).
2. Jane Jacobs, *The Economy of Cities* (New York: Vintage Books, 1967).

Chapter 9

1. The author observed this experiment in person in 1966, saw the attendants behind each child, and talked to the computer programmers and to the research staff.
2. To persons inclined to dispute this principle of instruction, let me point out that almost all educators pay at least lip service to the idea that the most important thing a student can learn is how to learn. He may be helped to learn how to learn by wise counsel and supervisors, but he will certainly never learn how to learn without making the basic decisions involved in the learning process, nor can he begin to learn this too early in life, which is not to say, however, that total freedom is ever possible or desirable.
3. Walter Bagehot, *Physics and Politics.*
4. Thomas Kuhn, *The Structure of Scientific Revolutions* (Chicago: University of Chicago Press, 1962).

Chapter 10

1. These calculations are based on projected public expenditures for education at all levels for 1971 of $50 billion. They assume an eligible population of 200 million and an average lifetime of sixty-

eight years. Projections of Educational Statistics, U. S. Government Printing Office. OE-10030-68.

Chapter 11

1. Paulo Freire, *Cultural Action: A Dialectic Analysis* (published at Cuernavaca, Mexico: CIDOC Cuaderno 1004, 1970).

———, "The Adult Literacy Process as Cultural Action for Freedom," *Harvard Educational Review* 40:2, May 1970, pp. 205–25.

———, "Cultural Action and Conscientization," *Harvard Educational Review* 40:3, August 1970, pp. 452–78.

2. Cf. for example: Jacques Monast, *L'Univers Religieux des Aymaras de Bolivie* (Cuernavaca, Mexico: CIDOC, Sondeos No. 10, 1966).

Chapter 12

1. *Griggs et al.* v. *Duke Power Company:* In this decision the Court forbade the use of scholastic requirements or tests that are not specifically related to the job. The immediate scope of the decision is limited to cases in which racial discrimination is alleged, but the language of the decision is broad and is sure to invite extension to other areas.

2. An oral statement made by Paul Goodman in the course of a seminar held by the International Association for Cultural Freedom at Aspen, Colorado, August 29 to September 3, 1970.

3. Testimony given before a U. S. Senate subcommittee on monopoly headed by Senator Philip Hart of Michigan contains estimates that monopoly pricing accounts for 25% of the gross national product. Almost regardless of how the impact of these prices on the poor is calculated, it comes to more than they receive in welfare and other benefit programs.

4. Thomas S. Kuhn, *The Structure of Scientific Revolutions* (Chicago: The University of Chicago Press, 1962).

5. Norman Cohn, *The Pursuit of the Millennium* (New York: Harper & Row, 1961).